T0369519

Marbles In Your Pipe

A Definitive Guide To Sales and Marketing in the Information Technology Industry

Adrian Noble

Marbles In Your Pipe
A Definitive Guide To Sales and Marketing in
the Information Technology Industry

iUniverse books may be ordered through booksellers or by contacting:

iUniverse
1663 Liberty Drive
Bloomington, IN 47403
www.iuniverse.com
1-800-Authors (1-800-288-4677)

ISBN: 978-1-4502-7446-3 (sc)
ISBN: 978-1-4502-7447-0 (e)

Print information available on the last page.

iUniverse rev. date: 12/17/2015

CONTENTS

CONTENTS

Introduction

"In order to make choices in life you must first have money in your wallet. If there is no money in your wallet, then somebody else makes that choice for you!"

In September 2008, when I sat down and decided that I needed to put my thoughts onto paper, I honestly didn't know what I was getting myself into. Suffice is it to say that it was a mammoth task and required plenty of blood, sweat, and tears before the book was finally launched in December of 2010.

In looking back at how much I had learned about sales and marketing *then* and then trying to put all these ideas, concepts, and methods together in a coherent form so that I could, in turn, teach all of you about what I had learnt in the hopes that you could take these forward and use them in your own careers - I had discovered that I *had too much material* to put together into one volume.

Comparing the "then" with the "now", and the fact that I have grown older and more experienced in my career, I now have *even more* to put together on paper and publish.

This being said it has become clear to me that writing is something that I enjoy and even though it becomes tedious at times I always feel that, when I write, I am teaching with you as my audience, and perhaps my students.

With plans in place to develop and publish the other books that will follow this one (I have to; there is *so **much*** to teach) it was decided between my publisher and I that we needed to revamp this book: update the information and polish the text. I still maintain that these are some of the sales methods that I learnt and used over the years and those of you who are quite experienced in sales might know this information. However, there is always room for improvement and you might pick up on something that you didn't already know.

The opening statement of this introduction is my life's motto and perhaps will always be that. There might be some of you who might adopt that slogan as one of your own and follow its principals. But whatever you decide you must always remember two things:

a. The life you lead is governed by how much you earn. It is an unfortunate statement to make but in today's society it has become a sobering truth. Your income decides where you live, and what you eat. It decides on what car you drive and where you educate your children. Without this commodity your dreams are limited.

b. Sales is the only profession in the world whereby you determine your own salary. But I must tell you; it's a really tough job; one of the hardest to do in fact. It requires patience, application, dedication, and discipline, but if you do this job well you will be rewarded, not only from the company you work for, but you will experience your own personal rewards as well.

One last note before I leave you – the title of this book is quite confusing until you understand what it is all about. With this understanding comes enlightenment, and all is explained in the last chapter.

Thank you for purchasing this volume and I am optimistic that you will enjoy the voyage. My greatest thanks is if you are able to learn something from this and take it forward.

Kind regards
Adrian Noble

May 2015

CHAPTER 1.
TYPES OF IT COMPANIES

In the IT industry there are different types of IT companies, each with a completely different focus. On some occasions a number of these companies combine their services to encompass two or more of these definitions, but to explain the differences and see where the dissimilarities are within each type, I have kept them separate in this section.

To understand some of the different terminology we need to quickly reference the following (found in different chapters):

Home Users -   As the name suggests **Home Users** apply to people who have computers in their homes. In today's society some homes have more than one computer and hence we find small networks contained within these households.

In my experiences I have found that the major concentration of these home computers is to be of gaming, music, movies, and the Internet. Invariably children are often involved when we focus on these industries so major concentrations of processing power, graphics, and sound (notwithstanding various peripheral devices such as joysticks, connectors for cellphones and cameras, and printers) are often the case.

It is extremely rare to find servers in these kinds of environments and this often influences the type or level of technicians you will be working with in your company. Level 1 technicians should suffice in this type of environment.

SOHO Business - SOHO stands for **Small Office, Home Office,** and basically refers to people who convert their small home network that was originally used for the children and the occasional email to friends and family overseas, to home-based companies. We have found, especially in South Africa, and I'm sure that the same is found in many other parts of the world, that many people are opting to run businesses from their home environments because of cost factors. Firstly, business premises are expensive to rent or lease, not to mention the costs involved with commercial electricity. Secondly, fuel costs are reduced because you do not have to travel to your workplace daily – you simply walk to the next room and your offices are there. Lastly, office relocation is fairly simple to undergo if the need arises.

Essentially, in terms of focus, the needs of this environment differ somewhat to the normal home environment in that the number of computers is somewhat the same, (there might be a few extra) but now the focus changes from games and music to office applications and accounting. The ever present Internet is still there, but instead of being used to search for school projects, games, music, and add-ons for cellphones, the Internet instead is used for business-related issues. Again, unless there are **vast** amounts of information being used, there should be very rare instances of dedicated servers on these sites. As an indication of network size in the SOHO environment, typically between 2 and 10 computers are found operating under these conditions, and are of the LAN (**Local Area Network**) type of topology. Level 1 (and sometimes Level 2) technicians are needed for these situations.

SME Enterprise - These are the **Small to Medium Enterprise**s, and these types of businesses form the backbone of the commercial industry and in South Africa, for instance, they form approximately 80% of the entire commercial sector in the country. It is for this reason that many IT companies concentrate on these types of businesses as they generate a steady flow of revenue on a monthly basis.

A computer base in the SME market can range from 10 computers up to about 500 computers, and we will typically find dedicated servers (and other supporting equipment) in these examples, so Level 3 Technical Personnel will be required to support this market. LAN's are definitely a given topology, but sometimes **Metropolitan Area Networks** (MAN's) and **Wide Area Networks** (WAN's) are also used.

Enterprise - The Enterprise market consists on those companies that contain hardware that are in the excess of 500 computers, and can, in some cases, number in the thousands!!! In every case that I have dealt with, these corporations have their own internal IT Departments, and so support from external IT companies becomes more specialised. For this we require the expertise of Level 4 Specialists.

Government - The Government obviously deals with the leaders of our country. Vast numbers of computers are required for each Department, of which there are several. Furthermore, we find that the Governmental Departments are regionalised (in South Africa we have 9 provinces, each with its own **Provincial Government**). These regions all then link back to the Head Office, or **Central Government** (again, in the case of South Africa, this location is in Pretoria in Gauteng).

In order to remain impartial and avoid favouritism for any particular IT company, the Government issues **tenders** so that numerous companies can attempt to bid for the contract. These contracts are awarded mainly on the **demographics** of a company (i.e. balance of employees for different races and disadvantaged people, such as physically disabled persons) and not on price, and typically, when selection occurs with numerous bids, the Selection Committee often disregards the most expensive response and the cheapest response, and then decides on the rest of the responses they have received.

Another thing to remember is time. The Government **always** takes a long time to make a decision about a solution (I have experienced deals that have taken up to two years and longer) so if you are looking at quick sales then this is definitely not the sector to focus on! However, if you are looking at a **huge** commission once or twice a year (probably to help you clear some of your personal credit card debts) then hammer this sector.

In terms of infrastructure sizes and required technical skill levels, these guys have some really funky requirements, so treat them as corporate and make sure you have some technical specialists available to assist.

Parastatals - These monsters are basically **huge** companies that are partially owned by the government, and normally are involved in offering public services.

They have their own board of directors, similar to privately owned corporations, but the Government has the authority to control the board if and when necessary.

Examples of these kinds or companies are (and I'm using South Africa here as an example):

Water Board - there are four such corporations, each one controlling a different region of the country.

SABC -   our television and broadcasting corporation.

Telkom -   our dominating land line telephone and communications operator.

There are others of course, but these should give you a general indication of this type of company.

Like the Government above, Parastatals work with tenders, and the processes are generally the same, including the lengthy sales cycle.

Treat these basically the same as the Government.

Before we actually look at each different type of IT Company out there we need to familiarize ourselves with some terminology so that we can better follow each designation. We will briefly cover the following:

- Topology
- Geographical Network Configurations
- Technical Support Levels

TOPOLOGY

In the following descriptions I am going to refer to the term **Topology**, so I need to give you this explanation so that you understand what's going on.

Topology refers to a physical structure of a network, and is often defined as to how the network is physically connected together. I seem to have had a bit of a problem with my former students in understanding this concept when I was a lecturer, so I'm going to try and explain it again here, and I hope you'll be able to grasp it.

Each and every Network Operating System has to conform to the OSI (**Open Systems Interconnect**) Model in order to be able to communicate with each other. This model was designed way back in the 1960's, and every piece of software written from then on that needed to connect to other computers has conformed in one way or another with this model.

This is a manual on sales, so I'm not going to explain each layer of this model – this you will find in good, technical manuals instead. What I am going to try to explain to you is the difference between a hardware network and a software network.

Take a look at the diagram on page 11. Here you have two computers that are connected together in order to communicate with each other (i.e. networked). The OSI model is a **representation** of what happens to data when it is passed from one computer to another. The user at one computer needs to send data to a user at another computer, so they type something into the computer. The data goes through each layer of the model, and in this the data is converted, divided into smaller packets, has little extras added to make sure the data is the same once it reaches the other computer, and after it is sent into the other computer, the packets are combined together and translated back into the original information, and eventually ends up as something readable by the other user.

The only time the two computers are connected is at the Physical Layer, and it is this layer that is the **Hardware Layer.** All the other layers are **Software Layers**.

In other words, a tangible piece of equipment, together with its connectors, is **Hardware.** The Operating System, Applications, Games, etc, are examples of **Software.** You are probably thinking that this explanation is mundane, but it is surprising how many IT professionals forget these simple concepts.

The connection between two or more computers can be **anything.** Hell if you can tie a piece of string between two machines and get the string to transmit electricity then the computers will communicate. **When we talk physical we are not**

talking just about cable. We are talking about **anything that allows the computers to communicate with each other.** The computers can have a cable attaching them, they can communicate via radio, infra red, satellite, cell phones, anything. If we could make them talk by the power of soap bubbles, we would! It doesn't matter how they are connected, but they are connected. Period!

When we address **topology,** we are looking at **ways to physically connect computers together.** We are not talking about what operating system they have, or the power of the computer, or what type of computer, or the size and strength of your mouse; we are simply talking about different ways to connect computers together.

In the following quick descriptions there are basically 4 different network topologies available, and combinations of these connection types are possible (and often done). Again, we don't care whether they are connected together with bowls of dog food, we are concerned about the structure of the connections.

In each short description (and accompanying diagram) I will explain where these topologies are generally used, so that you can have a clear indication of which one is used where.

Bus Topology - This topology is perhaps one of the oldest used and is not generally found today unless you were to come across an older network (sometimes found in schools with older machines) because of the problems this configuration used to give with respect to troubleshooting. This type of topology was capable of controlling up to 20 workstations; more than that, it became unmanageable. A Diagram is shown on page 11.

It basically consisted of a cable with terminating resistors on the ends, and then each computer was attached to this cable. A signal ran constantly up and down the cable collecting information from one computer and delivering it to another computer.

Star Topology - This is the mainstay of almost all networks today, and the majority of LAN's are connected in this fashion. A Diagram is shown on page 11.

The network consists of a centralized **switch** which gathers information from one computer and redirects it to another computer on the network. In order to increase the network, it is possible to connect switches together in what is known as a **daisy chain** configuration, which basically means that you connect switches in series, each with its own set of computers branching off.

It is possible to connect 5 switches in this manner before you have reached the maximum capabilities of the network, and a switch (depending of course on the brand and model) is capable of connecting up to 32 computers. This in effect gives you a total capacity of 32 x 5 = 160 computers!

Ring Topology - The Ring Topology (as shown on page 10) originally used copper as a connecting medium, but nowadays fibre optic has become quite popular. Due to the expense we really only find this topology with groups of servers (also called **Server Clusters**), but the redundancy it carries makes it an extremely stable configuration. In addition, with the use of fibre optic cable, the network can handle fibre optic lengths of a few kilometres, so **Metropolitan Area Network** backbones are quite possible.

Oh and here is another term you might come across, and is used frequently with servers. It is called **backbone**, and often describes the average throughput of a large network because the servers are the computers that perform most of the work, so their local network needs to be as fast as possible compared to the rest of the network.

Mesh Topology - This last one (shown on page 10) is encountered on a daily basis by everybody globally with access to at least a telephone, let alone a computer. Every time you make a call, or access the Internet, you are using this topology, whether you are all physically connected with cables (telephones, ADSL, ISDN, Broadband), or wireless (wireless networking, cell phone towers, satellite, radio) you will invariably be using this configuration.

Incidentally, although the diagram shows four computers connected together, in actual practice each "computer" can in itself be a **Local Area Network**. Thus the possibilities are endless.

Right! Topologies! Got it? OK! Now on to different geographical configurations!

It must be noted here that these terms refer to networks within a company, or conglomerate of companies, by definition.

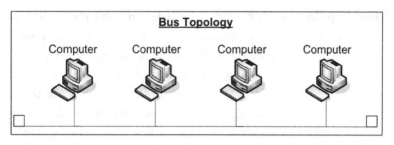

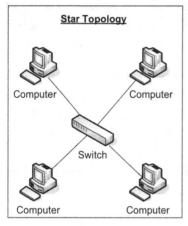

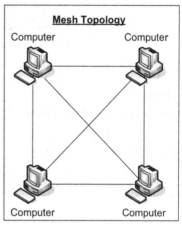

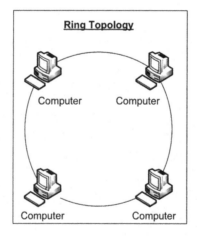

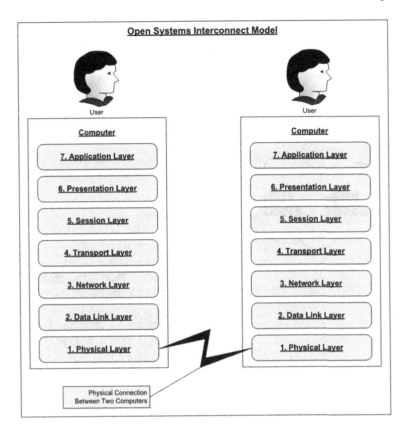

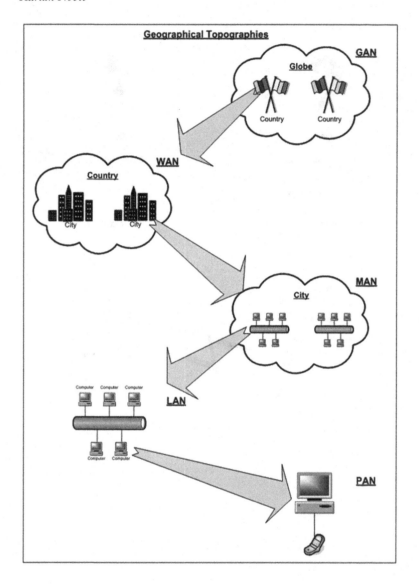

GEOGRAPHICAL NETWORK CONFIGURATIONS

PAN –   **Personal Area Network**. This refers to a network that is configured for a single person, and is often a category for people who have connected their computer (laptop, desktop, etc) to either a cell phone, smart phone, tablet or PDA so that they can synchronize data between the two devices.

LAN -   A very common term, **Local Area Network**'s, by definition, are those networks that are connected within office buildings, or in somebody's home, or a school, for example. Many different LAN's are connected together in different topologies, as discussed below, but in almost all cases you will come across some sort of LAN in your travels. Some people even refer to PAN's as LAN's, and hence the term is used quite loosely.

MAN -   This term is not widely used today, but a **Metropolitan Area Network** consists of LAN's connected within a city. An example of this would be a company who has their showroom in one location but the factory is in another position entirely but in the same city.

WAN -   A very popular topology, a **Wide Area Network** consists of LAN's connected within a country.

GAN -   **Global Area Networks** refer to networks that encompass the globe.

We often have the following possible combinations (as shown in the diagram on page 12) whereby **all** these network descriptions are used simultaneously in a single company.

TECHNICAL SUPPORT LEVELS

I have mentioned in this section various level of technical support that is required for each type of IT business, but we need first to define those technical levels to get a clearer indication of the basic requirements when the Human Resources Department of an IT company starts sourcing suitable technical personnel for the business.

There are basically four levels of technical expertise that are defined, and different levels are needed for the different types of companies.

Right, so first we discuss the different levels and then we cover which levels are suited for which type of company.

In any network we can sub divide it into four basic sections, being **workstations** (also sometimes referred to as **Desktops**), **cabling**, **servers**, and **developed applications**. By developed applications we mean those applications that have been specifically designed and developed for that particular company. Of course there are an almost unlimited number of commercial applications on the market, but in some case the requirements of a specific client cannot be met with one of these commercial products and hence the requirements of developers are needed to design the application to meet the exact requirements of the client.

Level 1 – Desktop Technician –	The **Desktop Technician** should have enough knowledge in order to support workstations and single computers, and in most cases we find that these technicians are new graduates from a tertiary college. Their job description typically involves with dealing with users who don't understand very much about computers, and often require assistance with fairly simple tasks.

I must stress that people are not stupid at all!!! There are many revolving anecdotes from technicians that have assisted average users and yes, we all laugh at them, and think to ourselves, "That person is dumb beyond belief!" but I need to clarify something here.

When we are young we all have dreams of becoming firemen, doctors, veterinary surgeons, pilots, dancers, singers, mechanics, and yes, computer geeks. Some of us (thanks to the grace of God) actually grow up to realise those dreams whilst the rest of us have to make do with second best.

When I was growing up I always wanted to be a Medical Doctor. My Mother was a Medical Technologist, my Father was a Histologist, and became a Senior Zoologist at a university in South Africa, so medicine was in our family.

So I entered university and tried a year of Zoology and Botany, bearing in mind that I never studied Biology at school. Well, hmmmm, all the processes of how the blood flows through the body, and the digestive system, was great, but do you think I could remember the names? Hell, no! It's a known fact that there are 206 bones in the human body and I think throughout that first year I remember exactly 10 (medical names now, not the layman terms). All the names of the arteries and veins, and the different muscles: forget it! Martian language comes to mind here! Plant life wasn't much better because I still, to this day, couldn't tell you the difference between Mitosis and Meiosis.

However I had another love. At the age of ten years old, and yes, I'm going to mention the school and the person, because it was this institution and this person (who sadly, is no longer with us, but very much remembered) who determined the course of my life, I was introduced to computers by the Computer School Master, Mr. Immelman, at Alexandra High School in Pietermaritzburg in South Africa. My Mother was involved with running the tuck shop at the school, and on Saturdays I often went with her to support the school's sport events.

Invariably I got bored and started wandering around the school until one day I came across Mr. Immelman's classroom which was filled with the most wondrous machines, with green (and orange) screens and keyboards and young boys sitting glued to them furiously pummelling away at those keyboards with such intense gazes that you thought they were controlling the world. These Radio Shacks and Apple II E computers were the start of my life, and Mr. Immelman nurtured me through those early years, and, well, here I am today! By the way, I ended up matriculating from this very school!

Some of you readers are sitting there thinking, "But Mitosis and Meiosis are so easy to remember! How come he can't remember them?", and this then brings me to my point here. Everybody has skills in different areas. Some people are absolutely brilliant at repairing motor vehicles; some people have the uncanny ability to tell you exactly what is wrong with your pet dog. Give some people your tax forms to consolidate and magically you receive your second Christmas present from the Taxman every year (I tried to do my own taxes one year and ended up with a lousy $40 rebate).

Everybody has different skills in diverse areas and some of them do not involve computers at all. Yes, we are all exposed to computers somewhere in our lives, but not all of us use them as tools for our lives; and it is these people you call stupid when they cannot grasp the concepts that are so natural for us.

So, when next you are performing first level support and are getting frustrated because the user does not understand what you are trying to explain to them, take a step back and ask yourself, "What do they do for a living? Can they be forgiven for their ignorance?", and once you think like this, take a deep breath and try again. You'll find that the experience will be more pleasant for both of you.

Level 2 –	These technicians generally have a bit
Network Technician –	more training than desktop technicians.

We often find that as young, fresh graduates start their first job as Desktop Technicians, they progress through to **Network Technicians** after a bit or working experience and, in some cases, a bit more formal training.

A **Network Technician** should be able to perform desktop support when necessary, but knowledge of basic networking now becomes more important to their job.

It is often at this level that a technician will become involved in cabling of a network. I have devoted a small part of this in the chapter on "Client Site Analysis" (Chapter 9) to mentioning a few pointers but this will by no means train anybody in proper cabling installations. I suggest some formal training in this field will be quite necessary in order to perform this task well.

As part of my background I was involved at an industrial company that dealt with Process Control and Automation for factories. I worked in the industrial security section and I learnt over the three years I was with them how to perform industrial cabling, which is a higher standard than data cabling. OK, I am not suggesting that you all go out now and find jobs that will teach you industrial cabling, but what I am suggesting is that, whilst you are a new **Desktop Technician**, you try and spend some time with the cabling guys on site learning the ropes, so to speak.

When I first started with this industrial company (I had been with them a sum total of two weeks) they were involved with a project with a major, prominent factory with something that is known as "Shut Down". Many factories slow down their production levels over the Christmas period, and it is at this time when many major factory upgrades are performed (take a look at the Year Plan on page 54). So here I was amongst a team of eighty electricians, welders, boiler makers, programmers, cabling specialists, and others. I was given a team of five guys and in three weeks we pulled approximately 27 km of industrial cable! I was then taught how to terminate the cable (in industrial terms terminating cables is to basically wire them to various electrical devices), and then I learnt rudimentary PLC programming. We worked solid, sixteen hours a day, seven days a week, for about five weeks, until that section of the factory was complete. Extremely heavy work, and at the end of it I was in prime condition physically.

In addition, you will also be involved in cabling cabinets, which house network devices such as switches, routers, and, in some cases, servers themselves. This is a completely different animal and my suggestion here is to spend a few hours with your cabling supplier and they explain the different aspects of this process with you.

In any case, cabling must be neat and tidy: your terminations must be straight and neat, and the overall inspection of the job must look professional. These are some of the things you will learn as you progress down this road.

The other side of begin a Network Technician is rudimentary work with servers, and for this you will need the proper training and certification. Once trained, you will start your journey down this road of working with servers and their little quirks. This knowledge will grow throughout the years, and is something that you never will know everything about, so make sure that you update your knowledge on an annual basis, and please, hoard as many computer manuals as you can!

I'm going to digress slightly here. In the chapter on "Client Site Analysis" I mentioned software drivers. Even though we are at a stage that Operating Systems contain most of the drivers that are required on installation (sound cards, networks cards, graphic cards, et al) and those that cannot be identified can be located on the Internet, you will come across situations whereby drivers are needed that cannot be obtained off of the Internet for various reasons, such as age of the driver, or just that there is no Internet connection available. Sometimes you will have to work with a machine that is using an older Operating System. Whatever the case, hoard as many software drivers you can. Create a folder on your local server at your offices and store them neatly and categorically so that they are there when you need them in the future.

Right, digression finished – we can continue.

Network Technicians will on occasion work with home users (some of them have small networks) but generally they are more reserved for the business sector.

Level 3 – **Server Specialist –**	These guys spend their lives playing with servers, network security, and generally specialised work that govern entire networks, from medium-sized installations to huge Enterprise operations.

Unless there is small request a **Server Specialist** would never even consider cabling other than working with a Server Cabinet, nor would they even consider being involved in local Desktop Support. **Server Specialists** sometimes even double up as assistants to **Business Analysts**, suggesting what equipment and solutions that will need to be implemented at a particular site.

These individuals are highly trained professionals (and yes, they cost a pretty penny to have on board) and as such they should be used wisely, because their knowledge is extremely vast.

Routers, Content Filters, Network Access Control Devices, Bandwidth Accelerators, and other, similar network devices all fall within the realm of the **Server Specialist**, and in some situations, these people generally focus on one or two different products, so in an extremely large and diverse project different specialists will be required. In these cases it is often preferred to hire these persons for the duration of particular projects, and so we often find **Server Specialists** are freelancers and are not affiliated to any one company; rather they become affiliated to those products they have dedicated their time to learning.

Level 4 – Software Developer –	This is the last category of technician that you will across, and these guys are a completely different breed of people. They don't cable networks, they don't fiddle with servers, or assist users with desktops; they are involved in defining the very applications and operating systems that run on computers.

In some rare cases Server Specialists have migrated over to perform this particular function, and in these cases these developers have a better understanding perhaps of networking and general, everyday workings of computers than those developers who have started their profession from day one, but the bottom line is you will be dealing with extremely gifted individuals who could instruct a computer to make a cup of coffee or wash the dishes if they so wish. We often dream of wizardry and magic, and wonder why it's not so prevalent in today's world – well, these developers are your wizards of the computer world! Trust me; I've seen some incredible demonstrations performed from some of these guys.

So now all of you are sitting there thinking to yourselves, "I want to be a software developer because they are highly paid and worth their weight in gold!", and some of you might make it to the top, but, and I speak from my experiences in university studying Computer Science, your mathematics and logic has got to be impeccable. You also need to be patient to be able to wade through mounds of coding looking for little errors. You also need to understand the average user so that your project is as User Friendly as possible.

With all this said, getting your teeth into this profession is a very exciting and rewarding challenge, and if you have the knack for it, then have a try at it. I've done some local development in my time and it's really enjoyable to see the code you've designed do the job it is supposed to do!

Like Server Specialists, **Software Developers** are normally freelancers, working from contract to contract, and although some of them are affiliated with Software Houses (explained later) most of them will take on extremely diversified projects, thus ensuring that the work is never tedious or repetitive.

Another aspect whereby **Developers** are similar to Server Specialists is in the choice of platform to develop in. There are so many different programming platforms available that one cannot hope to be proficient in even more than one or two platforms, let alone all of them. So again, when dealing with large projects, different developers are contracted where necessary to design different sections of the project.

Technician Level Descriptions				
Level	Description	Company Type	Network Type	Support Services
1	Desktop Technician	Retail, Network Company, Distributor	Single Computers/ SOHO Networks	Mainly End User and Home UserSupport
2	Network Technician	Network Company, Service Provider	SME Networks	Low Level Network Support, Cabling, Some End User Support
3	Server Specialist	Network Company, Distributor	Medium & Enterprise Networks	All kinds of Servers, Network Equipment, Server Rooms
4	Software Developer	Network Company, Service Provider, Software House	Medium & Enterprise Networks	Software Applications

TYPES OF IT COMPANIES

We have now familiarized ourselves with all the jargon necessary to get us to this point: discussing each different IT company.

I have identified six basic types but of course there are other people out there, whose options will differ from mine, and hence they will identify a few more, but these should suffice for our purposes.

For each company type we are going to analyze their strengths and weaknesses, and where their focuses are. We will also look at which kinds of advertising will suit the type best. There is another

21

chapter dealing with different kinds of advertising. In some cases I am referring back to material discussed in that section. Please bear that this section is not intended to teach you how to open and run your own IT business; there are several good books out there that specifically concentrate on this. Instead the intent here is to show you, as sales people, which company your abilities would be best suited for.

With respect to technical personnel we will look at which technician is required per company type.

Obviously these designations and specifications discussed below are not hard, fast rules, as there will be certain requirements that are needed from time to time that step out of these boundaries, but this should give you a good indication of what you will expect out there in the world.

RETAIL

Often, when people start thinking about forming an IT company, their minds automatically envisages a shop somewhere in a mall, with beautiful displays and lights; you can't move in the store for the number of customers littering the shop waving their credit cards ready to pay and thus rid your store of some stock. This dream is quite feasible provided you play your cards right and setup the business properly, and operate it tirelessly.

So the first thing to look at here is location, location, location! A retail business will have a shop front (also known in some circles as a **Showroom**) where a large part of the business is generated.

With the invention of the shopping mall it has become a prime hot spot for large congregations of people whose one train of thought in their minds is, "Spend, spend, spend!". Ultimately this becomes the ideal settling place for any retail business, but the major downside is affordability. Shopping malls (of which there are so many springing up now) spend an obscene amount of money in developing themselves that they (or actually, the Developers) need to recoup the money they spent, before they can start making a profit. The only way to do this is to hammer the rentals of the various shops, and we find that the average starting – out retail business battles with this initially, so the spaces become gobbled up by the larger chain retail groups.

So where to now? Again I will state this in another way: **a retail company gains almost all of its sales from public exposure!** And most of that exposure is simply walk-in business, which can only be gained if the public are aware that you exist.

Yes, advertising does play a part, and we will discuss that shortly, but walk-in business, or people driving (or walking past) your show room will take notice are remember where you are, so that when they need something they know where to go.

Knowing this then, if a retail company cannot establish itself in a shopping mall because of expenses the next best thing is to find a location as near as possible to a shopping centre. If people can park at the mall, and are in a spending mood, they will take the little extra effort to walk across the road to visit you.

This brings me to another point: **parking!** So many retailers open their businesses in a prime location; they establish good signage and advertising, and give really good prices and service, but they still lose, and this is because of parking. No parking, no business! This is an important point to remember.

The next thing to consider is the passing by aspect of advertising. Remember, a person driving past is concentrating on the road, traffic, and people on the side walk. They have perhaps between one and two seconds (depending on how fast they drive) to peer at your signage and identify you as a retail IT business. I have seen so many times before so many retails companies (and not necessarily IT companies) completely demolish their chances for success by using incorrect signage in front of their shops.

I have seen incorrect spelling (a definite killer in my personal opinion), gaudy colours which clash with each other and really demean the integrity of the business. I have seen writing so small, or bunched up together, that to identify any sort of contact details is impossible. Remember again, the guy is driving – you have got one second at most to allow him to locate a name and contact number.

Nowadays, with the Internet, a website address becomes a more valuable tool. People generally remember names better than numbers and a search on the Internet is always available if they cannot remember your website name correctly. Given this, it is surprising as to how many retail businesses (and even IT companies) who do not advertise their website address. If your company doesn't have an address, **get one!!!** You (or the bosses) are only crippling the business by not going this route!

And another thing – neon signage: hmmm, not good: makes you think of night clubs, party joints, etc! If you are looking at exposure in the dark hours then I would rather suggest a spotlight pointed at your shop front signage to illuminate it at night.

Next step – outfitting! Have you ever visited a jeweller's store? Course you have! What's it look like? Clean, neat, sterile, beautiful, ambient lighting; lots of shiny things to part your money on. What kind of clientele do you think they are aiming for? The wealthy, of course! The guys with the bucks!

I'm not saying that you should build a jeweller's shop, because you are selling computers, not jewellery, but rather make the environment warm and comforting, and exciting at the same time. Use colour, posters, etc, and make sure your shelves are full. Never have empty shelves: it reflects badly on the company. And make sure that the goods you display on your shelves follow logical order: in other words, combine the games with the joysticks, sound systems, and graphics cards. Don't stick them together with your business software, 'cause then you are just mixing up your clientele!

Some retailers like their Technical Department to be exposed to the general customer because then questions can be asked and the client can see how their computer is begin repaired. I personally have mixed thoughts about this, because have you ever seen the average Technical Department? It's one really bad looking stew, and I personally wouldn't like my clients to see that sort of thing, not to mention the discussions that occur between techies. Plenty of swearing and cursing going on in there! If you really want your Technical Department exposed to the sales floor, then please make sure it's neat and tidy, and try to control your technicians' language!

And another thing: make sure you have plenty of sales people on hand for assistance (they can also double up as security in the store) if required.

I'm going to do another digression here to illustrate a point.

Computer security is oh, so important in today's society but do you know how many retailers (and yes, other types of IT companies) I have walked in and I never see this happening.

I remember a couple of years ago I visited such a retailer and I was looking to purchase a computer on behalf of somebody else, and they gave me the usual quotes, and the usual sales banter, and assurances that the machine is of the highest quality available. They told me about their great backup support services and all the specials they have got running at that stage. But nowhere did I hear mention of the one thing I was hoping to hear.

I have visited many retailers before, and still I do not hear what I am looking for. Only one National Retailer has got this right, and only after I trained their sales personnel, so now I'm training you in the same way.

WHERE IS THE ANTI – VIRUS?

As a retailer you are there to offer your customers an excellent service, and also to make money, of course. The sale of anti-virus should be first and foremost on the sales person's mind. Firstly, it's a quick easy sale because the package is affordable. Secondly, everyone needs it.

Throughout this book you will see me mention **Kaspersky Anti-Virus**® and **Kaspersky Internet Security**®, because, in my opinion, they are one of the best anti-virus products on the market globally today, and they cater for such a wide variety of end users that it is impossible to make an excuse **not** to have one in your possession. Think about it, you've got children, Kaspersky Lab ®' has got Parental Restrictions. You have a Tablet or Smart Phone – Kaspersky Lab ® has a solution for you! And there are some really nifty features that you might want to try out. You have an Apple Mac, or Linux, or Novell ® – you have a solution for you! Look for a green and red display with what appears to be a green traffic light, and you will have found Kaspersky Lab ®' products.

How I trained the sales staff at the national retailer. I taught them to approach these customers and find out their needs. Some of them were obvious and then the conversation could steer in that direction; others were a little more difficult. In many case there were some customers that were purchasing computers, or parts to upgrade their current computers. Now, some of them should find out when the subscription was expiring. Once they had this knowledge they filed it somewhere and then when the time came to renew their anti-virus, then all the sales person had to do was to contact the client and sell them a new version.

For those clients who purchased new computers, this task was even easier. Invariably a prospect would have a quote from another competing company and would ask for a comparison quote from your store. I can almost guarantee you that some of those quotes do not include any sort of anti-virus. So now, grab hold of the sheet listing the labour charges involved for your technicians, and explain to the customer that there are over two hundred new strains if virus that are released into the Internet every day. Ask the client what their chances are in not getting infected by one or more of these viruses, essentially damaging the integrity of the computer, and resulting in them having to bring the computer in for repair, at the charges you have just shown them. For a very small additional fee they can load Kaspersky Lab ®' products onto their new system and prevent this from happening.

So I went a little further with the sales staff. Every person has a job, and has to work somewhere, so I got them to talk to the prospect about their work. One thing would lead in another and a lead was generated whereby the sales person could contact the customer's work, and hence sell them anti-virus as well. Small sales, I know, but if the first sale is done properly, then the client's workplace will eventually come back to the retail store looking for more.

This whole process is called **VAR Selling** and is discussed in chapter called "Value Added Reselling" (Chapter 6).

Right, on to techies! Most of the clients you will be working with this level will be home users, students, and those few people who require some home networking, and maybe even a SOHO office to work with, so you will need plenty of **Desktop Technicians** (Level 1) to look after all the clients.

My very first IT sales position was in an IT Retail company, of which there were two branches. To give you an indication of sales here, once a month we would all go to the Head Office to build and install computers for the next month's sales. In those days (early to mid 1990's) we were building between 400 and 500 computers on that weekend. Consider this: there are five working days in a week (six if you include Saturday – we worked on Saturdays) and there are four weeks in a month. So in twenty four days we sold between 400 and 500 computers within the two branches. This equated to between eight and ten computers sold every day per branch. And this happened on a monthly basis!

If we average that four of those computers had a problem (or two or ten) that meant that the technicians were dealing with four new jobs daily, not to mention their other work, initial delivery and installation of new computers at customers' sites, etc. Needless to say our Technical Department was extremely busy.

Most of the problems the technicians encountered were of the normal, desktop variety, and some of them were attributed to fault hardware, but it was not often that we had network problems, and thus we had to hire quite a few Desktop Technicians to cope with the demand. For network-related issues we had a **Server Specialist** that was roaming – he practically lived in his car with a laptop and cellphone and instructed the other technicians as to how to go about repairing the problem. For those few SME clients we had in those days he used to visit the sites if his assistance was needed.

Retail Advertising is one, huge headache, and it would be beneficial for an IT Retail Company to hire someone to focus primarily on this aspect of the business.

Retail sales are about volume, not profit. Most of the shoppers who visit retail stores are concerned about price. Of course quality is a factor but the unsuspecting shopper would not be able to discern quality and so for them it becomes a case of scouting around to various outlets to gather quotes and then sit and compare "apples with apples". You have got no idea how much irritation we used to go through in my first IT sales job because of the deals we lost from price, or we used to have the prospects come barging into our store to start haggling so that we had to reduce our price, or include something for free, etc. Sometimes it used to become so bad that we actually allocated a small measure of "freebies" aside so that when we had one of these types of customers we could just throw in a "freebie" quickly to sweeten the deal. After all that, free installations and configurations (at one stage we had to even include free training) had to be built in, and so we had to hire additional technicians devoted to this task. Also, fuel costs were our own.

In the end our profit margins were affected heavily with the sales of computers, and that is why the VAR method so important – those extras, such as the anti-virus, office package, games, joysticks, Internet access, etc is where the actual profit came from and not from the computer.

In any case, retail sales is all about volumes of sales, and in order to generate these sales you can't rely on just walk-in business (although this does make up a substantial part of revenue generated) so other forms of advertising has to be tackled.

In the chapter on "Types of Selling" (Chapter 4) we cover this in a bit more detail.

A retail store needs a web presence (we have already discussed this above) but what about those people that don't have access to the Internet, or they don't know how to use it? We need other ways to get people to know we exist.

Television and radio, although extremely effective, is beyond the pockets of almost all retailers, and so then are out as possible vehicles. Magazines are really good, because they are affordable and they cater for key markets. The only problem here is the quantity of magazines released. Normally these are only released once a week or once a month, and by then many prospects would have forgotten about you.

Flyers and leaflets, pamphlets!!! If you haven't read my thoughts on this in "Types of Selling" then I suggest you do so before continuing (page 81).

Newspapers seem to be a very good medium to gun for, and are a good advertising backbone of many large retail chains. They are cheap and are released on a daily basis, and a campaign lasting perhaps a week would be a very good idea to tell people about yourself and the specials you are running.

Billboards – I cover these in "Types of Selling."

Word of Mouth is very important to a retail business, and so you need to make sure that your services are of a quality that will impress your clients so that they want to refer you to others.

An interesting little concept I put together a few years back which seemed to work very well, and other companies have cottoned on to this idea (not from me obviously; I'm not that good) in their own fields are now offering similar concepts to their customers.

Here is how it works. Firstly the trick here is to incite the client to buy more from you, but you also want them to bring other customers to you as well. So you offer them a bonus scheme. When they bring a referral back to you they will receive a discount *on their next purchase*. The percentage discount is based on the amount the referral purchases: a higher purchase means more discount, but make sure you have a threshold so that the referral doesn't come in just to buy a mouse or disk and then your original client benefits from their discount.

Some retailers like to just give their customers money on referrals. I don't like this method because it doesn't generate further sales from that customer, and you have no guarantee that the money you give to the customer will be spent on goods in your shop. In the end, you'll lose money. Given the other method, you will most certainly generate further sales whilst gaining new clients.

Vehicles of getting this across could be anything to vouchers the referral must bring in (you might even want to give a discount as well to the referral for their initial purchase). You could give your customer a number which the referral must quote. This method is currently used in Network Marketing. Whatever the choice here, make sure you have a time limit or else these referrals could come to you a year or two later requesting the same thing.

In this type of industry cold calling (jumping on the telephone and phoning people for business) is a very poor way of advertising because the retail market concentrates on the home and not the workplace. Yes, there will be some work-related clients, but the bulk of the market will be from users satisfying their personal needs. Another poor method is advertising on others' websites. Not only does most anti-viruses block these (and also Spam emails), but the Internet knows no bounds when it comes to geographical locations, so unless you are part of a national retail chain, or you are offering online purchases, or some sort of mail order system, it is best to steer clear of this type of advertising. You will still need a web presence however but that will be your own web site, and not advertising on somebody else's.

NETWORK SPECIALIST COMPANY

These companies are focussed on business related clients. In general a Network Company would not even consider a personal or home-based client unless they are an important person within a business that is looked after by the IT Support Company.

As the name suggests, a **Network Specialist Company** is focused on looking after computer networks, and in this genre that are many, many different sub-categories to choose from. Often this company type will structure the size of client they can support by their internal staffing infrastructure, especially the company's Technical Department. Earlier in this chapter we briefly discussed the different types of networks in terms of size. We can add to this a different facet, and this is explained in another chapter called "Sector Analysis" (Chapter 2), but for purposes of this discussion we are going to bring some of those concepts in here.

Educational - As mentioned in Chapter 2 the **Educational Sector** uses computers for learning and not for commercial gain. Of course there will always be an Administration component of any educational institution, but these computers are generally quite minimal compared to the rest of the environment.

By this token then, educational networks are large, and are often in the excess of twenty or thirty computers per classroom (or laboratory, as they are called in some establishments). Depending on the size of the organization there might be one, two, or more of these laboratories leading to quite large networks indeed!

However, the nature and purpose of these networks is for teaching, and it is because of this that the demands of these networks are generally quite minimal. What I mean by **demands** is the type of applications stored on the workstations as well as the demands on the centralized servers. In some schools (I'm going to call them schools in this instance) there aren't even any dedicated servers, and we often find that the "server" doubles up as the teacher's computer.

So, in these types of networks we often find that the servers are mainly there to store data from the students (assignments, projects, etc) and provide a central place for printing. In some instances they are also used to provide Internet services to the students, although this tends to be abused and hence access is generally restricted.

Generally the workstations are not very powerful, and in some schools they are actually quite old and outdated, because time and again these computers are damaged or dirtied by the students. Frequently the data on the hard drives is corrupted leading to regular formatting and reinstallation. They become an administrative nightmare due to the garish attempts of learners trying to destroy the information.

It is often common to introduce these institutions to **Service Level Agreements** (covered later on in Chapter 11) because of the high level of network administration, and in some cases, semi-permanent administrators are sub-contracted to sites to assist with this high level of maintenance.

Discussing security factors in these environments, it is very important from the teacher's point of view to protect data (financial records, past, present and future examination papers, students' results) from the learners and so we frequently find two completely separate networks – that for the teachers and Administration staff, and that for the learners. The securities that need to be enforced for the students are restricted access to each other's' projects, and limited access to the Internet. What is extremely important is the presence of a secure anti-virus on each machine and on the servers.

Kaspersky Lab ® does a very good job of providing these securities and, combined with **Control Tools**, inherent in their business offerings, will prevent information from coming into the network from flash drives, CDROM and DVD disks, laptops, cellphones, and Tablet devices.

Medical -   This arena can consist of either small networks (in the case of private doctors' rooms) or large ones (in the case of hospitals and clinics). Regardless of the requirements on the servers (in the case of hospitals and clinics) the major concern here is **redundancy and quality**.

Think about it – you have a patient who is being operated on (let's say open heart surgery) and he is hooked up to a Life Support machine that is ultimately controlled by a computer, and then the machine's Operating System crashes!!! What then?

Another instance – someone in the Admitting Department is recording the personal details of an incoming motor car accident victim (their medical history, identity, etc) and the power goes down!!!

Here we concentrate on quality and redundancy. By quality I mean that the computers (servers, workstations, medical equipment) cannot be cheap at all (like the regular computers that are sold in the Retail sector). They need to be high-end systems that have guaranteed longevity. By redundancy I mean **everything** must have a backup. If one server is needed, two must be provided in a Master/Slave configuration so that if the one server fails for any reason the second server takes over until the problem has been rectified. By redundancy I also mean power backups. **Everything** must have an UPS (Uninterruptible Power Supply) provided so that if the power fails for any reason the electronic equipment continues to function until the power is restored.

That's why in every hospital there is some sort of backup power generator – to safeguard against power failures. But these generators do take a few seconds to activate and by this time most computers will cease to function.

In dealing with these environments it is important to bear these two things in mind – redundancy and quality.

Industrial and Mining - This sector is extremely specialized and IT companies looking into delving into this field need to make sure that they are well trained in **Industrial Networking**.

Industrial Networking uses equipment that is vastly different from the normal commercial cousins. For one thing, industrial environments are extremely harsh in many extremes. Firstly, the equipment needs to be able to function under massive power surges and dips (industrial mains power is not always the cleanest power available). Secondly, severe ambient temperatures affect the performance of numerous electrical equipment. Thirdly, the physical environment itself is harsh so the equipment must be able to take a couple of knocks without breaking. And finally industrial cabling is of a higher standard than normal computer cabling and it is expected by the client that computer cabling follows the same stringent standards as other cabling.

It is because of these factors that sales people operating in this sector will at first be quite horrified at the costs associated with industrial-based equipment, and the quantities involved, especially with cabling.

In industrial settings, everything is bigger. The roofs are higher, the buildings are longer, the machinery bigger, the staff more numerous, and yes, the chequebook is bigger, and industrial clients are willing to pay for the equipment as long as it works.

The most important aspect of these types of clients is "will the system work?" Factories lose hundreds of thousands of Rands (Dollars for our overseas friends) every hour they are unproductive and hence they cannot afford any sort of downtime. This is also why many industrial clients operate twenty four hours a day, and when working on site it is regarded as normal to be working in a live environment. This is also why an industrial client will take a long time before making a decision – they need to structure the implementations alongside their factory's normal operations, and they need to fully test the system before they can place their trust in it.

Technical personnel working in these conditions need to be industrially trained, and also, in some cases need to undergo physical examinations before they are allowed on site. In some cases technicians actually fail these examinations and are thus refused access to these sites, incurring extra expenses on the part of the IT Company because now qualified personnel need to be outsourced before the project can begin to be implemented.

Commercial - This is by far the most diverse sector of all and you will come across different networks of all sorts of shapes and sizes, with varying requirements from fairly simple to extremely complex applications. These could range from the simple (recruitment companies) to the extremely complicated (banks), but the major driving force behind this sector is the **need to make profit above all else.**

So why did I highlight this statement? Because so many IT companies (and sales people specifically) forget this basic premise and try to sell the client what they don't need in order to make a little more commission.

As far as Management is concerned whatever solution is implemented must be able to increase efficiency and productivity so that the business is able to increase its profits.

A commercial company is prepared to spend the necessary funds in order to have a solution as long as it meets the needs of the client and hence can be justified. Once thing to note here is frequently one of the decision makers within these types of organizations are the Financial Managers, Their primary objective is to ensure that the company is earning more than it is spending and hence a solution that is too expensive will often be rejected by the Financial Director, thus influencing an overall Managerial decision.

You will often find that many Network IT Companies focus on different areas of this sector such as SME networks (10 – 100 computers), Medium Enterprises (100 – 500 computers) and Enterprise networks (500+ computers). It is very seldom that a Network IT company who concentrates solely on Enterprise networks will adopt a client with a SME network because the company's technical infrastructure is not geared towards this kind of client – most of them are too highly specialized and hence their charges are such that the SME client cannot afford them.

Right! Now that we have looked at the different sectors in a little more detail we can concentrate on advertising methods within the Network Specialist IT Company.

Now, I'm going to ask you something and I want you to think about this. Think of yourself as a normal everyday commercial company (not necessarily IT, but anything). Ok, so you get up, get dressed and go off to work. As soon as you arrive you are immersed in work and involved in what you do. So when did you read the newspaper? Maybe just before work or during lunchtime. Did you read the entire paper or just the headlines? Maybe you skipped through to the Business Section, and then to the Sports Section. Maybe you read the paper before you went to work, when your mind was focusing on getting the kids to school, what bills needed to be paid, and what was required from you for the day. So you noticed an advertisement for computers. "Oooh," you say, rushing to find the nearest piece of paper to write the details down. "I must contact this company as soon as I get to work because they will definitely have what I need for the company I work for!"

Yeah, right!!! Throw me another banana!!!

How about this? You grab the nearest magazine on your way out and read it in the bus on the way to work. Think you will remember the advertisement you read in it when you get to the office? Maybe, but will you still remember it after your first 08h00 meeting? I think not!!!

What about this one? When did you ever watch television at the office? When did you ever remember any product being advertised when you were watching the box in the evenings?

My point is this – these forms of advertising, although seemingly quite attractive and appealing, will never work in this type of scenario. Ever!

Ok, so how about leaflets and flyers? Well, let's look at this for a second. You are in rush hour traffic; you are trying to get to work as quickly as possible, and are worried because you might be late. You stop at a traffic light, and some bloke shoves a piece of paper into your face. Are you actually going to give it more than a cursory glance? Never!

So then ask yourself – what sort of advertising will work with these types of clients? Meetings! And more meetings, and more meetings! The more face-to-face contact you have with a potential client, the more they are going to trust you and buy from you. And how do you get meetings?

Cold calling (or referrals, whichever comes first)!

This is the only way to successfully market this kind of business, and yes, it is also the cheapest.

On the technical side of things, you need a mixture of levels 1, 2, and 3 type technicians within the company. Your client base will definitely be much less than that of retail because you are no longer bulk selling for profit, but the requirements are a lot more specialized and stringent. In some cases you might even need a Level 4 Specialist, so either hire one or make sure you have one (or a few as the case may be) on hand that you can sub-contract when the need arises. And bear in mind that the cost of these specialists will ultimately affect the client's pocket, as their costs will be higher.

DISTRIBUTORS

Distributors focus on selling products to other IT companies who in turn sell them to the end user. By their very nature Distributors do not come into contact with the general public (unless it is a support issue and then it is preferably filtered through a third party IT Company).

There is a caption here that you will come across in your travels as a sales person: **Channel Sales**. This is the distributors' primary market and it basically means sales of products to various IT companies of different sizes and forms for the purpose to resell to the general public.

Channel Sales works on a different kind of sales strategy to normal IT sales in that you are working with fairly liked minded individuals who are generally as knowledgeable (if not more so) than yourself and this makes the concept of the products a little easier to put across. You will often find that in channel sales you need to be a bit more clued up in the products that you are selling (and yes, you will need a more in depth technical understanding as well) because the sales people you will be selling to are essentially in the same field you are and hence they are going to ask you some serious questions.

Many distributors will have to get involved with the importing and exporting of certain products so you will frequently find some sort of expert or team of experts within the distribution company you work for who deal with this aspect of the business on a daily basis, and this then brings me to my point here – in your quotes you will often have to deal with **Rates of Exchanges**, so make sure that you understand the concepts of converting between different currencies. In my past experiences as a Product Manager I had to deal constantly with the conversions between Rands and US Dollars, and I still, to this day, have difficulty in mentally converting the US Dollar to the South African Rand. My former resellers who operated outside of South Africa used to talk in US Dollars, and I always had to sit back for a minute and think what the equivalent was in South African Rands before I could continue my conversation with them.

Marketing is an interesting concept in the Distribution line, because you have to gearing your marketing strategies to accommodate IT companies and not the general public.

In Chapter 4 I speak about **Power of Leverage Selling**, and this becomes probably the most important type of selling you will perform in this business because you are "recruiting" the skills of other IT companies to sell your products to the end user. In my experiences the following types of marketing is highly beneficial to this type of business.

Presentations – These are covered in more detail in Chapter 12, but for the purposes of this discussion you will find that presentations are an excellent way to introduce your product range to a large audience. Again in my experiences as a Product Manager we used to host a Breakfast function whereby several potential resellers were invited to a product presentation and scored a free meal in the process. Although I was fairly educated in my product range, I always had my Technical Manager with me, because when the inevitable Question-And-Answer session used to commence after the presentation I used to get hammered with technical questions on the product range which I admittedly could not for the life of me answer. Remember your focus is on sales and not on the technical aspects of the product range you are marketing, so bear this in mind when you do host presentations: try to have some sort of technician with you to assist in answering questions of this nature.

Workshops – These form part of the training that you will need to perform in order to ensure that your resellers know enough about the products in order to sell them. I used to run two types of workshops, **Sales** and **Technical**, in which we would invite many resellers to our offices. I used to present the products in a more in-depth aspect to the audience and my Technical Manager would host a technical discussion. These workshops frequently used to span an entire day, and were an excellent opportunity for the resellers to really grasp the concepts of the ranges they would be selling.

Exhibitions and Conventions –	These are also covered in more detail in Chapter 12. Almost every type of industry runs conventions and exhibitions (also known as **Shows** and **Expos**) whereby the product ranges are presented to the general public. These become a superb way of promoting your product range (and your business) to some very prominent guests, some of whom are potential resellers, and some of whom are prospective end user clients. You will find that there is a fair expense in registering for these shows but the exposure you gain is vital to the successful selling of your range. Also included in this category are **Road Shows**, whereby you are performing a similar role but you are travelling to different sites around the country (and in some cases, the globe) promoting your product range.
Cold Calling –	Ok, this works well even in this type of business because potential resellers would really be interested in what you are selling. The big thing here is to illustrate to them how and where to find the opportunities to sell your products in their arena. If you can identify the potentials you will then become successful in convincing them to add your product range to their portfolios. I have found in the past that a combination of email broadcasting and telephoning seems to be the best strategy to use here.

Media Advertising – Right, back onto the radio, television, newspaper, and magazine advertising industry! Given the amount of hair products and cars and stuff that is advertised on the television, radio, newspapers, and magazines, you might be tempted to run a campaign of this nature. But there is something you have to remember here – not everybody wants a firewall, or a server. They do all need hair shampoo and something to drive around in, however, so you will find that these forms of advertising will be fairly weak on a return of investment. Where you will win, however, is advertising in **computer-related magazines**, because IT professionals like yourself will be interested in these magazines and hence be interested in your products. Even better, try to have a few articles published in these magazines because this allows your product (s) to be advertised in a more informative way (and sometimes is a lot cheaper).

Websites – These are as good as handing out product brochures to people because you can put all the information about your product range on your website. The only thing left to do is to steer people in the direction of your site and to do this you can use any combination of the above techniques. Yes, Internet Advertising is definitely a very good way to go here.

Technical Personnel within Distribution Companies varied depending on the types of products you are selling but in general you will need personnel that are specifically trained to deal with your products. If they are computers and laptops, those technicians will need to be trained to deal with **your** brand of computer or laptop, and not other brands. In some cases your technicians will be dealing with end users but in most cases they will be dealing with your resellers and hence they need to know their stuff, and know it well.

In some cases technicians will be requested to accompany resellers to certain clients to assist them is solving issues on site, but it is preferable to keep your technicians within your company and rather train the resellers' technicians instead because this will keep your technical base low. It is not often that your technicians are required to go out on site and those quiet periods where your technicians are inactive is simply costing the company for underutilized skills. To motivate your resellers to send their technicians on the necessary training (for a fee of course) it is recommended that the distribution company charge a high call-out rate for its technical staff. A reseller will accept this for one or two occasions, but over a long period of time the costs will add up and the reseller will realise that they will be better off in sending their technicians for the necessary training instead.

SOFTWARE DEVELOPING HOUSES

Now these guys are not your average IT Company. As the name suggests these companies concentrate solely on software development and I can tell you they do not come cheap!

There are many, many different kinds of programming languages, each serving different functions (some perform the same functions but in different ways). However, when somebody is trained to become a software developer they are usually trained in one or two programming languages; the rest of the languages are generally self-taught. What you will also find is that developers are specialized in one or two programming languages, and that's all! They might know a smattering of the other languages but they tend to choose a language that best suits their style of programming and they stick to it, and devote their entire lives learning more about their chosen language. It is for this reason that software houses normally hire people who are trained in different languages – they then are able to offer a wide variety of services to the end user.

This also brings me to my next point. Each programmer has a certain style of programming that is unique to their way of thinking and it is often fairly difficult for one programmer to pick up on another's work and continue with it in the same grain.

We all know that there are thousands of different commercial software applications on the market, and most clients are able to use these ready-made applications in their own circumstances, but there do come times whereby a proprietary application will need to be developed for a particular purpose, and based on this it must be understood that these developments are extremely expensive and time consuming.

Some very common developments are that for the Internet in the form of web pages, web sites, and applications that function over the Internet. Recently, with the technological advances of cell phones and mobile computing, much application development is being performed in this sector.

Another very common aspect of software development is in the form of databases, and has become and extremely lucrative opportunity as more and more businesses are requiring the electronic storage and easy retrieval of data.

Obviously, and this sector has been apparent from day one, Game Development is, and always will be, an incredibly demanding sector to deal with, and in most cases it is Game Development that governs the Retail Industry to provide more powerful computers to cope with the vast amounts of information and graphics that always accompany these types of applications.

Right, let's talk marketing here!!! Word of mouth, guys, and the Internet! Maybe a little magazine advertising (there are entire magazines devoted to games and applications) but mostly the Internet serves as the mainstay advertising medium for these types of companies, and referrals. I haven't seen any other form of advertising that has been successful for Software Houses (oh, and by the way, if you are wondering why they are called "houses" it is because they generally have a number of programmers who are dedicated to different languages and hence concentrate of different projects).

From a technical perspective, these guys are Level 4 Specialists, and are seldom called out to a client's site to repair damage. Most of the time the damage is repaired at the office and then the new "patch" (as it is called) is uploaded to the client's site and installed to fix any anomalies. And again I will stipulate, these Level 4 Specialists are damn expensive so end users need to make sure they do actually need the services of these guys, and are encouraged instead to find available commercial software that will do the same job.

SERVICE PROVIDERS

A Service Provider is an IT company that concentrates on selling services to clients, whether they are companies or individuals.

Two very common services providers you will come across in the IT world are **Telecommunications Providers** (cell phones, telephones, etc) and **Internet Services Providers** (also known as **ISP's**).

These companies sell bandwidth for Internet usage, and basic airtime for communications usage. Other forms of Service Providers are electricity and water, refuse removal, roads, and gas.

Any form of advertising works with these providers because they need to market their products to a wide range of people. The large Service Providers have sufficient funds to run marketing campaigns on television and over the radio, and these campaigns are often augmented by advertising in popular local magazines and newspapers. They even try using flyers and leaflets with little success or course, but these are tried anyway.

Cold Calling and Referral Marketing works to a certain extent, but Mass Media Marketing seems to be the preferred methodology. Also the Internet plays an important role.

Due the size of these companies, and the size of the customer base, we often find the existence of **Call Centres** which assist with general customer queries and sometimes technical queries. These call centres also, from time to time, deal with new customers who are entertaining the idea of purchasing their services.

Technician expertise varies within these companies and we often find all the levels of technicians operating within these companies. We also have a mixture between internal technicians and **field technicians**, whose job is to go out and visit clients who have problems with their services.

All – Purpose IT Company

The General IT Company tends to encompass most of these types of companies into their portfolios and because of this there are so many different variations that it is impossible to describe each and every scenario.

What we do find however is that many fledgling IT companies start off in this manner and as they grow and gain experience they tend to specialize into one or more of these categories. Some companies even develop different divisions to cater for different aspects of the market, and in this we can quite easily identify these types of companies as being "**XYZ Holdings**". When you come across this kind of name you will invariably find that these companies have different divisions, each with a different market focus.

Marketing and Technical vary depending on what these companies are focusing on so you will find varying sorts of campaigns and support bases.

Conclusion

Wow! There is a lot of terminology present in this chapter but it is necessary for you to know this information in order to go forward in this book and in your profession as an IT Sales Person.

You will learn later on in the book that in order to sell anything you need to know the products, and we formerly call this **Product Knowledge**. You can then deem the information in this chapter to be your introductory Product Knowledge in the realm of Information Technology and it will give you a good platform to build upon.

SUMMARY – CHAPTER 1.

Definitions

Home Users – People who use computers in their homes mainly for games, educational purposes, and the Internet, They are normally supported by Level 1 Technicians.

SOHO Business – These are companies who run from home-based offices and are normally extremely small is size (a few computers). They are normally supported by Level 1 or 2 Technicians.

SME Enterprise – These networks range from 10 computers to approximately 500 computers. Level 3 Technicians are required because of the involvement of dedicated servers.

Enterprise – Also known as Corporate. These networks are typically those above the 500 computer mark and will require Level 4 Specialist support.

Government – The Governmental networks vary in size from SME to Enterprise so any level of technician will be required depending on the network.

Parastatals – These companies are partially owned by the Government and are normally classed as Enterprise networks.

Topology

These are physical network structures. There are basically four types, namely:

Bus Topology – It consists of a cable with terminating resistors at each end and then each computer is connected in series along the cable. It cannot support more than 20 computers and is difficult to troubleshoot.

Star Topology – Possibly the most popular topology, this configuration uses a central switch or hub and each computer then is connected directly to the switch. It is fairly easy to troubleshoot.

Ring Topology – These structures are extremely reliable but expensive. It consists of a ring of cable into which each computer is connected. It is also fairly easy to troubleshoot and is normally used in **Server Clusters**.

Mesh Topology – The Internet is a good example of this configuration because each computer has more than one connection to another computer.

GEOGRAPHICAL NETWORK CONFIGURATIONS

Networks spanning over different geographical locations are given different names depending on their positions.

PAN – **Personal Area Network** which basically consists of a single computer connected with a Tablet, Smart Phone, or other mobile device.

LAN – **Local Area Network**. This term is typically given to computers connected together in an office.

MAN –   **Metropolitan Area Networks** are networks connected in a single city.

WAN –   **Wide Area Networks** connect within a country.

GAN –   **Global Area Networks** span the globe.

TECHNICAL SUPPORT LEVELS

The table below explains the different levels of technicians.

Technician Level Descriptions				
Level	Description	Company Type	Network Type	Support Services
1	Desktop Technician	Retail, Network Company, Distributor	Single Computers/ SOHO Networks	Mainly End User and Home UserSupport
2	Network Technician	Network Company, Service Provider	SME Networks	Low Level Network Support, Cabling, Some End User Support
3	Server Specialist	Network Company, Distributor	Medium & Enterprise Networks	All kinds of Servers, Network Equipment, Server Rooms
4	Software Developer	Network Company, Service Provider, Software House	Medium & Enterprise Networks	Software Applications

TYPES OF IT COMPANIES

Retail –   The **Retail IT Company** is normally located in shopping malls because they cater for the average shopper, and their main focus is on the Home User. They are normally distinguished by having elaborate shop fronts. Due to the nature of their business Level 1 Technicians are required, and maybe a Level 2 Technician might be required because they also focus on some SOHO networks.

It is very rare for a Retail Company to support Enterprise networks because these types of infrastructures are generally beyond their scope of support.

On more thing to note here is that profit is derived from bulk sales as profit margins are normally extremely low because of competition companies. Due to these extreme quantities of necessary sales Retail Companies concentrate heavily on mass marketing and advertising.

Network Specialist Company - These are companies that concentrate solely on business – related clients, and not home-based users. It is because of this fact that many such companies tend to specialize on various sectors, discussed below.

Technical Support requirements vary depending on the type of focus, but normally Technical Personnel of all levels are needed to support the myriad of networks out there in the marketplace.

Marketing and advertising is generally focused on personalization and it is uncommon for these IT companies to resort to mass marketing as a successful medium.

- **Educational** – Schools, Colleges, and Universities fall into this category, and these computers are used for teaching and not for commercial gain (although a small number of computers in the Administration Section of the institution does serve this role). Due to this these organizations house many machines, and hence financial consideration becomes extremely important when considering any sort of upgrade or change to the infrastructure.
- **Medical** – Hospitals, Clinics, and Doctor's Offices deal with people's lives on a daily basis, and it is because of this that the main focus here is on quality of product and redundancy, whereby there needs to be backup systems in place wherever possible so that there is absolutely no downtime experienced by the client.
- **Industrial and Mining** – Downtime in an Industrial client can result in considerable amounts of lost revenue, so their concentrations is on quality of

product more than anything else, and because of this these clients normally spend a great deal of time testing different products to see which will best suit their needs, not only for their present circumstances but for future development.

- **Commercial** – This is by far the largest and most diverse of the focus sectors, and will involve many different situations. However, given this fact, the main driving force behind companies categorized in this sector is the need to make profit, and hence any infrastructure that is considered must be designed in such a way as to allow the client to become more productive and efficient.

Distributors - These IT companies either import or manufacture products and then sell them to other IT companies who in turn sell them to the end user. This kind of selling is also known as **Channel Sales**. Technicians are normally highly specialized in dealing with these products.

On rare, isolated cases Distributors will work with end users, but for the most part their needs are best channelled through an appropriate IT company.

Advertising for Distributors are normally concentrated in a different way (as detailed below) to other IT companies.

- **Presentations** - Presenting the product range to functions such as reseller breakfasts are a brilliant way to promote the ranges to many prospective resellers simultaneously.
- **Workshops** - In order for resellers to properly sell and support the various product ranges **Workshops** are essential as they form much of the necessary Product Knowledge.

- **Exhibitions and Conventions** –These are superb events to showcase your product ranges, as many visitors who participate are the ideal clients for your offerings.
- **Cold Calling** – One of the major strategies your Sales Department should be employing is that of **Cold Calling**, because not much mass marketing is undertaken, and thus potential clients will not know of your company or your product's existence unless they are directly targeted.
- **Media Advertising** – About the only truly effective form of advertising for this type of company is to invest exposure in computer-related magazines, whether they are physical hard copies of on the Internet.
- **Websites** – Use websites instead of handing out product brochures and pamphlets. It save money in printing and distribution costs, and potential clients can obtain the information at any time. In addition, information can be quickly and easily updated if and when the need arises.

Software Developing Houses –	These company types concentrate purely on software development, and hence technicians that work for these companies are not network and hardware trained, and many do not focus their efforts on end user support. These people (often termed **Software Developers** or **Programmers**) normally leave end user support to other, third party IT companies. Their core focus is to develop the many commercial software packages that are on the market today.

Service Providers – These companies offer services to the end user, and a very popular example of this are **Internet Service Providers (ISP's)**. Again, diverse technicians are required because of the many different scenarios that are frequently encountered. Mass Marketing seems to be the best way to advertise the services offered. But the major criteria are firstly Internet speed and secondly price when consumers choose their service.

All – Purpose IT Company – Many IT companies start off offering anything and everything in their portfolio (much like a General Store) but as the company grows they tend to focus and become more specialized in one or more of the above categories.

CHAPTER 2.
YEAR PLAN ANALYSIS

The IT Industry often experiences an ebb and flow of revenue generation that hampers budget planning and eventual successful expansion. This is especially so in those IT Companies (ITC's) who prefer to specialise in certain categories instead of offering a broad spectrum of services.

By carefully analysing the Calendar Year, Sales Personnel can obtain a focussed strategy that will prove fruitful in generating a constant profit for the ITC.

The following analysis below refers to the diagram on the next page, and discusses the major events within various sectors.

Before we continue here, I need to point out something. In South Africa our School Year begins in January and ends in either November or, in some years, has finished early December. There are certain countries that also follow this pattern but there are also other countries who work opposite. In other words, their School Year begins in September and ends in either May or June.

For those of you who do experience this, it shouldn't be a big problem. Simply offset your Educational Sector in the diagrams by six months and it should line up for you.

In addition, seasons in the Northern Hemispheres and the Southern Hemispheres differs so the indications in the Insurance Sectors also need to be adjusted to suit those climates.

Year Plan - Sales Strategies

Sector	January	February	March	April	May	June	July	August	September	October	November	December
Commercial/ Corporate	Year End Upgrade	Tax Year End - New Budget Quotes	July Upgrade - Initial Quote	July Upgrade - Initial Quote	July Upgrade - Final Quote	July Upgrade - Final Quote	July Upgrade	Year End Upgrade - Initial Quote	Year End Upgrade - Initial Quote	Year End Upgrade - Final Quote	Year End Upgrade - Final Quote	Year End Upgrade
Education	Year End Upgrade	Service Level Agreements - Initial Contracts	July Upgrade - Initial Quote	Service Level Agreements Final Contracts	July Upgrade - Final Quote	Examinations - On-Site Engineers	July Upgrade	Year End Upgrade - Initial Quote	Service Level Agreements - Contact Analysis	Year End Upgrade - Final Quote	Examinations - On-Site Engineers	Year End Upgrade
Industrial/ Mining	Factory Shutdown - Upgrade	July Upgrade - Initial Tenders	Marketing to Industrial Sector	Marketing to Industrial Sector	July Upgrade - Final Tenders	Shutdown Upgrade - Initial Tenders	July Upgrade	Marketing to Industrial Sector	Marketing to Industrial Sector	Shutdown Upgrade - Final Tenders	Shutdown Upgrade - Final Tenders	Factory Shutdown - Upgrade
Insurance						Initial Marketing To Insurance	Marketing To Insurance Sector	Marketing To Insurance Sector	Insurance Claims Due To Electrical Storms	Insurance Claims Due To Electrical Storms	Insurance Claims Due To Electrical Storms	
Retail/ Domestic	Christmas specials - Returns/ Refunds	Easter Specials - Marketing	Easter Specials - Sales							Christmas Specials - Initial Marketing	Christmas specials - Marketing	Christmas specials - sales

COMMERCIAL/ CORPORATE

This sector is probably the largest in terms of actual clients, and is the main focus of most Support Companies. A close analysis of the financial year for these companies will allow for perpetual revenue generation.

The financial year begins at the end of February when the new tax year starts. In this month many companies develop requests for quotations for new systems and various upgrades. Although these quotations rarely lead to actual short-term sales they are important in establishing the allocated budget for the new tax year. Given this vital information the ITC is able to calculate potential revenue generation for the client throughout the year, and thus long-term financial planning on the part of the ITC is made available.

Within this sector two major projects can be developed and implemented. The first project, which for the most part is fairly minor compared to the second project, is normally implemented in the month of July. This month coincides with the all-important school holidays, in which many executives and other personnel partake in formal vacations to spend time with their respective children. Owing to this fact many companies within the Corporate Sector rely on skeleton staff to maintain the businesses, and thus overall productivity generally decreases. This in turn gives ITC's the opportunity to perform various IT restructuring within the clients' premises. Initial business relationships between clients and ITC's normally occur throughout the months of March and April, with introductory quotations, proposals, and project plans developed thereafter. During the months of May and June these proposals are then finalised, ordered, and relevant work schedules are drafted for the imminent upgrades.

The second project, which is by far the greater of the two, occurs during the month of December, and normally ends throughout the beginning of January in the following year. The beginning of December concludes the Educational Calendar

Year and the start of the Christmas vacation period. During this time nearly the entire Commercial Sector closes for business and involved personnel embark on formal leave. Major restructuring of the entire network infrastructure within the client's premises is a result of this period, and participating ITC's generally find this their busiest period. Another factor to bear in mind is that directly after this period is the end of the financial year, and thus outstanding budgets need to be justified. Most of these budgets are realised during this restructuring.

Again, initial quotations and proposals are generated during the months of August and September, and finalised during the months of October and November.

EDUCATION

The Educational Sector is by far the greatest influence on the productivity of all other sectors, as most working parents spend valuable time away from work with their respective children whilst the Educational Sector closes for various vacations.

As with the Commercial Sector, two major projects are developed, one during the month of July and the other during the month of December.

A few major differences occur between the Educational Sector and the Commercial Sector. Firstly, the Educational Sector's financial year generally starts at the beginning of October and thus initial marketing should occur during the months of August and September.

A second major difference is the actual nature of the client. Unlike the Commercial Sector, who uses the IT infrastructure for productivity, the Educational Sector uses it for learning. This often results in an extremely high level of maintenance and administration. It is because of this that many Educational Institutions prefer to enter into **Service Level Agreements (SLA's)** with the ITC's to ensure that regular support is given. Service Level Agreements are discussed in more detail in Chapter 11.

Lastly, possibly the Educational Sector's busiest periods of activity occur in the months of June and November when students are performing examinations. It is here that the Institutions will require the most support for the ITC. Often requests for permanent on-site engineers during these times occur, and thus most SLA's include these types of services.

INDUSTRIAL/ MINING

The Industrial, Mining, and Manufacturing Industry seems to mirror the Commercial Sector in terms of activity. There is however a major difference with respect to how they operate in terms of equipment and services procurement. The Commercial Sector seems to prefer the quotation and proposal format when considering bidding ITC's to secure contracts. The Industrial and Mining Sectors often rely heavily of the format of the **Public Tender**, and this is due to the sheer extent of the projects involved and the vast budgets that are affected.

It is this one factor that often deters smaller ITC's from participating in responding to the Tenders merely due to the fact that they do not have the necessary resources to support these imminent projects.

A popular school of thought that has emerged lately, and is proving successful in these ventures, is the combining of two or more ITC's to share the Scope of Work detailed in the tenders, and hence sharing the profits between the participating companies becomes feasible.

It must be understood that the establishment of a relationship in these sectors is a long term investment, because trust becomes an extremely important part of these negotiations. To these sectors, quality of the products offered is the principal importance, as downtime in the factories can lead to millions of lost income. Given this then, it is not often that these industries contemplate changing their infrastructures, because they frequently spend a lot of time testing various products in the marketplace until they find those that will suite their needs implicitly. Once these solutions have been implemented they will be loath to change as the downtime will affect their productivity and hence affect their profits.

During the Christmas period almost this entire sector ceases production from the 15th December until 15th January the following year, and it is during this period that any major restructuring is scheduled. ITC's therefore who wish to participate must be prepared for this time period.

INSURANCE

Although the Insurance Sector forms part of the Commercial Industry, it does have an interesting period in which increased activity is evident, and thus is highlighted in the Year Plan. In South Africa we experience our spring months from September until November. It is during this period that we experience major rainfall patterns throughout the country. These increased rainfall activities cause many electrical disturbances from lightning, which in turn often damages IT-related equipment.

If successful marketing is performed to the Insurance sector in the months preceding this event, then the **Loss Adjusters**, who are the companies that assess the damage first hand, will be familiar with your company, and hence will approach you for assistance in replacing or repairing affected equipment.

Interestingly enough, in this country we also experience heightened activities in the Insurance Sector during the Christmas Season for the simple reason that we have increased levels of criminal activity at this time.

Given that many people go away on holiday because of school holidays, and given that many poor people look at ways of increasing their cash reserves for Christmas, several thefts are reported as soon as the owners returns from holiday. Normally these reports start filtering through from the Insurance Companies in January and early February.

I have not indicated this on the Year Plan, but it is something that you should bear in mind.

RETAIL/ DOMESTIC

The Retail Sector normally structure their increased revenue periods to coincide with the school holidays, and we find that shoppers are most active during the periods of Easter and especially Christmas, when most workers receive their annual Holiday Bonus. Thus the Retail Sector plans certain specials that are offered at these times.

It is worth noting that the revenue increase does continue in January as many people return unwanted gifts or are willing to spend any money that has been given as Christmas gifts.

YEAR PLAN SUMMARY

The Summary illustrates the different areas of focus and refers to the diagram shown on page 61. Some of the terms here are discussed in separate chapters in this book.

Primary Marketing – This focus should be on canvassing for new clients, and establishing initial contact with them. Such practices such as physical canvassing, cold calling, referrals, and advertising should be applied during this phase. The client's initial needs are normally identified at this stage, and you should be qualifying the client to establish whether you can assist them or not.

Secondary Marketing – Once the initial contact has been made, further secondary marketing, whereby the respective clients are visited and on-site examinations are performed, should commence at this stage. You also need to establish whether their current financial budget can support any sort of project.

Initial Proposals –

Here the first draft of proposals are created. Also included in this category are initial contracts. These first proposals should be sent out to the clients and fully discussed so that, if there are any changes to be made, they can be identified and noted.

Final Proposals –

Proposals are finalised and agreed upon, and from which project plans are drafted and confirmed. It is at this stage where you should receive your orders and these also need to be consolidated and administered properly.

Primary Sales –

The bulk of the revenue generation for the IT Company is performed here as all projects are implemented. In this stage payments should be made or arrangements of how the clients will be paying for the work performed.

Year Plan - Sale Strategies - Summary

Focus	January	February	March	April	May	June	July	August	September	October	November	December
Primary Marketing		Commercial/ Educational/ Industrial/ Retail	Industrial	Industrial		Insurance		Commercial/ Educational/ Industrial	Educational/ Industrial	Retail		
Secondary Marketing		Retail	Commercial/ Educational/ Industrial	Industrial			Insurance	Insurance	Educational/ Industrial		Retail	
Initial Proposals		Commercial/ Educational/ Industrial	Commercial/ Educational	Commercial		Industrial		Commercial/ Educational	Commercial			
Final Proposals				Educational	Commercial/ Educational/ Industrial	Commercial				Commercial/ Educational/ Industrial	Commercial/ Industrial	
Primary Sales	Commercial/ Educational/ Industrial/ Retail		Retail				Commercial/ Educational/ Industrial		Insurance	Insurance	Insurance	Commercial/ Educational/ Industrial/ Retail

Conclusion

In order to achieve constant revenue throughout the year a careful analysis of this chapter should be performed and should be closely followed. But this analysis is a guideline only and should not be adopted as a hard fast rule. You will find that overlaps do occur and certain companies will not follow this Year Plan strictly speaking.

Summary – Chapter 2.

This chapter analyses different business sectors and allows the IT Company to focus of different areas in differing periods throughout the year. These sectors are:

Commercial/ Corporate – July, December and January are the months that this sector concentrates on major restructuring of their IT infrastructure, thus marketing and quotes should be performed at least three to four months beforehand so that these companies can budget for these projects.

Education – The School Holidays occur in July, December and January and any major restructuring projects are performed during these periods. Marketing and quotations should occur three to four months before these proposed events.

Industrial/ Mining – The major factory shutdown period is December to January whilst a smaller slowdown in activity occurs in July to coincide with the School Holidays. Impending projects are planned at least four to six months in advance to these periods.

Insurance –   Spring months are from September to November, whilst increased criminal activity occurs during Christmas. It is at these times that owners' computers are often damaged or stolen, so, if your company is affiliated with various Insurance Companies, revenue generation will occur during these periods.

Retail/ Domestic –   Easter, and especially Christmas are the times when shoppers often go in search of gifts, and so specials offered during these periods will show a marked increase in revenue generation.

Marketing in the different sectors should be concentrated on in different months of the year, namely:

January –   **Primary Sales** are concentrated on in the Commercial, Industrial, Educational, and Retail Sectors.

February –   **Primary Marketing** is performed in the Commercial, Industrial, Educational, and Retail Sectors. **Secondary Marketing** should be focussed in the Retail sector. **Initial Proposals** are normally prepared and delivered to the Commercial, Industrial, and Educational sectors during this month.

March –   The Industrial Sector should experience some **Primary Marketing** in this month, whilst the focus on **Secondary Marketing** should be concentrated on the Commercial, Industrial, and Educational sectors. **Initial Proposals** should be prepared and delivered to the Commercial and Educational sectors at this time.

April – The Industrial Sector should experience **Primary** and **Secondary Marketing**. **Initials Proposals** are sent to the Commercial sector, and the Educational Sector should receive **Final Proposals**.

May – This is the month that **Final Proposals** are delivered to the Commercial, Educational, and Industrial Sectors.

June – The Insurance Sector should experience your **Primary Marketing**, whilst the Industrial Sector will start receiving **Initial Proposals** for their December Shutdown. **Final Proposals** are delivered to the Commercial Sector for their December Shutdown.

July – The Insurance Sector will receive some **Secondary Marketing.** The Commercial, Industrial, and Educational Sectors are generating some **Primary Sales** due to their mid-year restructuring.

August – **Secondary Marketing** continues in the Insurance Sector, and **Primary Marketing** begins again in the Commercial, Educational, and Industrial Sectors. Also, **Initial Proposals** are delivered to the Commercial and Educational Sectors.

September – **Primary Marketing** continues in the Educational and Industrial Sectors, and **Secondary Marketing** begins in these same areas. **Initial Proposals**

continue their deliverance to the Commercial Sector. As the first spring rains occur, **Primary Sales** are experienced in the Insurance Sector.

October –   **Primary Marketing** begins in the Retail Sector in preparation for the December Specials. **Final Proposals** should be delivered to the Commercial, Educational, and Industrial Sectors in preparation for the December Shutdown. **Primary Sales** continue in the Insurance Sector due to the spring rains.

November –   The Retail Sector should now be concentrating on its **Secondary Marketing** phase in preparation for the December Specials. The **Final Proposals** will continue in this month for the Commercial and Industrial Sectors. Owing to End of Year Examinations, the Educational Sector cannot concentrate on any form of marketing. **Primary Sales** still continue in the Insurance Sector due to the spring rains.

December –   This month is all about **Primary Sales**. The Commercial, Educational, and Industrial Sectors are now concentrating on their infrastructure upgrades. The Insurance Sector becomes quiet as we are now experiencing summer and most of the rains have subsided. The Retail Sector is now concentrating on their December Specials.

CHAPTER 3.
SALES STRATEGIES

You can never hope to succeed in sales unless you have some sort of strategy as to how you are going to target the market out there.

So many sales people start off their careers with a concept of "let's throw a whole bunch of stones at someone and hope that one of them will connect!"

Take a look at history. A well organized, disciplined army faces the battle in formation. The army's soldiers march in straight lines and fight in unison. These armies frequently were the ones that won the battles (although not always) but a rabble who fights in a bunch without any organization whatsoever normally is the one that loses.

You need to be well organized and disciplined in your approach. You need to develop a strategy and then test it out. If it works after a few tries then it is a good strategy. If not, then you need to alter the concepts and retest.

As an example I have given you three strategies in this chapter to look at for inspiration to develop your own. Obviously you can use these strategies at will, but what I am showing you here is an example of how to build your own.

In developing your own, you need to firstly decide on a type of market you want to pursue. Then you need to study that market to discover what will be important to them, and how you can benefit their business.

These strategies are not the easiest to create, and the only way you will know if it works or not is to test it out. Develop one and then try it out for a week of two. Speak to some people about it and see what they think. As I said before, if it is working that you have a good strategy. If not, then you need to accept that there is something wrong with it and alter it accordingly. If necessary, ask others their opinion, especially if you use a strategy on a potential client and the turn you down. Ask them what reason they have for not going with your strategy. Their answers will give you a good insight as to where the problems in your plan lie.

But ultimately the bottom line is: you need to do the research in order to design a plan that will be beneficial for all. Take a look at these three strategies and then see if you can come up with some of your own.

SCHOOLS

I have always maintained that schools are an excellent form of income for any IT company although many people have said that this is indeed not the case. There are a number of reasons for this. Firstly, schools are fairly cash strapped because they rely on the school fees of the student (or from their parents, to be more accurate). The law states that a child cannot be denied an education even if their parents cannot afford to pay the school fees. So this leaves a school in a quandary – they need the fees in order to maintain the running of the institution.

One of the most expensive budgets for any school is the provision for Information Technology within the institution, and there is often a compromise in supplying the students with state-of-the-art technology.

Also, many schools are reluctant to provide new technology because (and this is unfortunate) the lack of respect on the part of the students with regards to new equipment – students tend to either break the new equipment or dirty it and we find that within an academic year at least half of the new equipment installed needs to be replaced from damage.

Right, so, given these factors many IT companies baulk at the prospect of servicing schools because admittedly there is generally little profit gained. Many schools will haggle for the cheapest equipment and solutions on the market, even though these might not be the best quality devices. Labour charges have to be compromised in order to install the solutions for the cheapest possible price. So then you have to ask yourself – where is there profit to be made in these ventures?

Ok, let's look at this closely for a minute. The average school has approximately 500 to 600 students (most often it is more, but let's be modest and work with these figures). Now each student has parents (obviously). These parents must have jobs, either working for a company or managing their own. Right?

So if we implement a solution or product or range of products into a school we can then motivate the students to advertise our products and/or services to their parents. This in turn will mean that the parents will introduce our offerings to the companies they work for. If the companies are interested they will then come back to you for similar solutions. This means that you will receive referrals back from the school. Makes sense?

I'm going to use an easy example to illustrate this. An easy sale is to provide a good anti-virus product and I mean a good product!!! In one section I discuss briefly network security, and in today's society security is of paramount importance.

Anti-virus is a fairly quick and easy sale, and basically **everyone** needs it, whether they have computers at home or the office, laptops, or even Smart Phones and Tablet devices. As long as the device is exposed to the Internet, it is vulnerable to all sorts of malicious attacks. This makes the sale an easy one.

Right, so what we do now is to offer a special to all the students of the school. You've just implemented a solution to the school and they are extremely happy with the results so now what you would like to do is to be able to market to the students.

Some schools are quite willing to assist you in furthering your company, but some schools might want a piece of the action. In this case you could then offer the school a percentage of the profits, or free technical support, or whatever. As long as the school feels they are gaining something they will be more than happy to allow this sort of thing to happen.

Alright, so you have the permission from the school to go ahead with the project, so what now?

The easiest way here is to create a voucher or coupon that can be handed out to the students. The first thing here is to offer a discount to the students for their personal computers and/ or mobile devices if they come to you with their voucher. The second special you can offer is for their parents' companies (or workplaces); that is, when a company approaches you with one of your vouchers you honour their discount.

These company discounts can be anything from a range of products to a complete network overhaul, provided you stipulate that the special offer only applies to those products and/or services that are offered at normal prices. It would be suicide to your company if a prospective client uses their voucher to purchase goods from you that are already on special.

Another thing to note here – please, please make sure that some sort of expiry date appears on the voucher, otherwise they could be returning vouchers to you a year or two down the line and then you do not have the stock on offer anymore! In addition, placing a time limit on the vouchers lends a sense of urgency so the sales will come in quicker.

As it stands you probably will receive approximately a 10% return on your vouchers. That's about fifty odd sales that you have gained. And remember, that client will probably come back to you for more purchases at a later stage.

Now here's a curveball on this idea. Some students will disregard your voucher, either because they don't have a computer at home, they already have what you've got to offer, or they just don't have the money to purchase anything. Some students even just throw the voucher away.

So how do we get those vouchers in? By offering something the students want! The "in" thing today for teenagers is MP3 players. They are hot and happening and they are all the rage. So how about offering a "lucky dip draw" when they hand their vouchers in at your company? This should bring the vouchers in. We need to make sure that we receive their contact details so include some of these details on the voucher. And then, and this is the tricky one, you need to get hold of their parents. Asking for the parents' details is not always the easiest thing in the world to do, because some students will not bother to fill this information in on their vouchers. Some students can't even remember where their parents work!

So how do we do this? Again,

"Lucky Dip Draw!"

You already have some sort of contact details for the student (most often it will be a cellphone) so all you need to do is call them up and mention that they unfortunately did not win, and then ask how your special offer can benefit them. What do they need or want? In any case, once you have drawn them into the conversation ask them how you can get in touch with their parents. They should give you some sort of contact details, and then you have won your way through to your ultimate goal!

A couple of things to note here. In most schools of today students are not allowed to carry their cellphones, or their instruments must be switched off whilst they are school. This then forces you to only contact them in the afternoons when they have arrived home from school.

Also, in some cases the students might only give you their home telephone number, in which case you are then forced to either phone in the evening or on a weekend. Remember though, this only happens some of the time. In this case you need to remember that nobody wants to be bothered with business-related issues after work, or on weekends, so your conversation needs to be a brief as possible. You could perhaps say something like:

> *"Dear Sir/Madam, this is X from Y Computer Company. I'm terribly sorry to worry you at this time but there is something business-related that I would like to discuss with you, and I would rather not discuss it now. Would you mind giving me your work telephone number and I will call you back during office hours to chat about this?"*

Sometimes the prospect will be more than willing to hand out some contact details to you. At other times they will request more information in which case you can begin your sales pitch to them. Either way you will (in most cases) gained some valuable sales leads from your voucher.

Increasing Technician's Productivity

Generally speaking 99% of technicians (engineers for some people) are on fixed monthly salaries. This means that if there is no work coming in to the company their expertise is wasted – they sit around in the office waiting for work to come to them. The Technical Department has to rely on the Sales Department to generate incoming work for them to do. If the Sales Department is lacking in their ability to perform this task, then this is an exorbitant waste of the company's money.

So how do we get around this? How do we inspire the Technical Department so that they are working all the time?

I was working at a company as a Business Development Manager and Management came up with an idea on this topic. It was fledgling at the time and we worked together and came up with a solution that actually worked extremely well, and because of this the company as a whole grew quite dramatically in a short space of time. As far as I know they are still employing the concept to this day.

So how does this work?

Well, basically a Sales Person sells products and/or services to clients whilst a Technician sells their time and expertise in installing, configuring, maintaining, and repairing existing solutions.

Knowing this fact we then need to come up with a concept that allows a Technician to increase their salary in such a way that they become motivated. And this is what we did.

We negotiated with the technicians so that, for every hour they spent on site, they receive 50% of the labour charge. This was over and above their normal base salary. Thus is a technician spent two hours a week on site resolving issues, they were paid for ten hours of labour. We encouraged technicians, when they were in the office, to use the telephone to contact the company's former clients requesting work from them. The result – we never saw our technicians. They used to come into the office in the mornings, hit the 'phones for an hour, and then they were gone for the entire day.

We also noticed a marked improvement in completed Technical Job Cards (all the information filled in, and signed correctly) because the technician could not claim their bonus pay without completed job cards. We also noticed a marked improvement on settled accounts with respect to labour, because the technicians would not receive their bonuses until the client had paid for the work performed.

We had one such technician who had just started with the company and we introduced this scheme to him. In his first month he was cracking over one hundred hours of labour, and this became consistent each and every month thereafter; each month he would constantly perform over one hundred hours of labour a month. And this gentleman was ruthless: he **never** left the client's site until his job card was signed, and when he went back for payment, he would sit in Reception the entire day if necessary until he either had a copy of an Electronic Bank Transfer or a cheque (*check* for our USA readers).

We then went one step further with this. In another section we will discuss Service Level Agreements, but basically, by way of explanation for this discussion, a **Service Level Agreement** (abbreviated **SLA**) is a monthly retainer a client pays to an IT company for their services on demand. An SLA client always has a first preference when it comes to scheduling technicians versus non-contracted clients, but we found a few problems when assigning technicians because one particular technician generally familiarizes themselves with a particular site, and hence when one of these clients sent in a request it was preferable to assign the same technician. But this method didn't always work and sometimes we found ourselves having to send out alternative technicians to these sites.

So what we did in this case was to assign a technician to a particular site, and in return they received 10% of the monthly retainer as part of their monthly salary for the duration of the contract. This in effect meant that now a technician was able to increase their basic salary, and also meant that they would ensure that the client renewed their contract.

In the case where an alternative technician had to take care of a site on behalf of the assigned technician, these salary amounts were calculated and transferred to the alternative technician's salary. This then meant that the originally assigned technician ensured that they were always available for their client so that they did not lose out on their salaries.

We had to go further with this concept because we discovered loopholes in the structure we had put in place.

The Sales Department became complacent because they maintained that they were not receiving any benefits by negotiating work for the technicians and so we noticed a marked reduction of labour charges being quoted from the Sales Department.

So we added a clause to this structure.

The technicians were receiving a 50% bonus for every hour of work they performed on site. In order to include the Sales Department In this scheme we said that if the labour was as a direct result of what the Sales Department quoted then they received a 5% bonus from the Technician's portion of the payment. This in effect meant that the Sales Department received 5% and the technician received 45%.

One last note on bonuses here! In order to further increase the technicians' productivity, you could award bonuses for hours worked. In other words, an average working day consists of eight hours (plus one hour for lunch). Assuming a technician works on site six hours daily, they can quite easily rack up at least a hundred hours a month (six hours daily multiplied by five days a week multiplied by four weeks in a month equal one hundred and twenty hours). You could then assign a bonus for reaching the one hundred hour threshold, another for reaching the one hundred and twenty hour threshold, and yet another for exceeding the one hundred and twenty hour threshold (and with this the technician will be working through lunch). Just make sure you have an agreement signed with the technician so that you don't violate any labour laws.

BULK SALES PERSONNEL

Sales Personnel are one of the major backbones of any business because they determine how much new business comes into a company. Without the Sales People no company can exist for very long, but the whole process of hiring these people are time consuming and costly, not to mention the fact the top, really experienced Sales people are often extremely expensive to employ.

This does not mean however that you should not embark on this process at all! On the contrary, employing a really experienced sales person is a definite asset to any company! This strategy is designed for those times when you need sales personnel quickly and are cost effective to ensure that the company receives some incoming revenue.

So here we go on this one!

Contained within the offerings of most IT companies are products which are fairly easy to sell. One of these product ranges is anti-virus as we have mentioned above, so we will use this as an example.

Most graduates from Computer Colleges struggle to find employment due to the fact that they are "green" (i.e. lacking in any, or very little, work experience) and companies are reluctant to hire these people.

So what you do here is to visit these campuses and become friendly with the lecturers. Once you have established a relationship with them request a list of their current graduates. Once you have this list you then have a source of potential sales people.

Now remember, these graduates are fresh out of college so the majority of them have little or no work experience and they are looking for practical work knowledge that they can enter onto their Curriculum Vitae so that they become more employable.

It would be short-sighted on your part to offer the graduates fixed base salaries. After all, they are untried people in the job market with little or no experience to give you an indication as to their performance. Some of them might be better suited towards technical performance, whilst others are wonderful sales people. Some even are not even performers at all, and only studied the course because they needed some sort of tertiary qualification. These people unfortunately will never become proficient in the IT industry; their interests lie elsewhere. You cannot determine the strengths and weaknesses of your prospective graduates until you have tested them in the work environment.

Knowing this you **must** employ at least ten people because general statistics say that for every ten people you should find at least one diamond in the rough. The others start losing interest and they generally do not perform.

So what do we do here?

Offer them a generous commission on any sales they achieve for the company. Perhaps you could go as far as to give them a small cellphone and petrol allowance, and allow them to use the office telephones in order to give them a chance to secure some sales. However, you need to give your graduates some direction as most of them have no idea how to sell or how to focus on sales. This is where the anti-virus products I mentioned earlier come in.

I have discussed this in another chapter but you are reading this chapter first (obviously – you are reading through this book), I am mentioning it again here. If you use anti-virus products as a vehicle for your prospective graduates, you need to educate them a little, so this short explanation will help you.

Everybody in today's society needs some sort of anti-virus protection on their computers, whether they are home computers, work computers, servers, laptops, or Mobile Devices (Smart Phones and Tablets). The amount of White Collar Crime has dramatically increased in the last decade and is becoming increasingly prevalent as we migrate further into this Information Age.

To define White Collar Crime, Edwin Sutherland (in 1949) described this as:

"A crime committed by a person of respectability and high social status in the course of his occupation."

So what this means is the stereotypical criminal, complete with a balaclava and a weapon, bursting into banks and warehouses and loading up goods and cash into a getaway car, is now fading into the background. These new criminals are respected business people, accountants, computer experts, Directors, and so forth, and are discovering ways of stealing money from companies with the use of computers. There is an entire chapter devoted to this (take a look at Chapter 15), but this short explanation should do for now.

There are 2 families of products: those for single computers and Mobile Devices (also called Personal Security Products) and those for networks (also called Corporate Security Products). You could start your new employees on the Personal Security Products and, once they have become quite proficient with these, start migrating them onto the Corporate Security Products.

In addition, and this is what you are going to have to teach them, there are always opportunities with each prospective sale.

While they are selling their anti-virus to a potential client, get your employees to question the prospect on what type of computer they own, what it is used for, etc. Also, does the prospect have children and do they use the computer for schoolwork, etc. By doing this your sales person is now investigating ways of selling other products, from upgrading the computers, to new printers, replacement cartridges, new and improved Internet contracts, to games (including joysticks). A good sales person will always find an opportunity to sell something even if the prospect is not interested in the product(s) you are offering in your primary sales pitch.

There is a definite no-no here! I was, at one stage, involved as an Operations Manager for a company who sold advertising spaces in a Business Directory. The Owner's ex-wife was also involved in the company performing freelance sales. She decided to employ a young gentleman to assist her, and he would gain some commission for each successful sale.

Ok, so this lady was worried that he was not performing well, and asked me to spy on his sales abilities. I tailed him the one day, and he was basically selling the advertising spaces to people he met on the street, and when they declined the opportunity, he then started presenting them with cellphone covers, plastic jewellery, and other paraphernalia that the prospect obviously didn't want. Needless to say he was fired on the spot! Have you worked out why?

Never, ever, cross sell! Never try to sell somebody a product and service and then switch to a completely unrelated product range unless the prospect has indicated an interest in that area. In addition, even if your product ranges are all related to computers, never sell more than one set of products unless they are related to each other.

Let me give you an example here.

You approach a prospect with anti-virus and he says that his computer at work has already got a solution. After a bit of questioning you discover that their network security is not of the highest standard, so then this gives you a perfect opportunity to sell network security-related products. This does **not** however give you an opportunity to re-cable his entire company, not until you have at least performed a decent site inspection (covered in another chapter). Keep the products related!

Right, back to our discussion on your graduates. Being enterprising youths there are many ways in which to sell the anti-virus products. They could (after obtaining permission or course) setup a table at a local shopping mall on a Saturday and offer discount for all purchases done on that day or even approach people whilst they are having their cars washed. Anything to make it fun! Obviously you will need to provide them with marketing materials, some products, and some contact forms whereby they can capture the prospect's details for later sales.

In the case where your employees gain a prospective client who requires solutions at their workplace, and you obviously feel that the sale might be beyond their skills at this early stage, make sure you are available to go with your young sales person and assist them in closing the sale. Of course they will receive their commission, but this helps them in observing experienced sales people in operation, and will bolster their confidence.

Once you have worked with your graduates for approximately three months, and have established your star performers, you can then decide to offer them a base salary with commission.

CONCLUSION

These are a few of the myriad of different sales strategies there are out there, and if you develop a good strategy based around a type of industry then you will assuredly become quite successful.

Some strategies, if developed and implemented properly, can result in a good few months' worth of work before the plan has exhausted itself.

Apply these examples by all means, but try to develop your own based upon your own experiences and your target market.

SUMMARY – CHAPTER 3.

You will never be successful unless you start to develop strategies in order to target certain markets.

The best way to start is to sit and analyse a market of your choice to see what is important to them, and then concentrate on delivering products and services to augment their primary focus.

The three examples given in this chapter are:

Schools - Schools have a good number of students, each of which has parents who work somewhere. Furthermore, most of these students have computers at home. Structure sales based on those students with certain discounts to entice the students to purchase. Also, offer come sort of discount system so that the students' parents' will approach you for support for their computer networks at their workplace.

Technicians' Productivity – Most technicians work on fixed salaries which can affect their overall motivation. By offering them a percentage on the hours they work, they will feel that the harder they work, the more money they can earn. In addition, give the technicians percentages on Service Level Agreements provided they look after those sites. This will effectively increase their base salaries.

Bulk Sales Personnel – Hiring many Sales Personnel can affect a business financially so instead try to approach college graduates who are willing to work on a commission-only basis. In this way you can increase your sales without having to worry about paying salaries, because their payment will be directly based upon their sales performance.

CHAPTER 4.
TYPES OF SELLING AND FORMS
OF ADVERTISING

There are many different ways of selling your products and services to clients but the main point to always remember here is: **nobody will ever purchase anything from you if they don't know you, and who you represent!** This might seem an obvious statement but it is surprising how many sales people seem to forget this so easily.

Looking at other sales books written by far better people than myself, I come across this similar statement in every single one, and so I need to make the same observation here as well.

> *A client will not buy from you if he doesn't trust you.*

New, inexperienced sales people are so often discouraged when they contact new companies in the hopes of being able to do business with them, because of the amount of rejection they receive. After a few days of this these new budding talents often just give up hope and tell themselves that this profession is just not for them. Of course, one must remember that in any profession sales is perhaps one of the hardest to perform, but it is also the most rewarding when you get the formula right and the sales start flowing in.

It's amazing at the incredibly high levels of staff turnover in companies who undertake Telesales as one of their marketing strategies, because these sales people contact literally hundreds and thousands of prospects in the hopes of obtaining a few sales. Most often, and this comes from personal experience, the operator on the other end of the phone line is so bombastic and forceful in their speech, not to mention extremely fast or intelligible in their sales pitch, that you, as the prospect, lose at least half of what they are saying and you end up either giving in to them, telling them just to leave you alone, or putting the 'phone down, just to get rid of them. Quite simply, in my personal opinion, it is probably the worst way of selling, and I find no confidence instilled in me at all when I am contacted by these types of sales people. Others might think differently, I'm not sure, but this is my personal opinion.

Going back to this statement then, we need to be able to have the client trust us before they will buy from us and in an initial telephone call to them, for example, the trick here is to schedule a meeting with them so that they can see who you are and who you represent. It is a known fact that people tend to form an opinion of another person within the first thirty seconds of them meeting each other, and based on that their initial decision whether to trust you or not will be derived from that initial contact.

In other sections throughout this book we go into this a little more, but it is enough for now to say that in order to be able to create any substantial business with a client we must ensure that they are both familiar with you and with the company you represent.

In this chapter we look at the different forms of selling, and different types of advertising, in order to achieve this goal. We will look at the merits and demerits of each type, and where they are best suited.

PROSPECTING FOR NEW CLIENTS

This subject is otherwise known as **Cold Calling**, and is basically the process whereby you contact potential clients literally out of the blue. They have never met you before, they probably don't know about your company, or they are currently using another Support Company, and you need to convince them to change over instead to your Support Company.

This is quite an important section, and because of this I have dedicated the entire of the next chapter to this art form. I therefore suggest you complete this chapter and then go on to the next chapter to learn about Cold Calling, or Prospecting for New Clients.

POWER OF LEVERAGE SELLING

Word of Mouth Advertising is still the most cost effective and popular form of selling in any market, because it primarily uses the power of the human's emotions and the basic need to communicate with others as its vehicle. Think about this for a second. You have just experienced a movie that has just been released on circuit, and you personally thought it was excellent. What's the first thing you want to do after leaving the movie theatre? You want to tell a friend about your experiences. You probably want to tell more than one person and then you almost certainly want them to experience the same movie for themselves so that they can compare their experiences with yours. This is natural human behaviour, and the movie industry has been using this type of advertising ever since its inception in the early 1900's.

Many companies have brought this concept into other industries and have exploited this natural human trait to generate revenue.

How?

A company has a product or service to sell. Right! They have various choices of marketing but they decide on Word of Mouth Advertising to sell the product for them. By selling their product to a person (or people), and then offering to pay that person a portion of the proceeds to sell the product to another person, the company has in effect created what is commonly known in today's industry as **Network Marketing**. Now I must make a differentiation here for clarification. There is another, similar mechanism called **Pyramid Schemes** whereby very similar marketing concepts are used. The major difference here is there is usually somebody (or some bodies) at the head of these schemes that ultimately financially benefit quite substantially from the efforts of others, and normally the main product involved is money itself without an actual product or service being involved.

Such Pyramid Schemes are for the most part illegal and one should avoid them wherever possible. As long as there are products and/or services involved, and the concepts are ethical with respect to business practices, then there should be no reason why you should not employ a similar scheme in your sales strategy.

In another section we deal with the concept of the **Distributor**, and for the purposes of this discussion I'm going to borrow the concept as an example to illustrate this selling strategy in action.

A Distributor purchases or manufactures products and distributes them to other companies (called **Retailers** for this conversation) to sell to the general public.

Let's assume you work at the level of the distributor. Your job then is to enlist the services of, not the general public, but the Retailer, who will sell them to the general public (also known in IT circles as **End Users**). Now think about this for a minute.

Paul Getty was an American Industrialist who used this concept, and this quote from him you will find in many sales books:

> *"I would rather earn 1% of 100 people's efforts than 100% of my own."*

This notion forms the basis of this type of selling.

There are nine hours in a standard working day (eight if you include lunch). Let's assume that you are spending an entire day (eight hours) telephoning people for new business. The average call takes approximately five minutes, and you would need to allow ten minutes for before and after preparation (ideally). If you were to work solidly, without taking any breaks (other than that for lunch) then theoretically a possible thirty two calls could be made in this time.

An average sales team normally consists of two to four people (sometimes, more, sometimes less, but we are working on modest averages here). Let's assume that instead of you phoning clients for new business you instead involve a third party IT company who enjoys your products and is motivated to sell them to end users, and their sales staff contact the public instead. Well, those thirty two calls per person are now multiplied by two or four people resulting in sixty four to one hundred and twenty eight calls per day! And this frees your time to contact even more IT companies to do the same thing!

Do you now see the power of this type of selling? By working with third party IT companies not only do you have access to their sales personnel (indirectly of course – you could never order them around, but instead you could motivate them with incentives), but you also have access to their entire client database which could quite easily be much larger than yours.

Does this make sense to you?

ADVERTISING IN MEDIA

Depending on the type of IT company you are involved in, active advertising does work in some cases. However, the important things to know about this type of selling are firstly it does require a budget, the size of which depends on the type of media used. The second thing to remember is it is much like picking up a whole bunch of stones in your hand and throwing them at the frog in the road in front of you – some of them are going to hit their mark but also a lot of them are going to miss and are wasted. Let's look at three common categories.

Television and Radio - By far the most expensive type of advertising available in this category, television and radio attract possibly the largest audience in the shortest space of time than any other form of advertising. With television it is quite possible to reach millions of people with a single thirty second advertisement, and the combination of visual and audio effects on the potential buyer's sub-conscious makes it still the most effective form of advertising yet. However, almost all IT companies do not use this type of advertising because of the costs involved which can run into hundreds of thousands of Rands (Dollars for our overseas friends) for a single campaign.

Coming a close second, but not as effective, is the use of the radio. It is by far cheaper, but the audience is not as large and the visual impact is lost. Some IT companies, to my knowledge, have used this type of advertising.

Newspapers and Magazines - For IT companies this is by far the best form of advertising because it is fairly affordable and reaches quite a few people localised in the area of the IT Company. Furthermore, unlike television and radio, the reader can refer back to the advertisement as many times as they like without it having to be repeated constantly.

Flyers, Leaflets and Pamphlets - Mmmmmm, this, as far as I am concerned, is possibly the worst form of advertising for any type of business in any country. Yes, it is the cheapest form of media advertising, but the number of leaflets or flyers that need to be printed, and the intensive labour involved in handing them out, does not lead to any economical solution by any means.

Firstly, they irritate most people, whether they are stuck on cars' windshields, or shoved in drivers' faces at intersections, or jammed into mailboxes (also traditionally known as **Junk Mail**), the return on investment is about 0.5% if you are lucky. And then, and I have come across this frequently, there are often spelling and grammar mistakes on the flyers that really demeanour a company's reputation.

Before you **even consider** this venture, I want you to seriously put yourself in the client's shoes here. Would you actually spend a large sum of money on a computer from a company that has just manhandled your car whilst you are shopping in order to stick some piece of paper on your windshield? And God forbid it starts to rain, and all the ink (because they have used a cheap inkjet printer to do the job) has now decided to run and smear all over your bonnet. How does that sound to you?

How about this one? Given the amount of hijackings that occur on our intersections, and the fact that by law you are supposed to be watching the road at all times, would you consider taking a flyer from some character on the side of the road and sit and read it in earnest?

No, seriously guys please do not ever even consider going this route, ever!!! Have I got your promise? I hope so!

Retail Selling

In another chapter we analyze different types of IT companies, and one of these is retail. In case you haven't read that chapter yet, or are looking for a bit of a refresher to your memory, I'm going to repeat some of what was said here.

An IT company who chooses to compete in the retail market has its own set of challenges to face.

Firstly, the location of the shop is extremely important because you would want to attract a good number of shoppers as they wander past your company (also known as **Walk in Business**). Many IT companies of this nature opt for location in shopping malls because of the high volume of potential clients these centres naturally attract. The downside of this is the high rentals payable to the mall.

Secondly, the owner of such a company must be prepared to fork out quite a substantial amount of capital in order to create a shop environment that is pleasing to the shopper's eye, is secure, and relatively easy to manage. Then, money needs to be spent on stocking the environment with items that will sell fairly quickly and will attract buyers.

Given this quick background we now look at selling in these environments. Retail selling consists of high volume, low profit. Shoppers, when purchasing in this state of mind, are more concerned about price than anything else. Of course quality does become an aspect to a certain extent, but a retail business relies on a shopper's impulsiveness to buy on the spot without too much deliberation in order to meet its turnover.

In addition, proper merchandising plays a very important role in attracting a buyer to the items you would like them to purchase. Your shelves should be colourful, neat and appealing to look at, without seeming cluttered or disorganized.

There should be ample sales staff on hand to give assistance when needed, because these types of shoppers expect a high level of service when they need it.

On this note, I have noticed frequently that retail IT companies seem to follow a trend, and this is largely due to a number of reasons.

Owing to the fact that retail involves volume sales, an owner of such a company would like as many staff on the "sales floor", as it is generally called, to cater for as many shoppers as possible. These sales staff generally seems to be relatively inexperienced in their product knowledge and one finds that three or four of these types of people can be hired for the same price as a fairly experienced sales person. In most cases the retail store would not experience site evaluations or external meetings with potential clients; instead most of the sales generated are done within the confines of the retail store.

In addition to this we often find that the level of technical expertise follows the same trend as that of the sales personnel: the technicians involved in retail stores are often of Level 1 status (as discussed in Chapter 1), and these technicians seldom leave the store to visit clients.

A couple of tricks to this kind of selling. Knowing that the shopper is impulsive, you need to make the experience a "no-brainer"; if you let the shopper think too much about their purchase, then generally you have lost the sale. Also, Value Added Reselling plays a big part here.

Quick digression to explain what **Value Added Reselling** is (abbreviated **VAR**).

When you sell a computer to somebody, then that's exactly what they have got – a computer. They take it home, plug it in, and then great!!! A Computer!!! Now what do we do with it? It would be nice if we had some games to play with, and maybe a joystick. Oh, how would my voice sound if I can record it on the computer? And I really want to put all my mother's recipes onto the computer. I wonder how I can put last year's photographs of the beach onto the computer and then print them out.

VAR is the art of selling a client more than just a computer; you sell them a solution. By interrogating the client about their needs and wants you can find out exactly what they desire and then sell them on that. Not only do you satisfy their needs, you also increase your turnover, and ensure that he client is happy and will eventually come back to you for additional purchases. **VAR** is **HUGE** in the retail market, and mastery of this skill is extremely important. I have put in a separate chapter on this subject (Chapter 6).

So back to our discussion. A shopper's credit card is generally bigger than your entire shop, so get them to use it! Find out if they have kids, and their ages. If they are very young you might want to look at some educational software to teach them the basics of language and mathematics. If they are older, get the shopper to invest in Internet, an encyclopaedia, and a colour inkjet printer so that they can produce their school projects. And don't forget to sell them some sort of word processing package for typing purposes.

Find out if the parents are looking at doing some of their work at home in the evenings and on weekends. If so, an Office package will be needed, and again, a printer is required.

If the family like to go away on holiday, a good digital camera will be a definite bonus.

If nothing else, there is always a product that can (and should) be included with each computer sold – an anti-virus package. In Chapter 6 we go into this in more detail, and I will explain the differences between anti-virus packages.

INTERNET SELLING

Over the last fifteen to twenty years the Internet has definitely become a force to be reckoned with. In fact, a number of years ago, Bill Gates, the Founder of Microsoft ®, even said:

> **"Businesses who do not do business on the Internet will soon go out of business!"**

And this gentleman was quite correct in his statement. Most businesses in today's society have some sort of web presence, and with the advent of many different commercial web site creating software, it has become quite easy to design your own masterpiece.

I personally think twice about trading with an IT company who does not have a web presence, because technology is our game and we should be using it to its fullest as an advertisement to our clients. If they can see what is capable with technology, then even the most conservative of companies will be more willing to accept new solutions.

But there is more to the Internet than just websites. Let's take a look.

Websites -   You cannot feasibly have an IT company without having a web site, so grab some software and design the thing.

Once you learn the tools of having the site indexed correctly with the popular Internet search engines, it speaks for you twenty four hours a day, seven days a week, three hundred and sixty five days a year and, if designed correctly, will even sell your products for you and bring you the proceeds of the sale directly into your bank account. Any company, especially IT companies, should have a web presence, and even when you are approaching a potential client, always visit their website to glean some information about who that company is and what they do. The information you gather from these sources can be well used during your sales pitch.

A few very important things to note about web sites.

Firstly, the **domain**. This is extremely important to get hold of, because this is what people are going to be searching for when they look in your direction. A few hundred Rands (a few hundred Dollars for our American friends) will secure you this domain and as long as you renew it yearly, it belongs to you for life.

Mark Shuttleworth amassed an incredible fortune by simply selling his domain. OK, admittedly, it's what he built up under the domain name that made it so valuable, but nowadays the transaction of selling domain names is very easy to do compared to the traditional selling of businesses.

Secondly, **indexing**. Make sure that it is indexed as much as possible so that when somebody does a search your web site is listed within the first page. Most people will not bother to scroll to a second or third page of search results within a search engine so it is vital to appear on the first page.

The next point to note is that of **content in the site**. It is preferable to enlist the services of a professional opinion, because, like a receptionist of a company, people often make up their minds with the first impression. If they see a gaudy, disorganised website, with spelling mistakes, and pages under construction, then generally speaking you won't hope to see too much business coming from it.

And another note here. Unless you are setting up a merchant website (one in which people can purchase and pay for goods online) try to keep prices out of the picture. Not only does it become an administrative nightmare to keep your prices up to date constantly, it also allows those penny pinchers the opportunity of judging your company, not by the quality of your work, but by the prices you offer.

Email Campaigns - Email, in my opinion, is probably one of the greatest communication discoveries of this century, because of the potential it offers to communicate almost instantaneously with almost anybody around the world, and at a fraction of the costs associated with conventional telephone calls. I personally have discovered that a considerable amount of my sales time involves emailing, and I can even use email to setup appointments and close sales deals.

I have included a short synopsis on this topic, but I have also expanded on this in Chapter 17.

But, with every good idea comes the potential to exploit, so inevitably email had to follow suite on this one with unsolicited email, or **Spam**, which basically is an electronic form of flyers and leaflets (as discussed above), or **Junk Mail**. People put together an advertising email and broadcast it to many people (sometimes numbering in the thousands) which generally degrades valuable Internet bandwidth which could be used for other legitimate forms of communication.

Authorities take a dim view of this type of exploitation, and if you are involved in spamming you could run the risk of having your email address permanently cancelled.

If this tool is used correctly on the other hand then it can be an extremely powerful advertising medium to use for sales. Broadcasting bulk email messages is very useful to impart useful information but you need to use **mailing lists** in order to do this without running the risk of being accused of being a spammer. Basically, a mailing list is a list of people (and companies) who share common interests, and who obviously know you (or the company you work for) and would therefore be interested in the information you would like to impart to them. Sending out bulk emails to these lists of people (sometimes called **subscribers**) is legal, and provided you include an option for them to unsubscribe from your mailing list with the emails you sent, you are more than welcome to work with these sorts of campaigns.

Just a couple of things to remember here when dealing with email campaigns. Firstly, in order to reduce the amount of spam received into a person's mailbox, most people run Spam Filters that bock out unwanted email. These filters use a series of keywords (and due to the very nature of some of the words used I'm not going to mention them here) and the filter scans each incoming email to see if it contains any of the keywords stored in the filter's database. If emails of this nature are found, they are generally moved to a Spam, or Junk Email folder in the recipient's email client and it might be days sometimes before the intended recipient actually attempts to look at the email before deciding whether it should be deleted or kept.

If you are going to broadcast an email, make sure that you have composed the message in such a way that it will not flag the incoming Spam filters on the receivers' computers. To get an idea of the contents of these lists search for them on the Internet or search through Anti-Spam Filters for examples. By the way, if you go to www.Kaspersky.com you will be able to get more information on this.

The next point to know is that of the size of the email. A simple email can be broadcast to many people without using a lot of bandwidth provided you ensure that the contents of the message are kept simple, without large amounts of graphics or pictures. Another one to avoid is to broadcast emails with attachments, which generally contain files that are substantially larger than the average email size.

The last point to note here is the difference between the "CC'" field and the "BCC" field that are used when sending messages to more than one person simultaneously.

"CC", which stands for **Carbon Copy**, allows you to send the same message to other people at the same time. However, all email addresses that are listed in the "CC" field will be displayed when the email is received. With broadcast emailing this is not a good idea, because you would not like your subscribers to know who else is competing with them for the same information, especially in business. After all, they all have the same common interests.

"BCC", which stands for **Blind Carbon Copy**, works the same way as Carbon Copy except that the list of recipients is hidden from view when the email is received. All that is shown is the original email address the email was sent to (normally listed in the "To" field).

And this brings me to my final point on this. When you embark on email broadcasting, send the email back to yourself, and place all your intended recipients in the "BCC" field. That way all the receivers will see is an email addressed to you.

Online Newsletters - Online newsletters are quite a good way to advertise your goods and/or services over the Internet to a group of interested people. Basically a newsletter is like an Internet version of a newspaper or magazine, with various numbers of subscribers who pay a small monthly (or yearly) fee in order to be able to access the posted information. You, as the sales person, have the ability to advertise in these sites (for a fee of course) or you can even write articles and post them to the organizers of the website for consideration and editing.

You will find many different groups on interests and, depending on your target market, you can advertise in any number of newsletters, even if you personally do not subscribe to the actual newsletter itself.

On the converse side of things, creating and managing one yourself is a different matter entirely and, unless you are prepared to devote a substantial amount of time to maintaining it, or hire somebody to do the job, it is best to steer clear of them, even if the incoming revenue from potential advertisers looks attractive.

REFERRALS

This is the ultimate way of selling, when people contact you because they need products and/or services from you. This is by far the cheapest way of selling (it actually doesn't cost you a cent) because people are contacting you, and not the other way around.

Now how do we get here?

Well, if your company has done a superb job with your previous clients they are going to start talking to other people, recommending your business to them. Also, those clients you have assisted with in the past: if they were happy with your service they will then come back to you with their new requirements.

In the chapter on CRM (Chapter 13) I discuss ways of going that extra mile when it comes to customer service. These methods form an important part of referral selling, so I would advise you to go through that chapter and apply some of those methods – they will pay off in the end.

Another aspect of referrals is your advertising campaigns. If they have been well presented, then people will also come looking for you.

A few other points to note here.

If you have performed a good service to a client and they are very happy with your company, ask them for a letter of Referral or Reference. Most people will be more than willing to spend a few minutes drafting a document that you will be proud of, and something you will be able to show other sceptical clients in the future.

Another similar concept here is that of Reference Sites. If you have performed a service to a well-known or large client, ask them if you can use them as a reference site. Again, most clients would be more than willing to allow you to refer to them when you are marketing to other future prospects. In fact, many large companies actually request references to make sure that the company you work for has the experience to be able to cope with large projects.

Lastly, when contacting a client on a cold call, regardless of the outcome of the contact, ask them if they could refer you to some people, or give you some names of people that they think might be in need of your services. Thus, even if you did not get that company's business, you haven't completely wasted the phone call because now you have some more companies to contact.

BILLBOARD ADVERTISING (INCLUDING VEHICLES)

This is an interesting way of advertising because there are mixed opinions to this form. Some people like it and some people don't. I personally have found definite pros and cons with this type of advertising.

Let's first look at billboard advertising and then we will move onto vehicles.

Firstly, billboards are hellishly expensive but not as much as a fully-fledged campaign with television, radio, or magazines.

Provided the material on the billboard has been designed in such a way as to allow drivers to absorb the information in the few seconds that they are driving past, it will be effective. However, a big downside of this is that only a small percentage of the population will be able to see the billboard at all, because most people drive the same routes every day. The only difference here is people who have to travel a particular route for varying reasons such as meetings, deliveries, or social visits. Other than that the same people will be viewing the billboard on a daily basis. Of course the one benefit of this is that viewing the same information regularly means that the driver will eventually remember the information being imparted, but what then? The billboard will eventually become stagnant and boring.

This then brings me to the other side of the coin here. In order to make a long lasting impact on people the billboard needs to be changed on a regular basis advertising the same company, but with different information and designs. This means that the costs involved in this type of campaign escalates dramatically.

Vehicles (buses, cars, trucks, trains, etc), on the other hand, do not have the problems associated with being in one spot, as they are constantly moving. However, there are other problems that are coupled to this type of advertising.

Firstly, unlike billboards that can be changed constantly, once you have branded a motor vehicle, it is very expensive to change the design and artwork. Once the design is there, it is there to stay, or at least for a long time (a minimum of three months is quite feasible). Those people responsible for the design need to ensure that it is good and hard-hitting because a driver might only see the vehicle once in his or her lifetime and whatever information is begin imparted needs to be structured in such a way that it makes an impact in less than a second.

The second thing, if the vehicle is involved in an accident, then the campaign is basically over until another vehicle can be sourced and branded. Obviously the insurance will pay out for the accident (unless you never took out insurance on the vehicle or the extra branding) but time is a major factor here. The same is true if somebody vandalizes or steals the vehicle.

Once the campaign is over, the value of the vehicle is marred by the damage on the paintwork by the branding. Such a vehicle, if ever sold, will need to be resprayed to eliminate all traces of the former designs.

With regards to trucks that travel over long distances, unless the company who the branding is designed for is a national corporation, the effects are generally lost if and when the lorry leaves the local area. The same can be said of intercity buses and trains.

But, on the other side of the playing card, if the design is created well and striking, the impact becomes memorable and the campaign can become a marked success.

CONCLUSION

In order to become a success in your profession of IT sales you are going to have to try several different methods to see what will work and what will not.

Again I am going to stipulate this: you need to study your client (or the particular industry they work in) in order to gain a complete understanding on how they operate, and what makes them tick. Once you have gained this vital knowledge you can plan a sales strategy that is tailor made for their needs based upon what is important to them.

With regards to advertising different methods will need to be employed depending on the type of client you are targeting but budgets do unfortunately become a deciding factor here when you tap into the right method to use. You need to carefully balance the advertising campaign with the return of investment, and the best advice I can give you on this is – talk to some professionals in the advertising game as to what will work and what will not before you commit yourself to a particular project.

SUMMARY – CHAPTER 4.

A client will not buy from you if he doesn't trust you!

Many sales people become discouraged because of the amount of rejection they experience whilst trying new sales techniques until they find the ones that fit their industry and their personality the best. Here we look at different methods of selling.

PROSPECTING FOR NEW CLIENTS

Otherwise known as **Cold Calling**, this is an extremely important part of selling, and it is because of this that Chapter 5 is devoted to this topic.

POWER OF LEVERAGE SELLING

Word of Mouth Advertising is probably one of the most effective forms of selling because it primarily uses the power of the human's emotions and the basic need to communicate with others as its vehicle.

Power of Leverage Selling is employing the selling techniques of others to sell your products and/or services to others on your behalf, and you benefit from their efforts as well as you own.

Network Marketing uses these techniques by selling their product to a person (or people), and then offering to pay that person a portion of the proceeds to sell the product to another person by simply talking about their personal experiences with that product.

ADVERTISING IN MEDIA

In some instances active advertising in the public media is necessary depending on the type of IT Company you are working for. The important issue to note is that it does require a fairly substantial budget.

Television and Radio -	This is the most expensive advertising media to use, but it also reaches the largest audience in the shortest possible time.

Many IT Companies do not use this form of advertising because of the budgets involved.

Newspapers and Magazines -	This seems to be the most popular form of advertising used by the IT industry because it is reasonably affordable, it reaches a large amount of readers localised to the IT Company's area, and people can refer back to a prior advertisement as many times as they like.
Flyers, Leaflets and Pamphlets -	The rate of return from this type of advertising is so low that it becomes a hindrance more than an advantage for the company and hence should be avoided wherever possible.

RETAIL SELLING

Due to the fact that price is a major issue in the Retail Industry, volume selling is extremely important and active media advertising becomes a major part of the success of this industry.

Most business is achieved by shoppers visiting the Retail Store, and thus the shop needs to have a positive aesthetic aspect to promote shoppers to visit them.

Proper merchandising is also important as it plays on the shoppers' psychological urges that will promote them to purchase.

Due to the fact that volume sales are vital to the survival of the Retail Industry sales personnel must learn to sell as much as possible to the potential buyer whilst they are still present in the store. In Chapter 6 there is a discussion on Value Added Reselling which addresses these issues.

INTERNET SELLING

This has become more and more prevalent over the years as society turns towards this medium to purchase products and services.

Websites -	In order to be successful companies must have a web presence in the form of websites. You must have a domain name that will be easy to find,

and you must have it properly indexed with the popular search engines so that people can find it easily.

The design of the site needs to be professional and easily understood. If it too cluttered then visitors will not be able to find what they are looking for.

Pricing on websites should be omitted because it requires a substantial amount of administrative work and people who shop for price and not for quality of product might overlook your offerings if they are more expensive than your competition.

Email Campaigns - Emails offer the potential to communicate to almost anybody around the world, and at a fraction of the costs associated with conventional telephone calls.

Spam or unsolicited email does however mar the beneficial aspects of this type of selling and various authorities do get involved when you participate in the act of spamming.

Broadcasting emails or copies of emails sent to many people simultaneously should only be sent to **mailing lists** which are lists of receivers who accept the communication you send them.

When sending out emails you need to be aware of **Spam Filters** which will block certain emails containing offending keywords or phrases in the subject line or body so you need to word your mails in such a way as to be deemed harmless by the recipient's spam filters.

Also, when broadcasting, be mindful of the size of mail being sent.

Carbon Copy ("CC") allows you to send the same email to more than one person simultaneously but all recipients in the sending list will be visible.

Blind Carbon Copy ("BCC") performs the same function but hides all the recipients' email addresses

Online Newsletters - These newsletters are like an Internet version of a newspaper or magazine, with various numbers of subscribers who pay a small monthly (or yearly) fee in order to be able to access the posted information.

The downside is that they require a great deal of administration in posting new articles on a regular basis.

REFERRALS

This is the best way of selling, when people contact you because they need products and/or services from you, and is by far the cheapest way of selling.

If your company has offered a good service in the past then former clients will revisit you for further requirements and they will also unwittingly promote your company to other potential prospects.

Ask your large and well-known clients for references on work you have performed for them in the past.

When cold calling on prospects request of they have any other people you could contact and ask your prospect it you could use them as a reference.

BILLBOARD ADVERTISING (INCLUDING VEHICLES)

Billboard advertising is expensive but not as much as a fully-fledged campaign with television, radio, or magazines.

The information must be presented in such a way that people driving past are able to absorb it in a couple of seconds and the billboards must be positioned alongside major thoroughfares so that they gain as much exposure as possible.

Billboards need to be changed or updated frequently so that the information remains fresh as they will be viewed by the same peoples frequently.

Vehicles have the benefit in that they are constantly travelling around so that their exposure becomes greater but the information cannot be updated as readily and if the vehicle is involved in an accident then it will affect the advertising campaign.

CHAPTER 5.
PROSPECTING FOR NEW CLIENTS

Often when faced with the prospect of gaining new clients, many sales personnel baulk at the task and often wonder where to actually start, and hence do not start at all. Experienced personnel, having practiced this for years, tend to not have the same problem. This chapter serves in assisting you in prospecting for new clients.

I have been involved in Sales over the last twenty one years and I have learnt, through reading, learning from others, and my own experiences, that there are certain concepts to be learnt when dealing with clients.

A note here – some sales people refer to their prospects as "customers". For personal reasons I have never been fond of this term, and hence I always tend to rather use the term "client". You will therefore notice that I mostly use this preferred term when discussing prospects.

This chapter is basically divided into 4 parts:

- **Identifying the client** – Finding out the client's needs. In order to be able to sell your goods and/or services, you **must** be able to find out these needs.
- **Contacting the client** – Telephoning the client to arrange an appointment to meet with them.

- **Establishing the client** – What to do during the actual sales interview, and what to look for from the prospective client.
- **Supporting the client** – What to do after the sales interview; follow-ups, proposals, etc.

Due to my history in the Information Sector, I have based this chapter and the entire book on the IT sector, but there is no reason why you cannot adapt these techniques to other sectors, whether you are selling cars, furniture, insurance policies, or whatever. The sales techniques are basically the same.

Please bear in mind that this subject of discussion is by no means exhaustive, and additional reading material is highly recommended. There are many accomplished authors of Sales training manuals and other Self-Help titles that are more qualified and learned than myself; I have simply placed my own personal experiences into these pages in the hopes that you can gain some information from them.

For the sake of identifying a company you represent, I have used the name "ABC Computers" where applicable. If such a company exists then please can I express my apologies, since the use of such a name is purely coincidental unintended? Similarly, I am using the name of Mr. Smith during proposed discussions. Again, the use of this name is entirely coincidental.

IDENTIFYING THE CLIENT

The first step in obtaining new clients is to establish the client's needs. In doing this it becomes extremely important to understand the nature of the company and what their focus is.

There is absolutely no point in grabbing the nearest telephone directory (or nowadays, with our friend the Internet, running a search for Business Directories in any particular area or industry) and contacting the first one hundred names you find there. I can almost guarantee that you will come to a sticky end!

Prospecting is an art, and if performed correctly and intelligently it will lead you to guaranteed success at a minimal cost. So now where does that leave you?

Well sit back for a moment and think about the company you are going to contact. You need to figure out what the company does, and hone in on that. By this I mean concentrate on what they do, and how you and computers can help them achieve their goals.

Take for example Recruitment Companies. Their core focus is finding jobs for people. How is this achieved? By advertising, either in newspapers or over the Internet.

What will the company require to access the Internet? Well, firstly, an Internet connection is required. This means that they will need an **ISP** (**Internet Service** Provider) and probably a registered domain. Then a computer capable of accessing the Internet is required (an **Internet Server**). This server will require a modem or other similar device to access the ISP. The Recruitment Consultants will require email addresses so that candidates can send messages and/or CV's to them. The server will then have to become a **Mail Server**, capable of receiving emails from the ISP and distributing them internally.

As soon as the server can access the Internet the internal network is subject to a host of Internet attacks. Viruses and other malware can affect the network, so the server will require an **Anti-Virus** solution. Email can be spammed so an email **Spam Filter** is necessary on the server. A **Firewall** solution will need to be provided to prevent hackers from gaining access to the internal network. In addition, Industrial Espionage has become rife in today's society, so the internal network will also need to be protected from internal attacks, either from employees stealing information, or candidates entering the premises with wireless devices capable of accessing the company's network.

Further to the point on internal attacks, what about the consultants attempting to use the Internet for personal gain at the company's expense, such as personal emails? This means that a **Content Filter** will be required on the server.

How will candidates know the company exists on the Internet? Well, the company is going to require a Web presence, which means that they are going to need a **Web Site** developed and maintained. As mentioned earlier, the Recruitment Company should have a registered domain hosted with their preferred ISP.

What about candidates who don't have access to email? A faxing solution will then be required on the server, both to receive and to send faxes. And candidates who visit the company? Well then a printing solution is needed on the network.

What about all those CV's coming in via email? They are going to have to be categorized. This means that a database solution is required on the network.

And the data will need to be stored, and so a backup solution must be present in the server. What happens if the mains power turns off whilst the data is being backed up? Well then an UPS will need to be installed on the server. How about lightning strikes? Lightning protection will then need to be placed on the modem.

How does the company manage its finances? This then means that an accounting package will need to be installed on the network, and the company's financial records will need to be backed up on the server.

Let's take another example- a Tool Manufacturer. What does the company do? It manufactures tools. How? Well, first the tool will need to be designed. This is going to require designing software (a CAD package). Then materials will need to be obtained for the tool, therefore a Bill of Materials package is required, as well as ordering of stock. How are all those parts categorized? Well, they are going to have to be stored in a database that can be accessed at the factory.

What about the finished product? Well, the database is going to have to be accessed by the Sales Personnel, so stock control becomes important. How do they sell the tools? Advertising, either by brochure, newspaper, or by the Internet. How do they access the Internet? Etc...

Do you catch my drift? The important thing when marketing to clients is to work out what they need and then offer them a solution. IT sales are not just about selling a bunch of computers to a company. It is about selling them a solution that will make their lives easier. And in order to sell a solution you have to be aware of their needs.

What is the core focus of any business? To make money, or course!!! And in doing so what is the business's primary concern? To increase productivity and efficiency! What is then our job? To offer them a means to increase their productivity and efficiency by giving them tools to do their job.

What does all this then mean? Well, in order to offer solutions to potential clients you have to study them. There is no point in contacting a hundred clients with no clear focus as to what you have to offer them. Rather focus on ten clients and find out what their business does and where you think you can help them. Then you are guaranteed of success. With most companies advertising on the Internet, a simple browse through their website will give you an incredible amount of information as to their core focus. Most companies like to tout their Vision and Mission statements on their home pages. These will give you insights into their core focuses.

Remember also that most clients are ignorant when it comes to Information Technology, and what the market has to offer. That is not their primary concern. Their focus is on other issues, just like your focus is on computers. What happens when you are sick? You go to a doctor. Why? Because that doctor has spent years studying the human body and how to fix it. How does the doctor gain more knowledge about the human body? By practicing medicine and gaining experience. They also read medical journals to find out other ways to perform certain procedures. What then is the doctor's focus? Medicine, of course!!! That is the field they are experts in. What do you do? Computers! And how do you gain more knowledge? By practicing and studying computers. You are an expert in your field, which are computers.

OK, once you have sat down and thought about how you can help a client, the next step is in approaching the client.

CONTACTING THE CLIENT

This is the tricky bit, because the wrong approach will be disastrous. Firstly, you have to bear in mind that you are now going to be dealing with people, and not machines. They have feelings and opinions just like yourself, and that is going to influence their decisions as to whether they want to talk to you or not.

And that brings me to my next point. Decisions!!! This is the key factor when approaching new clients. You want to approach the Decision-Maker in the company. There is no point in gabbing away with the Receptionist, because he/she probably has no clue as to what you are talking about, and the Receptionist definitely does not sign the cheques, and hence does not make the decisions about the company!!! So who to talk to in the company? Well, think about it for a moment. Who controls the money in the company? The Accountant! OK, there's a start. But maybe there might be a Financial Director (FD). OK, that's even better. But the FD probably has little knowledge about IT, so that's a bit of a dead end, unless you really want to educate the FD about the finer points of Information Technology.

Well then maybe there is an IT Manager in the company? Great, because then it means that you will be talking to somebody on your own wavelength! But what happens if the company does not have somebody dedicated to looking after the computers? Well, then the only option is to approach the person at the top, the Managing Director (or MD). This is going to be a bit daunting, because that person has spent years in developing his/her company, and is going to be sceptical about how you are going to help him/her. Also remember that the MD is probably an extremely busy person, so you cannot waste their time. Whatever you say must make an impact, or else you will end up as "just another salesman" in their minds.

Remember that the company belongs to the MD. He/she has spent a long time in building the company, and has spent many hours of precious time and a lot of money is creating that company. And for what purpose? To make a profit, and hence generate money!!! So what's the bottom line? To help them make more money!!! The MD doesn't care about helping you make a sale; they care about making their business bigger and better, so you have to find ways of helping them achieve their goals. Of course you want the sale, because that means money in your pocket, but you have to think in terms of what that client wants. After all, ultimately they are going to spend their precious money on the solution you provide for them, in order to generate more money. Give them the wrong solution and they will never deal with you again.

The reason why I am stating this now is that there are so many sales personnel out there who will try to sell a farmer a sports car when in actual fact all he really needed was a bakkie (a truck or van, for those of you who don't live in South Africa). Give them the right solution and they will come back to you.

All this boils down to one thing: attitude!!! Open any sales manual and every one will tell you: "Cold calling is an attitude!" It is not an art or a science, it is an attitude, and your attitude should be one of: "How can we help you?" and not of "How can I help myself?"

In summary so far then, you firstly need to establish who the Decision-Maker is in the company. The easiest way is to ask the Receptionist who looks after the computers in the company. That person in charge of the IT is ultimately responsible as to making sure that the tools of the business are running smoothly. If not, they will be in trouble, and hence that person will always be on the lookout for better ways of doing things, and having things run. That's where you come in, because you can provide them with better solutions. Once you have the correct person, the next step is in actually talking to them.

This is the fun part, because you have to convince them that you are there to help them. They don't know that when you first say "Hello", so you have to prove it to them. How is this achieved? Number one is, smile on the 'phone. This might seem a strange concept, but it comes across. Remember, you are an ambassador of ABC Computers, and you work for a winning company, and because of that you are also a winner. Number two is, you must believe in both your abilities as a specialist, and in the products and services you are selling. Number three is, be loud on the 'phone. I don't mean shout at the person, who will probably think you are completely nuts; I mean speak clearly and completely, so that they can hear you, and don't rush your speech. The thing is, you are probably nervous out of your wits, but the person on the other end of the telephone can't see you and hence won't see your nervousness: it's your voice that's the key. Sound confident and you've cleared the first hurdle.

Sometimes the receptionist will ask why you wish to talk to the person in question and at this point you should introduce yourself as a representative of the company, and state that you might have solutions to offer to make his/her job easier.

A big rule here! If the person you are trying to contact is not available, NEVER leave a message for them to phone you back!!! Rather contact them at a later stage. I learnt this once from an experience I had. I wanted to market to a certain company whom I had never contacted before and the lady I needed to deal with was unavailable. I left a message for her to phone me back. Bad mistake! When she eventually did contact me back she berated me and found that the entire practice of her having to contact me in order for me to do business with her was bad manners. The result was that I never managed to do business with this client.

In addition to this, the whole practice of leaving messages is never infallible. Sometimes the person on the other end of the line takes the information down wrong. Either they spell your name wrong, or your telephone number, in which case the prospective client never reaches you. In other cases they forget to pass the message on to the intended recipient resulting in the lost communication. And they frequently give the prospect the incorrect message, telling them that you want to sell them vacuum cleaners instead of computers. Familiar territory? Has this ever happened to you?

To digress a bit on this, I have learnt, with today's' technology, a nifty little trick in message passing. This will be covered in another chapter in further detail but it is suffice to say that if you can obtain your prospect' email address, then you could rather send them an email with your intended message. In this way **you** could word it to suit your marketing strategy, and you can ensure that they receive all the information in the correct way.

When you finally reach the person in question, introduce yourself and the company. ABC Computers is a Network Security Solution Provider, and you should state this to the person. What this basically means is that we as a company help streamline and protect computer networks in order for them to run more efficiently. What you are looking for is to setup an appointment with the involved person. Say something like," I would like to setup an appointment with you to see how we can be of service to you." Offer them a choice of days and times when it would be convenient for them to meet with you.

The most important thing here to remember is that you must be in control of the conversation, and hence you should try to decide for them. If you ask them when they are free, then you are letting them decide. Rather give them a choice of days, and then a choice of times. Follow this conversation, for example:

YOU: *"Good morning Mr. Smith. My name is X, and I represent ABC Computers. I understand that you are a busy person, so I won't take up too much of your time. Our company provides Computer Network Security Solutions to companies such as yours to*

> *help make your job easier. I would like to setup an appointment with you to further discuss this and see how we can be of service to you. I am free next week Tuesday at 2:00pm or 10:00am on Wednesday. Which day would you prefer to meet?"*

There are a few important things to note regarding the above conversation. Firstly, not once was the word "sales" mentioned. This is important, because often people do not like to be bothered with salesmen. Secondly, the conversation is blunt and to the point. It is impossible to explain the entire company to the person. Rather leave that for the interview. Thirdly, the person was given a choice of times, thus the conversation is in your control.

If the person already states that their company is already supported, or are involved in a service contract, then request that they consider ABC Computers the next time they upgrade or alter their network. Request their contact details, and don't forget to give them yours. Request also if they have any referrals or contacts that they know of that might benefit from our services. Most people would be more than willing to impart a few names. Always check before phoning these new people that the person you contacted can be used as a reference.

If the contact wishes for more information, give it to them. We basically secure computer networks, and offer a wide range of products and services that, combined together, will create solutions that increase productivity and efficiency.

Once contacted, make as many notes as possible (i.e. 'phone numbers, name, email address, etc.) Often vital details are overlooked, and hence another 'phone call will be required to complete the information.

Also, when establishing appointments, don't forget to leave your contact numbers, just in case the contact has a problem at a later stage with the appointment.

Oh, and if the client ask you questions that you don't know the answers to, be honest and respond with, "I am not too sure about that. I would rather obtain more information, so that I don't give you the wrong information. Can I take some details down and get back to you?"

On most occasions the contact will query you for more information. Don't worry, because that means that the person is interested in meeting with you. Answer their questions honestly and truthfully, and when the questions are finished request the appointment again. Let's analyze the above conversation again:

YOU: "*Good morning Mr. Smith. My name is X, and I represent ABC Computers. I understand that you are a busy person, so I won't take up too much of your time. Our company provides Security network solutions to companies such as yours to help make your job easier. I would like to setup an appointment with you to further discuss this and see how we can be of service to you. I am free next week Tuesday at 2:00pm or 10:00am on Wednesday. Which day would you prefer to meet?*"

MR. SMITH: "*So what exactly does your company do?*"

YOU: "*We secure companies' networks in order to increase productivity and efficiency. In doing so we combine a wide range of products and services together to provide solutions. It would be best if I rather spent a few minutes with you and discuss this further. Which day would you prefer to meet?*"

MR. SMITH: "*So basically you sell computers. We already have somebody who already supplies us with computers.*"

YOU: "*Well actually Mr. Smith, our company sells Network Security solutions based on technology. These* *solutions, once implemented correctly, requires little maintenance on our part to your benefit. All I need is a few minutes of your time to fully illustrate this, but I am only free next week Tuesday at 2:00pm or 10:00 am on Wednesday. Which time would suit you more?"*

MR SMITH: *"How about 10:00am on Wednesday next week?"*

YOU: *"Great. Please may I leave a contact number just in case there is a problem? Thank you for your time and I look forward to seeing you next week."*

In the case of the client having a contract with another Support Company, the conversation might be something like:

MR. SMITH: *"So basically you sell computers. We already have a contract with another company."*

YOU: *"Oh really. If you don't mind me asking, are you content with their service?"*

MR. SMITH: *"Yes, we are happy with their service."*

YOU: *"That's fine. Would it be possible if I could contact you again when the contract nears completion?"*

MR. SMITH: *"Yes, that's fine. Contact me again in six months."*

YOU: *"Thank you for the opportunity. I would like to leave my contact details with you for future reference. One last thing; based on the information I have given you, would you recommend ABC Computers to* *other companies whom you think could benefit from our services?"*

Most of the time the contact is more than willing to give you a few names as referrals. Don't forget to ask his/her permission to use him/her as a reference first. Make a note of when the contract nears completion, and phone the client again.

ESTABLISHING THE CLIENT

OK, so you have successfully established your first appointment/s, and you are feeling good about yourself, and you should be, because that person is no longer a stranger to you. The next step is in preparing for the appointment and the actual appointment itself.

Before doing anything else, make a note of the appointment in your diary. I personally use Microsoft's MS Outlook ® for this function, because as well as being able to enter the appointment itself in Outlook's Calendar, I can at the same time store all the relevant contact details for the new client. At the beginning of each day the first thing I do is look at both my task lists and my calendar to see what's in store for the day. There is another important item mentioned here: the Tasks List. These can be anything from drafting a quote to researching information to paying your electricity account. Use this tool: it becomes invaluable to you.

When scheduling multiple appointments, try to space them at least two hours apart, unless you know beforehand that you are not going to spend a lot of time there or the two consecutive appointments are geographically close to each other.

Many a time I have scheduled appointments too close together, and have had to phone ahead to the next appointment in apology for being late. Rather have the time in-between the appointments to reflect and refocus.

There is a time old strategy that, if performed correctly, will give you unbelievable results. It is known as the 5-3-2-1 strategy and works like this:

5 – Visit 5 clients a day
3 – 3 must be new clients
2 – 2 must be previous clients
1 – Receive 1 order per day.

Although this strategy takes a while to implement, striving towards it will make you successful. If you space your appointments two hours apart, then the following is possible:

08h00 appointment 1
10h00 appointment 2
12h00 appointment 3
14h00 appointment 4
16h00 appointment 5

And you will have seen your 5 clients for the day. In-between appointments the time can be used preparing quotes and gathering the information required to create the proposals.

Try to leave the time after 16h00 open for all your administrative duties, and after lunch on Friday afternoons – nobody likes to discuss serious business on a Friday afternoon. You might also like to leave this time open for marketing ventures – phoning more clients for appointments.

Anyway, back to the appointment. On the day of the appointment always phone the client beforehand to make sure they are still available for the appointment. Sometimes emergencies come up and the person is not available. Sometimes the person actually forgets the appointment. In any case, a quick 'phone call is a lot cheaper than petrol in the tank.

Once you reach the company, make a note of neighbouring companies, and jot down their contact details displayed on their billboards (if applicable). These become new leads for you, and because they are close by, this becomes a definite selling advantage to you, because your company's engineers can go from one company to the next within minutes. Some neighbouring companies become friendly towards each other, and if you make a good impression at the client you are visiting you can always use them as references to their neighbours.

Always dress formally before meeting a new client. Remember, first impressions are always lasting, and as a representative of ABC Computers, you have a high standard to uphold. For the men, a tie and collar is important, and for the ladies, a suitable business look is required. If you have a blazer, use it. It is always better to look overdressed than underdressed in these types of scenarios. NO JEANS! NO SNEAKERS! NO WAY! NOT EVER! You never approach a potential client dressed in this fashion. The only time this type of dress is partially acceptable is during installations, and even then formal overalls and safety boots are preferred.

Try to arrive ten to fifteen minutes early for the appointment, and enter reception ten minutes early. There is an important reason for this: time in the lobby. By sitting for a few minutes before the appointment you can obtain a lot of information about the company. Firstly, listen to the switchboard. Is the receptionist being inundated with calls, or does she/he have time to play card games on the computer. What is the general atmosphere with the people gathered in the lobby (if any). Are they sad, anxious, or jovial? Look around. Can you identify incorrectly laid cables? What sort of paintings or certificates are on the walls? Try to make a mental note of all this information, and add the notes to the contact stored in the database when you get back into the office.

PUT YOUR CELLPHONE ON SILENT BEFORE YOU REACH RECEPTION!!!

Another note to add: your breath. Attempt to refrain from smoking fifteen minutes before the interview, and watch the alcohol levels the night before. Ditto on the garlic in last night's dinner. If clients detect bad breath then they generally don't like to deal with you in the future. If necessary keep a tube of toothpaste in the cubby-hole of your car. Nobody knows its there and you can always be assured of that fresh, clean white smile.

A bit of a side-line note here regarding alcohol: if you are a non-drinker, then you should be fine, but if you are a drinker, then take careful heed of these pointers. There are some clients who prefer doing business over a few drinks. Some of them might be your 16h00 appointments. NEVER match a client's drinking habits. If you become drunk whilst in the company of a client, then you probably will lose that client. Look at this for example: the average man gets pretty much on his way after four beers, and normally they want you to match their pace. You can, but alternate each beer with a soft drink, or soda water. That way you have had the same amount to drink, but instead you have consumed only two beers, and diluted the same with an equal amount of soft drink. Most clients don't even notice this strategy, and it helps.

Once you meet your contact follow him/her to a designated meeting area. Always thank them for giving up their time to see you. Wait for the person to sit before you do.

Here's a helpful tip. If beverages are offered, always request a glass of water. Outright refusal of any beverage might be considered rude, and an acceptance for tea of coffee might take too long, and also affects your breath (in some cases). By accepting a glass of water you have made your host feel more at ease, and you are not obliged to finish the glass of water, just in case you are not thirsty.

Right, what you now need to do is to establish the meeting and to explain your company's procedures regarding site evaluations and proposals. Always start off by asking a little bit of information about the company you are visiting, and spend a few minutes discussing this, then explain your site evaluations. If at all possible try to perform one right then and there, or if the client does not have the time, schedule one within the next few days. Don't take any documentation into the meeting with you if you can help it – by handing over brochures and other typed information you are simply distracting your client from what you are discussing. Rather explain and make notes as to what documentation to bring for the next meeting.

This accurately tells you what the person is interested in instead of giving them reams of brochures that they probably are never going to read, and this will simply increase your printing costs.

Listening is extremely important when dealing with meetings. After all, you are there to help them, not the other way around. When you go to the doctor, who explains where the pain is? You, or the Doctor?

Explain briefly your company's procedures, as stated above, and then pass the ball into their court by throwing a question at them. Something like this might help:

YOU: *"... and that's what ABC Computers does. Now that you know a bit more about us, how can we be of service to you?"*

By opening the client up, you are probably going to be bombarded with problems, questions, and requests on new products or services on the market. Calmly discuss each issue and MAKE NOTES with each issue. If you can't answer the question, be truthful and state as such, but gather the information regarding the question and research it when you are back at the office.

One important thing here: in whatever book or device you are using to store notes don't read information in there pertaining to other issues. The client will feel that they are not important and that you are ignoring them. Always make eye contact. That also makes the client feel important. Never answer your cellphone (it should be on silent anyway): it breaks the mood of the meeting.

Once you have concluded your meeting thank the person for their time and give them a follow up date (i.e. *"I will phone you in 2 days to let you know."*) AND STICK TO THAT FOLLOW-UP TIME.

The next step is drive (or walk) away. Go around the corner or something but don't hang around the parking lot writing in your book or attacking your cellphone. Some clients wait just inside reception to watch you leave. You don't want them to wait. And don't light a cigarette (if you smoke) until you are away from the premises.

One last thing! Unless you have physically performed a network evaluation your initial meeting shouldn't take more than thirty minutes. If you go over that then it means that you have given too much information, or have lost the reason for the meeting in the first place! Subsequent meetings can (and perhaps would) take longer as you start establishing good relationships with your clients, but the first meeting is always introductory, and that is its purpose.

OK. The last step. Supporting the client.

SUPPORTING THE CLIENT

After you get back to the office you haven't finished. Now comes the task of preparing the proposal. Information needs to be gathered, prices need to be obtained, and everything needs to be formatted and looking good.

Here's a quick tip when shopping for prices. If you have seen more than one client during the day, and have a few proposals to generate simultaneously, group the required items together per supplier. That way you can obtain the information you require for a few proposals from a particular supplier in a single 'phone call. Hey, every penny counts when it comes to profit. Obtain all the necessary information, including prices first before committing yourself to the actual proposal creation. Here's another quick tip. Do the shortest proposal first and send it out. Then use it as a template to create the next longest proposal, and so on and so forth. Don't forget to save each proposal in their specific directories in your hard drive on your work computer, as you will need to refer to them in the future. As you progress through you will find that a lot of the information overlaps and hence can be used in other proposals, thus saving you valuable typing and preparing time.

Concerning delivery of proposals: it obviously is always better to hand-deliver your proposal to the client. That way you can sit and discuss it and if the client has any questions they can be answered right then and there. Alternatively email is also a good delivery system. Try to steer clear of faxes if possible. For one thing the quality of the proposal is always affected, and for another if the proposal is fairly lengthy, (more than five pages) then some clients get put off by having a long stream of paper billow out from the fax machine.

A proposal of up seven pages can be stapled and delivered. If it is over seven pages, however, then a plastic quotation folder is preferable. It is more professional when delivered in this way.

Another handy tip – when hand delivering proposals always take an additional copy for yourself. That way if there are notes to be made you can alter your copy and bring it back to the office for updating.

If you have not physically hand delivered the proposal to the client, but instead emailed or faxed it, wait a few hours and then contact the client to confirm receipt of the document.

If you are able to discuss the proposal with your client when you deliver it, then do so. It allows the client to fully understand exactly what is required, and if there are any pertinent questions they can be dealt with.

After the proposal has been delivered, wait a few days depending on the size of the proposal. If the client is requesting one or two items, normally two days should suffice. If the proposal is substantial, then give the client about three days. Major network restructuring involves big cash, and the client usually has to confirm the project with a few people in the company. That means that the client will need to schedule an internal meeting with his/her colleagues to consider the options. Also, most companies will obtain a few additional quotes from our competition to see who the best in the field is. This also takes time. Don't worry; just be patient.

Once the proposal has been accepted, and you have received an order number, then the actual ordering of stock or, as in the case of services, the scheduling of relevant engineers, takes place. At this stage it is always a good idea to contact the client and inform him/her as to delivery ETA's (Estimated Time of Arrivals) for the order. This way the client can prepare their respective company for the onslaught of ABC Computers engineers and/ or stock.

If the order is delayed for any reason (out of stock, unavailable engineers, etc) LET THE CLIENT KNOW!!! Although the client might not be happy, they will appreciate the effort on your part to at least communicate with them and keep them informed. After all, they are investing their hard-earned cash on you and the company you represent.

CONCLUSION

The art of prospecting is a time old tradition throughout the sales community and in most cases becomes the entire starting point of your success. The important things to note about this are:

1. Remember to research your potential prospects so that when you contact them you have your focus set on their wants and needs.
2. Always try to smile on the 'phone when you contact them. Never rush your speech, and always speak clearly and definitively.
3. Don't become discouraged by negative responses. Out of every ten attempts you should receive at least one positive response. If not then analyse your tactics and modify them.
4. Once you are successful in making the appointment stick to it and never be late for the meeting.

5. Always give your prospective client a good impression as to the professionalism of the company you represent. Make sure your appearance is of a high standard and ensure that your product knowledge is as extensive as can be.
6. Communication with your client is essential. As long as your client is informed frequently as to the status of their queries they will be happy.

SUMMARY – CHAPTER 5.

Often when faced with the prospect of gaining new clients, many sales personnel baulk at the task and often wonder where to actually start, and hence do not start at all. Cold Calling is an important aspect of sales and does take a lot of practice but is essential to your survival as a sales person.

IDENTIFYING THE CLIENT

In order to be able to sell your goods and/or services, you must be able to find out your client's needs and by doing so you will be able to better understand how you can help the client achieve their goals. The core focus of any business is to make profit and your function is to offer them a means to increase their productivity and efficiency by giving them tools to do their job.

If necessary visit a company's website, or read about them in magazines and newspapers to obtain a better perspective about what their focuses are.

CONTACTING THE CLIENT.

You want to approach the Decision-Maker in the company. It could be the Managing Director, the Finance Director, or the IT Director, but these people will ultimately make the choice as to whether to support your proposal or not.

When contacting a prospect try to schedule an appointment and try not to mention the word "Sale" in your conversation. Also, try not to discuss your entire meeting over the telephone.

ESTABLISHING THE CLIENT

You need to schedule your meeting in your diary, whether it is handwritten or on computer.

Make sure when scheduling multiple appointments that you space them at least 2 hours apart giving you time to prepare for the next meeting.

Use the 5-3-2-1 strategy if possible:

5 – Visit 5 clients a day
3 – 3 must be new clients
2 – 2 must be previous clients
1 – Receive 1 order per day.

Make sure to confirm on the day or the day before that the appointment will still take place.

Ensure you dress formally for your meeting and guarantee you arrive at least fifteen minutes before your meeting.

3Switch your cellphone off or put it on silent before you participate in your meeting.

Refrain from smoking before your appointment.

Make sure you take notes as you discuss different issues but don't read notes made earlier that do not pertain to the meeting at hand.

If during the meeting you don't know the answer to a question then be honest and say so – don't lie to the client.

SUPPORTING THE CLIENT

Once you have finished the meeting and you get back to the office you need to prepare the sales proposal. Information needs to be gathered, prices need to be obtained, and the proposal must be comprehensive and professional – looking.

Try to hand deliver proposals so that you can discuss it with the prospect and take extra copies with you so that you can make any alterations.

Once the proposal has been accepted you need to prepare for the orders. If there is a problem with delivery of stock or services then notify the client so that there is proper communication between you and your client.

CHAPTER 6.
VALUE ADDED RESELLING

There is a popular misconception amongst IT companies that assumes if you sell a computer to a client then that is all they will need. However, clients for the most part are unaware of what they are buying and what exactly is out there in the marketplace. Many people arrive home with their brand spanking new computer, and they eagerly set it up, plug everything in, and switch it on (or the technician will deliver and install the system on your behalf). But what now? I have a computer, so what can I do with it?

Normally, a client will sit and play round for a while (perhaps an hour or two) but then they become bored with finding out about the Operating System, and they will look for more inspiration and stimulation. But you haven't provided anything else for them to do, so the system sits until they go back to the computer shop for something else. On the way they see another computer shop and decide to stop in "just to look around" and they end up spending money at your competitor!

I equate this type of selling to somebody purchasing a DVD player but no movies to go with it. If the sales person at the Department Store was astute they would have tried to include one or two movies in the deal so that the customer has something to do when they get home. If not, the customer most probably will go to the nearest video store to hire some movies, and then the Department Store would have lost out on some extra sales.

The term **Value Added Reselling** (or **VAR**) is assigned to those companies that offer holistic solutions in order to ensure that the client's every needs are met with respect to what they are purchasing, and in today's society it is vital to the survival of the IT Company to take on this mantle as well.

In this chapter we look at the concept of providing extra service and sales, and we look at a few typical examples of add-on products.

ADD-ONS

When a client buys a computer they are essentially purchasing a tool to perform various tasks, such as providing a communication medium (through the Internet and email), supplying education to their children (through various encyclopaedias and also Internet searching), allowing the customer to work from home (using products such as Microsoft Office ®, accounting packages, and other, more specialized packages), using it for security purposes (with the addition of CCTV) or entertainment, in the form of DVD's, music, and games.

Given the cutthroat market of computer selling, there generally is not enough profit to be made from selling just the machine. Where an IT company's profit comes from is providing supplementary products to accompany the computer at the time of purchase.

As a sales person, you need to talk to the potential buyer to get an idea of what they are hoping to use the computer for. If they mention they have children, then you know they will need some sort of Word Processing software so that the kids can type up school assignments and projects. In addition, a printer is a definite purchase because the child will need to print their work to hand in at their school. The Internet is also necessary because information needed for these assignments will nearly always be found on the Internet.

Reread the last paragraph again. What do you notice? Did you see that given a response from the client I managed to come up with three offers to assist them? And that could become three extra sales.

Let's take another example here. Ok, here is the scenario. A retired historian had decided to purchase a computer because he would like to write a book based upon a particular section of history. Ok, so what do we need here? Well, definitely a Word Processing package to type up his book, and perhaps a printer so that he can print it out in manuscript form. He will definitely need the Internet so that he can do some research and email people for information.

Ok, one more example. A student at university would like to take up a part-time job as a DJ at various parties (weddings, birthdays, etc). Ok, so he needs a computer. Great! What else will he need? Definitely a good sound card with advanced music mixing facilities. He is also going to need a headphone set. Speakers – not necessary unless he purchases a good system. Most musicians will obtain these from a specialist music shop. He is going to need a DVD writer and music software so that he can burn music CD's for various parties. Lastly, he will also probably use the Internet to purchase songs and search for other music to use. A last possibility is to offer him a microphone so that he can run karaoke events.

Where am I going with this? The trick here is to analyze your client's needs and then offer suggestions to fulfil them. Some of the suggestions the client will probably not even be aware of, but, if you know your products well, you can apply them to different circumstances.

Furthermore, you need to focus on different occupations and deduce what they would do in their job. If it's a Post Master, they will need a database and communication. If it's a Beauty Salon, they will need digital cameras to take photos of sample hair dos, and an accounting or billing system to charge the customers with.

You need to focus on different scenarios and occupations and realize what these people would typically do or need in order to get their jobs done. Once you have this information it becomes easy to apply it to the products you have in your portfolio in order to meet their needs.

A popular term that has been adopted for these extras is called **Add-Ons**, and you will come across this term (or similar) in almost every aspect of your life, when you decide to purchase something. Walk through a supermarket and you will see this all the time. What is based at the teller? Shelves of chocolates, sweets, and cool drinks! What sits above the fridges in the Meat Section? Bottles of Barbeque sauces and various herbs and spices!

You will come across this concept wherever you go, so why not start adopting it to your own salesmanship?

EXAMPLES OF ADD-ONS

Here we look at some examples of different add-on products that can be offered to various clients in various situations. This list is by no means exhaustive, and there are such a myriad of different scenarios that almost anything can be added onto a purchase in order to create a solution.

a. Internet - Possibly one of the most popular add-on products on offer today, access to the Internet has become part of normal everyday life for most people, and there are various packages available that will connect people in a matter of a few hours. There are various options available which include:

Bandwidth - This term refers basically to the speeds you will experience when you are connected to the Internet, and to put it into another perspective you could equate this to the lanes on a highway, and the maximum speed you are allowed to travel on that highway.

When you use a highway, you share the road with other drivers, who also need to use the same road to reach their destinations.

We relate this to the cables that connect us to the Internet: other users are also using the same cables to do the same job.

The size or width of the lane refers to the size of vehicle you can use on the road. This would relate to the data packet size you can use to transfer data.

Ok, now if I have confused you here, then let me digress slightly and explain this a little better.

Let's assume you have a file of 1024 kb that needs to be transferred over the Internet. Operating Systems work on 32 or 64 bits, which means that 32 bits of information can be processed at any given time. That file then would need to be spilt up into packets of information, or chunks, and fed to the processor one at a time. The same process happens with networking, and with the Internet. The connecting devices on either end of the connection can only process a certain amount of information at any given time, so the 1024 kb file is divided into data packets and fed through the connecting devices piece by piece.

Right, back to our discussion!

Each highway has a maximum speed limit. In South Africa this is 120 kph (approximately 74 mph). This does not necessarily mean that you will drive your car at 120 kph all the time. Sometimes you will drive at the speed limit, and sometimes you will drive a little slower. This is the same with the Internet. When we talk of **speeds** we are talking about the **maximum possible speed** that your data can travel. Depending on the circumstances, such as the strength of your connection (especially when working with wireless connections) and depending on how busy the "highway" is, your resultant data transfer speeds will differ but will never exceed the maximum data transfer rate, or "speed limit". This is why sometimes when you connect to the Internet your connection is slow; there might be many other users who are also connected at that time.

Connection type - There are various ways to connect to the Internet, both wired and wireless. Originally, some ten to fifteen years ago, we only had a choice to connect via cables. Nowadays, with the advancements in technology that we now experience, we have the luxury of experiencing wireless connections, thus allowing us the ability to explore the possibilities of mobile networking.

There are now quite a few connection types and protocols that are available, and I have given a brief description of each so that you know the differences between them.

Physical – These different standards refer to physical cabled connections to the Internet, and range from copper cables to Fibre Optic cables. Copper cables uses two data transmission types, being **analogue** and **digital**, whilst Fibre Optic cables only uses **digital** transmissions. I have listed them in alphabetical order.

ADSL - This acronym stands for **Asymmetrical Digital Subscriber Line** and is a form of **DSL** (explained below). It uses a high frequency signal over a telephone line allowing it to coincide with voice calls which use low frequencies. This means that voice calls can be made at the same time computer data is being sent over the same line.

If we look at distances typically ADSL cannot exceed further than 4 km although reports of up to 8 km can be achieved depending on the grade of copper wire used.

The name **Asymmetric** refers to the fact that the downstream data flow is much larger than that of the upstream flow. This makes the concept ideal for home users because very few users would consider uploading data to another computer. This is normally reserved for dedicated web servers. The faster downstream is more attractive to these types of users because this is the service that is the most commonly used.

Analogue - This was the original medium for users to gain access to the Internet, thanks to a certain gentleman called Alexander Graham Bell who invented the telephone in the 1800's. He never would have dreamed that his invention would be used for this kind of application! As the name suggests, the transmission type that is used is called **Analogue**, and works with something called **frequency modulation**. Ok, I'm not going into an entire discussion here about electronics, so I'm going to try to explain as easily and quickly as possible to try to help you understand.

Take yourself and go and sit on the beach and watch the ocean. It generates waves that advance onto the beach and then recede back into the sea. One such wave, from its advancement to its recession, is called a **cycle**. When the weather is calm the waves perform their cycles at a fairly lazy pace, but when there is a storm they become faster and faster (and yes, bigger as well) and the cycles of waves increase dramatically. This phenomenon in electronics, of the number of cycles per second (electricity flows a hell of a lot faster than the ocean, believe me), we call the **frequency**, and if a device is transmitting at a certain frequency, or cycles per second, then the receiving device must also be able to collect the information at the same speed.

Analogue signals use these frequencies to transmit information. Digital is another animal, however!

A computer uses bits to create data. Let's equate this to light switches. A light switch has two states. It can either be **on** (1) or **off** (0). These are absolutes. A switch cannot be half on, or half off. It's either on, or it's off! Final!

The electronics inside computers take strings of light switches and, using different combinations of on's and off's we can relate them to different things. To just show you a very simple example, let's take two switches.

Switch A	Switch B	Number
Off	Off	0
Off	On	1
On	Off	2
On	On	3

If both switches are off, we can translate this to mean the number 0. If Switch A is on and Switch B is off, we can translate this to mean the number 2. And if both switches are on, this then is the number 3.

To put things into perspective, computers use billions of these switches, each with different combinations, and basically that's how we get our data. Incidentally, this is the basis of **Binary**, the number system that is used by computers.

Digital Transmission uses combinations of these numbers in different sizes to transmit data. I mentioned earlier about 32 bit Operating Systems. A single switch is a bit, so 32 bits would mean 32 switches combined together to get various combinations. The transmitting and receiving equipment must send and accept the same number of bits (by the way, in computer language, we call these strings of bits **words**, so 32 bits is the **word size** of the device – it has a word size of 32 bits) in order to understand each other, and this then will hopefully assist you in the bandwidth table shown above to understand the different speeds.

Now that we have got all of this out of the way, let's continue. The human voice is analogue in nature, and the telephone lines, or rather, the sending and transmitting equipment at the telephone exchanges, is designed to use analogue signals in order to transmit the information. But computers can't understand this language. We need to convert the signals to digital.

Enter the modem! Otherwise known as a **Modulator/ Demodulator**, the modem takes the digital signal from the computer, converts it to analogue, sends it over the phone line, and when it reaches the other side, the receiving modem converts the analogue signal back into digital and gives it to the receiving computer. The modem is also known as a **Dial-Up Modem**.

That's basically the concept behind the modem which has become the platform for almost all electronic communication. And this technology is still used today in remote locations where only phone lines exist and nothing else.

Incidentally, this is a bit of useless information for you. One of the names given to this "protocol" was **POTS** which stands for "**Plain Old Telephone System**".

> **Broadband -** This term is an abbreviation of **Broadband Internet Access** and is basically a high data rate Internet access system which is compared with normal dial-up modems used in Analogue connections.

Modems use a maximum transfer rate of up to 56kbps but with Broadband you can gain maximum data transfer rates that can exceed 256kbps, making it a much more versatile system to use.

There is another benefit to using Broadband over dial-up modems. Modems use the entire telephone line for Internet usage, which means that you cannot make a phone call while you are connected to the Internet. Broadband on the other hand **shares** the phone line and thus you can surf the Internet and make phone calls at the same time.

> **DSL -** To put this one in a nutshell **Digital Subscriber Line** (formerly known as **Digital Subscriber Loop**) provides digital data transmission over the wires on a local telephone network. Now this differs to the technology offered by dial-up modems, which convert the digital data from the computer into analogue signals and then

transmits them over the phone lines. DSL does not convert at all, but rather maintains the original digital coding.

This means that it can coincide with normal voice calls because they both use different data types (DSL uses high frequency whilst voice calls uses low frequency). In other words you can surf the Internet and make voice phone calls at the same time.

Right! Speed! Depending on the line conditions, the implemented service levels, and the DSL technology, maximum speeds can range from 256 kbps to 24'000 kbps.

There are two standards that use this technology and explained elsewhere in this section, **ADSL** and **SDSL**.

ISDN - The **Integrated Services Digital Network** is a telephone network that operates in much the same way as Analogue networks in that a dial up connection is performed to connect to a particular exchange and then either voice or data is transmitted. The major difference here is that **ISDN** is **Digital** meaning that the quality of signals is of much higher quality than analogue.

There are three kinds of service-related interfaces that are offered, namely:

Basic Rate Interface (BRI), **Primary Rate Interface (PRI)**, and **Broadband – ISDN (B-ISDN)**.

To explain the functionality we will define the BRI, where there are two **B-Channels** and one **D – Channel**. Each B-Channel is capable of transmitting 64kbps of data each, whilst the D-Channel is used for the carrier signal, and is a way of ensuring the data transmitted properly.

If a voice call is being made and the Internet is being surfed at the same time, the two B-Channels are shared between the different types of signals, meaning that you will have 64kbps available for the Internet. However, both channels can be combined to allow a 128kbps throughput for data.

PRI and Broadband-ISDN use combinations of these 64kbps channels to increase bandwidth, and the reason for the term **Broadband** is simply that the up-speeds and down-speeds are the same.

Leased Line – A **Leased Line** is a direct communications connection between two places. There are no "dial-up" requirements as this connection is permanent. You could theoretically equate this to connecting a network cable from one computer located in one town to another located in another town. This permanent connection can be used for both telephone and data services (Internet included).

SDSL - This is similar to ADSL (explained above) but the major difference is the fact that the upstream and downstream data volumes are the same, meaning that it becomes more attractive to the business sector, as both services are required. However, the physical technology required for this type of service is more expensive than with ADSL, so the consumer must expect to pay more for their subscription. The name, by the way, stands for **Symmetrical Digital Subscriber Line.**

Wireless - Recently (some odd fifteen years ago, could be longer than that; I'm generalizing in this time span) the Technological Gurus designed the Wireless connection, because they were probably fed up with begin tied down with cables all the time. Understandably, Radio has been around for almost a century, and Satellite was designed during the Second World War, but radio has been exploited by so many other applications that it becomes unstable for decent data transmission, and the cost of using satellite to do the same job proves to be too expensive (the people that shot the satellites into orbit have spent a good few billion Dollars to get them there, and they need to recoup their costs) so the Gurus designed other cheaper methods to do this job, and they are listed below. I have listed them in alphabetical order.

WARNING!!! You are about to be hammered with some seriously hectic acronyms!

Bluetooth - This protocol is not strictly used for the Internet per se, but I have included it here just to help you understand what it is all about. In the chapter on Types of IT Companies (Chapter 1) I discussed **Personal Area Networks (PAN's)**, and it is this protocol that makes this topology possible.

This wireless protocol was designed to exchange data over short distances (about ten or so meters, although some people claim to have been able to connect up to a hundred meters using a Class 1 protocol) between fixed and mobile devices, such as cellphones and laptops. It was originally designed to replace the cumbersome RS232 serial data cables.

EDGE - This acronym has quite a long one here - **Enhanced Data rates for GSM**

Evolution. Ok, so basically it is a backward-compatible digital mobile phone technology that offers improved data transmission rates and is offered as an extension to the standard **GSM.** To go a little further it is also considered to be a 3G technology, and using various compressions and encoding techniques it almost triples the potential of GSM/ GPRS networks.

GPRS - **GSM** mobile phones (discussed below) are the most common instruments of their kind used globally and they use the **GPRS (General Packet Radio Service)** system to transmit data. The **GPRS** core network is the centralized part of the **GPRS** system and also provides support for **3G** and **WCDMA** based networks (also described below).

GSM - The **Global System for Mobile Communications** standard is the most popular standard used globally, and apparently the GSM Association estimates that over 80% of the global market are using this standard, allowing for communications between different Mobile Phone Operators. Furthermore, the signals are all digital in nature giving a better clarity of speech, and allowing the simultaneous of data transfer.

HSDPA - This toy (the full name being **High-Speed Downlink Packet Access**) is basically an enhanced **3G** communications protocol giving the user higher data transfer speeds with greater volumes. Current uses support download speeds of up to 14.4 Mbps.

3G - This is the **Third Generation** of telecommunications standards and general technology for mobile networking. 3G networks allow network operators to offer customers a wider range of more advanced services while achieving greater network capacity through improved spectral efficiency.

3GPP - In your travels you might come across this term being bandied around so I have included it here to give you a bit of an insight.

3GPP stands for **3rd Generation Partnership Project** and is a collaboration between groups of telecommunications associations, to create a third generation (**3G**) cell phone system specification that meets with the **ITU**'s (**International Telecommunication Union**) requirements. This standardization includes Radio, Core Network, and Service architecture.

4G - This is the **Fourth Generation** of telecommunications standards and general technology for mobile networking and where it adds to **3G** is it offers broadband Internet access to **Laptops** with **wireless modems**, **Smartphones**, and other mobile devices incorporating **Mobile Web Access, High Definition Mobile** and **3D Television,** and **Cloud Computing.**

WCDMA - This **Wideband Code Division Multiple Access** basically is an air interface found in 3G networks, and is used to communicate with other systems.

To give you an example of what I mean here, Microsoft ® and Novell ® are both network Operating Systems for computers, but they do not "talk" to each other over a network without an interface. The **IPX/SPX** network protocol was thus developed that allows the two systems to liaise with each other. We could, in this instance, equate the **WCDMA** to the **IPX/SPX** protocol, allowing these phones to communicate with other phones that have been developed using alternative technology.

Domain and website hosting - These make nice birthday gifts! Huh? Have I lost you for a second? Ok, let me explain!

When we search for websites we use domains to find where the websites are.

Some of you readers are saying, "Yes, but I know this stuff already!" However, as I have said before, there are readers that **don't** know how this all works.

So I'm explaining it!

In basic terms (because this is not a technical manual)!

Basically there are bunches (or clusters) of servers in several countries throughout the world that the Internet is based on. These servers hold the base domains, for example:

.com (Commercial)
.org (Organizational)
.co.za (Generic for South Africa)
.co.uk (Generic for United Kingdom)

For instance, in South Africa we have a cluster of servers in Cape Town called **SAIX** (**South African Internet Exchange**) and these systems hold the base domains. When other servers connect to these (and somebody pays for the service) we have second level domains, such as:

Kaspersky.com
Microsoft.com
Kzntreasury.gov.za
Mweb.co.za

Many ISP's purchase the right to host domains (they buy licenses for this privilege) and they can have a second level domain and then charge clients to host their domains on these servers. Mweb.co.za is one of South Africa's biggest ISP's.

With regards to domains, anyone, and I mean anyone, can own a domain. I could for example have adriannoble.co.za if I wish provided somebody else has not already purchased that domain. There is a small initial fee to register a domain in your name, and then a yearly renewal to keep the domain active.

These domains can be hosted on any computer anywhere in the world, which is why I said earlier that they make very good birthday presents. In the United States of America this is a common practice because the domain will remain with its owner for life provided they renew it annually and the owner will be able to host it anywhere in the world.

Once you own a domain you can develop a website, have it hosted on your ISP's server, and have it attached to your domain so that when somebody types in adriannnoble.co.za your website appears.

Search Engines such as Google, categorize your websites according to certain keywords so that when somebody is searching and the keywords match your website, your domain will appear in the Search Results window. Of course you need to submit your website to these Search Engines in order to have them indexed, and if you wish to appear in the first ten search results (which is normally the ones that browsers will select when searching) you might have to pay for the service.

Now you might think, "What is the significance of owning a domain?" We have a South African by the name of Mark Shuttleworth who owned a domain and built an entire company from his garage based upon authenticating Digital Certificates which are used to verify the authenticity of certain websites. Almost all of his business was conducted over the Internet, and when he sold his domain (and his database) he earned in the excess of $5 Billion from the sale! For a simple name!!!

By the way, **hosting** means that the website and domain reside on your ISP's servers, which are connected permanently to the Internet with enough bandwidth to cope with the amount of traffic that could be generated when people visit your site. You can host your own domain and website locally if you are permanently connected and you have purchased a connection that is big enough to cope with the incoming and outgoing traffic that might be generated as your website becomes popular.

Although you can use software such as *FrontPage*® (discussed below) to design your website, it is best to enlist the advice of professional Website Designers because they know what works and what doesn't. They are aware of which combinations of colours are pleasing to the eye and which combinations irritate others. They also know the layouts that are the most appealing to browsers. My advice? Put one together and then ask a professional to take a quick look and let you know where you have gone wrong. You can also embark in allowing the designer to develop the project from scratch, but then you (or your client) must be prepared to pay dearly for the service, because these designers are in great demand, and they are expensive!

Emails and aliases - In order to communicate with the world, and in most cases, to conduct business properly in today's society, people need email addresses. Most of your Internet packages you purchase from ISPs have email addresses included as part of the deal. Some package deals also include **aliases**. So what are these things?

Let's look at an example to understand how this works. You own a small business and you have two people working for you. You have ownership of a domain and you need some email addresses for all your staff.

Email addresses always have the format of <u>someone@</u> <u>somewhere.anywhere</u>, so your email addresses will look something like the following (assuming your domain is xcompany.com):

<u>adrian@xcompany.com</u>
<u>sales@xcompany.com</u>
<u>reception@xcompany.com</u>
<u>info@xcompany.com</u>
<u>accounts@xcompany.com</u>

These emails are aliases of the domain xcompany.com.
If you do not have a domain you can always use your ISP's:

<u>adrian@mweb.co.za</u>

There are instances whereby companies have a domain (<u>www.</u> <u>xcompany.com</u>) but they use their ISP's email address extension instead (<u>adrian@mweb.co.za</u>). So when does this scenario happen?

In order to use your domain as an email extension you need an email server attached to your domain for your company's exclusive use. The server can either be located at your premises (in which case it is a **local** email server) or at the ISP (called a **remote** email server) but the server is specifically assigned to your company and no other. If not then you need to share the ISP's email server with other users, and in this case you will need to use the ISP's email address extension.

b. Anti-Virus - There thousands of new strains of malware that attack the Internet on a daily basis, and because of this having an *Anti-Malware Software Package* is as important as having an Operating System. But it still astounds me that so many sales people do not include these packages as a standard when somebody purchases a new computer. Take for example Kaspersky Lab®, which offers three families of products to cater for any situation. Let's take a brief look at these, but before we do, we need to mention a very important aspect of Kaspersky Lab ®' protection that is inherent in every one of its products – **Cloud Protection.**

Kaspersky Security Network ® - Every single user of Kaspersky Lab ® products, from the consumer to the business, can take advantage of this **Cloud Protection** as an added form of protection.

Kaspersky Security Network (KSN) is a complex distributed infrastructure dedicated to processing depersonalised cybersecurity-related data streams from approximately 80 million voluntary participants around the world. **Kaspersky Security Network** not only allows users to detect and block previously unknown threats, but also helps to locate and blacklist online attack sources, providing reputational data for millions of known websites and domains, applications (black- or whitelisted) and so on.

Whenever a user installs one of the **Personal Security** products (discussed below) onto their computer, one of the screens during installation asks the user if they would like to "participate in the *Kaspersky Security Network*", which is enabled by default, as home users are advised to take advantage of the cloud-assisted protection. Business users can configure the settings via *Kaspersky Security Center*®.

So, why the concentration on the **Personal Security** users? Well, let's think about this for a second. It is the home user that is at the forefront of exposure to various forms of malware present on the Internet. Many personal users are not aware of the dangers of visiting dubious websites to download pirated software, videos or music. In businesses, generally speaking, systems are configured to restrict access to various information and prohibit downloading for personal gain.

So how does all of this actually work? In every single Endpoint installation, whether it is a Personal or Business Security product, and regardless of the platform used, there is a local instance of a signature database which contains special records (signatures) of blacklisted URLs and domain names, executable files, and contents of SPAM emails (SPAM is discussed in Chapter 15).

Let's use an example to illustrate the method of how the *Kaspersky Security Network* ® (*KSN*) works. You have just downloaded an application from the Internet and you wish to install this onto your home computer, which is protected by a Kaspersky Lab ® product. The first thing that happens is your system checks to see if it has any information regarding the application, and whether it is safe to install or not. If there is such information in the local signature database, your computer will respond according to this information. If the application is **trusted** (*whitelisted*) then you will be able to install it successfully. If it is **not trusted** (*blacklisted*) then you will be prevented from installing it, because the application probably contains some sort of malware that will perform damage to your computer software.

If the local signature database cannot find any information pertaining to the application it then goes and checks in the *KSN* to see if there are any records and copies these to its local signature database. It will then decide the outcome based on this information.

If in fact there is *no* information present in the **KSN,** your local product will allow the application to install but it will use a number of its proactive defensive technologies, among which ***Host-Based Intrusion Prevention System, Automatic Exploit Prevention*** and ***System Watcher*** (discussed below) to monitor every aspect of the application's behaviour as it installs and executes. Any suspicious behaviour detected will force the application to close. With any event a record of the application and its behaviour is recorded by the local database and this in turn is uploaded into the *KSN.* This information becomes available to other *KSN* users within minutes.

With this technology in mind, let's look at the products.

Personal Security – This family of products caters for the individual user and are ideally suited for the average home user. With the addition of **Tablets** and **Smartphones** into our everyday lives, the latest editions of the Kaspersky Lab ® **Personal Product** range are able to install onto the Windows, Apple Mac, Android, Windows Phone, and iOS platforms.

The below table lists the three main products in this range and gives a list of comparisons between the three offerings. I have included a brief description of each feature to help you understand a little better.

The three popular products in this family are:

- *Kaspersky Anti-Virus 2015* – This is the basic package and offers the consumer the full multi-award winning *Kaspersky Anti-Malware* engine as well as a personal firewall. Users who are on a tight budget, do not access the Internet very often, or just require a good Anti-Malware package should choose this product. It supports the Microsoft Windows ® platform.

- *Kaspersky Internet Security Multi-Device 2015* - This is a fully featured personal computer protection offering for those users who access the Internet often and require complete peace-of-mind that their data is protected against malicious and damaging attacks.

Owing to the fact that several home computers are accessed by the entire family, there is also *Parental Control* built into this package, giving parents the ability to limit or control what their children are accessing and when.

As well as supporting the Windows ® platform, *Kaspersky Internet Security 2015* also supports the Apple Mac ®, iOS ®, Windows Phone ®, and Android ® platforms.

- *Kaspersky Total Security Multi-Device 2015* – Formerly named *Kaspersky PURE,* the *Kaspersky Total Security Multi-Device* product really has a complete Personal Security Protection platform offering, as well as all the features of *Kaspersky Internet Security 2015,* additional features included are **Password Manager, Backup, Encryption** and **File Shredder.**

The package also supports Windows ®, Apple Mac ®, iOS ®, Windows Phone®, and Android ® platforms.

	Kaspersky Anti-Virus 2015	Kaspersky Internet Security - Multi-Device 2015	Kaspersky Total Security - Multi-Device 2015
	Essential Protection	Premium Protection	Ultimate Protection
Proactive Defense	XXX	XXX	XXX
Antivirus	XXX	XXX	XXX
Tweaking of computer security settings	X	XX	XXX
Personal data protection	X	XX	XXX
Parental control		XXX	XXX
Application Control and Safe Run		XXX	XXX
Firewall		XXX	XXX
Dangerous website blocker		XXX	XXX
Anti-spam		XXX	XXX
Network security management		X	XXX
Password Manager			XXX
Data backup and recovery			XXX
Protection for Android devices		XXX	XXX
Protection for iOS		X	XXX
Protection for MAC		XX	XXX
Protection for Windows Phone		XXX	XXX
Public Wi-Fi protection		XXX	XXX
Webcam Protection		XXX	XXX

Below is a brief description of each feature.

- **Proactive Defence** – To effectively counter threats that behave "intelligently" in their attempts to bypass the defences of traditional technologies, Kaspersky Lab® has developed a multi-layered security solution, which includes an important module, *System Watcher,* which monitors applications for any deviant behaviour. To name a few examples, *System Watcher* incorporates the *Behaviour Stream Signatures* and *Automatic Exploit Prevention* subsystems, which are designed to roll back **Ransomware** attempts and usage of software vulnerabilities, respectively.
- **Anti-Malware** – With the award-winning *Kaspersky Anti-Virus Engine* that is provided in all of Kaspersky Lab ®' products, and coupled with the several reactive

and proactive mechanisms, as well as regular signature database updates, all further empowered by cloud-assisted *Kaspersky Security Network* users are sure to have one of the best security products looking after their valuable data.

- **Tweaking of computer security settings** – With the basic *Kaspersky Anti-Virus 2015* product you are still able to configure some basic controls on the computer. However, with the more advanced products like *Kaspersky Internet Security* and *Kaspersky Total Security Multi-Device* there are **advanced** options that can be accessed to allow a more configurable secure environment.

- **Personal data protection** – Kaspersky Lab ® have built in several features to assist in protecting your personal data from being compromised. Some of these features include:

  - **Safe Money** – this unique technology adds extra layers of protection whenever the user is accessing banking websites thus preventing theft of credit card details, passwords, and other personal information.

  - **Secure Keyboard** – When a bank or payment website is opened this technology automatically prevents and kind of *keylogger malware* from accessing data typed on the keyboard.

  - **Virtual Keyboard** – When required the **Virtual Keyboard** can be displayed on the screen allowing the user to enter confidential information using mouse clicks instead of the keyboard. This helps prevent *keyloggers* from reading data entered via the keyboard.

  - **Encryption** – With *Kaspersky Total Security Multi-Device* users have an option to encrypt their important files into password-protected data vaults.

- **Parental control** – These tools are designed to keep your children safe when they go online. They enable parents to prohibit their children from seeing inappropriate content, limit the amount of exposure to social networks as well as controlling the disclosure of personal information, limit online purchase and the downloading of games and other applications.
- **Safe Mode** – When the web browser is working in Safe Mode, untrusted applications have no access to the transaction process, including clipboard. In addition, the browser is constantly scanned for any unexpected or untrusted modules.

Kaspersky Lab® also includes two other features – Rollback which, in the event of any sort of infiltration, allows the user to "rollback" the computers' Operating System to before the incident's occurrence and then 'block' the attack. There is also **Anti-Blocker** technology that assists the user in unblocking the computer if it is being blocked by a *Trojan* – by using a predefined key combination that allows bypassing the blocking screen and running the necessary disinfection.

To go a little further, Kaspersky Lab ® is one of the few products that protect against **Rootkits**. These are small pieces of software that are able to penetrate the Operating System's low-level system processes and hide themselves from detection before the AV is loaded into memory. *Kaspersky Lab® Anti-Rootkit* technology is not only able to prevent the installation of known or even unknown rootkits (with the help of *System Watcher*), but it can also detect and disinfect the rootkits, which penetrated the system before Kaspersky Lab ®'s solution was installed.

Many forms of malware try to copy entries into the system's Registry, thereby activating whenever the Operating System accesses the Registry for various reasons. Kaspersky Lab ® protects the Registry against these forms of attack.

These technologies also scan **Macros.** A **Macro** is a small set of commands in an Office Application such as MS Word (discussed below) that runs each time the application starts. Typical Macros could be things like setting the margins, font type, and font size whenever the application starts up. For example, Newspaper Publishers format all their text into columns so that they fit onto the page of the final printed newspaper. A Macro could be designed that will automatically setup the columns every time the Word Processor starts up. The **Proactive Detection** technologies scan all **Macros** to ensure that nothing deviant occurs.

- **Firewall** – A **Firewall** controls the flow of information in and out of a computer and provides a secure "perimeter" for the computer. In addition, the **Network Attack Blocker** detects suspicious activities and blocks external attacks.
- **Dangerous website blocker** – Before loading the contents of a website, the Kaspersky Lab®'s **URL Advisor** first checks the reputation of a web-site that user is trying to reach, either in local cache or in the *Kaspersky Security Network*®. A Colour-coded icon displays to indicate whether the site is "Trusted", "Suspicious" or "Dangerous".

The multi-platform Kaspersky Lab® **Safe Browser** detects and blocks phishing web-sites that mimic the real web-sites and attempt to run malicious code or conduct fraudulent activity.

- **Anti-spam** – With the influx of SPAM email (covered in more detail in Chapter 15) Internet Service Providers are hard-pressed to stem the tide of this unsolicited mail, especially when considering the fact that each subscriber is unique in their personal definitions of what constitutes SPAM mail. Offered in both *Kaspersky Internet Security* and *Kaspersky Total Security Multi-Device* the consumer can use

Kaspersky Lab ®'s excessive knowledge of SPAM email contents or apply their own settings. The engine, which operates with most popular email clients, is intelligent in that, once you have "taught" it with some sample emails to begin with, it begins to "learn" other mails that are similar and automatically quarantines them.

- **Network security management** – Using the My Kaspersky Account you are able to check the security status of all your online devices that are running Kaspersky Lab® security software, as well as manage your product licenses. If you are running ***Kaspersky Total Security Multi-Device*** you are also able to activate and configure security features.

- **Password Manager** – Passwords can be managed for applications and websites. Also included are ***Identity Cards***. These are virtual information facilities to help automate the completion of web forms and they contain a range of personal information such as name, identify number, address, birth dates, and credit card information.

In addition, the ***Password Manager*** securely stores and synchronizes your passwords for access from your PC, Apple Mac®, Android® phones and tablets, iPhones® and iPads®. You only need to remember a single **Master Password** and all relevant passwords for that application or website will become available.

- **Data backup and recovery** – Backups of your documents and photos can be scheduled and automated for supported platforms.

In addition, the ***File Shredder*** is included. When you delete a file from your hard drive traces of that file still remain on the drive. Using specialised software it is possible to restore that deleted information to its original condition. With Kaspersky Lab®'s *File Shredder* it purges the data completely from the hard drive.

- **Protection for Android®** – 96% of mobile malware is aimed at this operating system, for the simple reason that **Android** ® is an Open Source platform. What this means is that anyone can develop code for the system without having to acquire special rights or permissions. Hackers and malefactors thus have an easy time developing malware for this operating system. In addition, Android users can take advantage of the whole range of remotely activated anti-theft commands: Device Lock, Data Wipe, Locate, Alarm, Mugshot, and SIM Watch. If needed, it gives the opportunity to review logs of recent device activities and status of anti-theft commands, and their subsequent results.

- **Safe Browsing for iOS and Windows Phone–** Kaspersky Lab ® is providing the iOS and Windows Phone user with protection from phishing links with **Safe Browser**. In addition, the digital life of iOS users is further simplified with Password Manager.

- **Protection for MAC** – Although the share of Mac-specific threats is low compared to that of PCs, it is constantly rising, so having a security solution is not a luxury, but a necessity.

- **Insecure Wi-Fi notification** – Kaspersky Lab®'s **Wi-Fi Security Notification** automatically verifies the current connection that is being used and warns the user if the network they are trying to connect is unsecure or compromised.

- **Webcam Protection** – Available for Windows ® based computers, this innovative technology prevents unauthorised access to your webcam so that you or your surroundings cannot be spied upon.

Business Security – Since 2007, Kaspersky Lab® has been developing its business product range based upon the concept of the **Open Space Security**, for the different types of computers available, namely *workstations, file servers, mail servers, internet gateways, collaboration servers,* and *mobile devices.*

With the evolution of malware and a rise in mobile computing, Kaspersky Lab ®, rethought the concept of endpoint security and redesigned their business offering.

The current **Kaspersky Endpoint Security for Business** line provides the freedom to choose one of the four tiers. The focus is placed on *how much security is required* by the customer rather than the *same security for different types of computers.*

Looking at the table below we will examine each of the four tiers and what they encompass in terms of features. However, before we go into this we need to first mention the **Kaspersky Security Center®**.

Kaspersky Security Center® - This software package, which was formerly known as the **Administration Console,** is the central point of control for entire product range. Installed and configured on a central server (Windows XP ® and above are supported) it deploys configurations, licenses, software packages and updates to all the endpoints in the network. It gathers the updates via Internet connection and stores them locally so they can be reused multiple times thus saving bandwidth.

Various tasks can be configured in the **Security Center®** to monitor and manage all the endpoints in the network.

It is also able to use the **Kaspersky Security Network®** for various queries from its networked computers – if it's enabled.

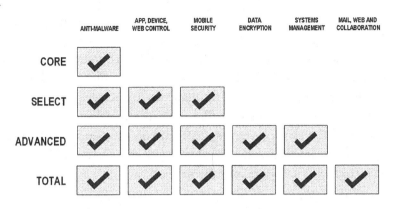

With the four tiers discussed below each level becomes accumulative in features from the previous level.

- **CORE** – This basic tier offers the endpoints Kaspersky Lab ®' award-winning Anti-Malware engine and is suitable for the protection of systems in **peer-to-peer networks.** These types of networks do not have any dedicated servers. Instead each workstation acts as both a **client** and a **server** depending on the requirement.

This tier does *not* offer protection for servers or mobile devices. It also does not contain any *Endpoint Controls* (see below).

Another good use for this tier of security is in *hybrid* networks where various third party solutions are already in place offering differing forms and layers of security.

- **SELECT** – This bundle provides protection for workstations, file servers, and mobile devices, and incorporates a full **Mobile Device Management** facility. It also contains three very important features in its *Endpoint Controls.*

Endpoint Controls – In a business environment, (academic environments are also included here) productivity is a core focus and employees (or students in the case of academic situations) need to concentrate on the daily running and development of the company. Time wasted in playing games, accessing social networks, and engaging in activities that are counter-productive need to be taken into consideration. There are also several risks involved with people who are unaware of the levels of security required by the company, and having the power to be able to manipulate their local security software on their endpoint could result in the leaking of valuable information to the outside world, or introducing malware into the network.

The ***Endpoint Controls*** were designed so that IT administrators of the company running Kaspersky Lab's business solution can maintain the security policies of that business, and there are three such controls:

- **Application Controls** –Users within the corporate network can be restricted from the usage of various applications available in the infrastructure. The main purpose of this control is to ensure that no malicious or potentially unsecure application is run within the company, but it also can be used to prevent the usage of applications that are unwanted by the company, for any reason.
- **Device Controls** – Protecting the corporation's data is very important and Administrators look for different ways to secure their network. One area that can become potential breaches in security is that of allowing external devices to gain access to the network or the endpoints. The **Device Controls** limit usage of USB ports, printers, Bluetooth, Infra-Red, and Wi-Fi, as well as other external sources.

Let's look at an example of how such a breach could occur if proper controls are not in place.

You are a sales person and you have been offered a lucrative position in another firm. You have been promised a definite increase in salary combined with additional benefits. However, one of the criteria for the new employment position is that you provide the new company with an existing client database.

Now, in the "old days" people made use of *Floppy Discs or Stiffy Discs,* and *Compact Discs* to externally store and transport information. All of these drives had flashing lights and each made some sort of mechanical noise whilst they were in operation so anyone passing by would notice that the drives were in operation. In today's world, with the ubiquitous usage of the *USB Memory Sticks,* there are no flashing lights or mechanical noises so a user can quietly insert one of these devices, copy information, remove it, and place it in their pocket and walk away.

With Kaspersky Lab®' **Device Controls** however the Administrator could be as specific as to *only* allow a specific *USB Memory Stick* with a particular serial number to gain access to a particular USB port on a given endpoint to copy only a file with a particular file extension, and give it only 45 minutes' worth of access.

Looking at another, similar example, the same sales person could instead print out that entire database, and walk out of the company with the hard copy in his or her briefcase and nobody would notice unless the System Administrator restricted access to the company's printers.

- ○ **Web Controls** – The Internet has become a very real integral part of our lives and a great part of our lives is spent connected to and using the Internet for various activities. It is also one of the most vulnerable starting points for malware infiltration.

Given the amount of resources the Internet has to offer it is quite easy for anyone to spend considerable time exploring and in a work environment this becomes quite detrimental to the overall productivity of the company.

The **Web Controls** allow Administrators to limit access to the Internet in various different ways such as limiting time spent on social networks, controlling actual websites that can be visited, and clamping down on the ability to access Webmail email accounts. Data transfers can also be controlled and prohibited if need be, and this will prevent any sort of data leakage.

- **ADVANCED** – For those businesses that require even more security the **ADVANCED** level is ideal for providing additional tools to enhance these requirements. As well as containing all the features offered in **SELECT** the following are now added:
  - **Encryption** – Using a 256-bit AES algorithm, entire hard drives, folders, or files can be encrypted and managed by the *Security Centre.* When encrypting the entire drive pre-boot login screens are possible and 2-stage authentication is possible and configurable allowing not only passwords to gain entry but Smartcards and Security Tokens as well.
  - **Systems Management** – Explained also below in the *Targeted Solutions* this suite of tools really augment what was only achievable in the past by additional third party applications. Features such as Third Party *Patch Management, Vulnerability Assessment, Hardware and Software Inventory Management, Remote Operating System Deployment and Remote Tools, and License Inventory Management* assist in offering a complete Endpoint Security Solution, and not just an Anti-Malware product.

By combining all of these tools into a single unified solution all configured and managed by the *Security Center* the consumer is guaranteed of a comprehensive solution developed with the same code base and incorporated into a single management console. This reduces the costs involved in purchasing additional packages and running tem on separate dedicated servers. It also reduces the administration and training as everything is incorporated into a single console. In addition, because the entire system is developed by the same team there are no concerns about compatibility issues.

- **TOTAL** – There are three types of servers that frequently connect outside of the internal network to transfer information, and these pose potential threats to the contained environment. These three servers are:
    - ○ **Email** – Email is one of the most popular forms of communication and the presence of Email Servers is very common. However, with a substantial amount of Spam, Phishing, and data leakage occurring via email, it is necessary to be able to scan incoming and outgoing emails at the server level.
    - ○ **Internet Gateway** – This server type, as the name suggests, is the link to the Internet from the internal network. In some cases it is also known as a *firewall* and its function is to control traffic flow. However, it may be required to scan all traffic flowing through the server, for any sort of malware, without slowing down the flow of traffic; this is what *Internet Gateway* does as part of the **TOTAL SECURITY FOR BUSINESS.**
    - ○ **Collaboration** – Microsoft **SharePoint** ® is one of the leading brands in collaborative software (another older system was known as **Lotus Notes®**) and with the amount of traffic flowing to and from these servers from distributed sources there is a very real need to secure the traffic. The data leakage prevention feature is also available as an add-on feature to Collaboration Security.

A more detailed explanation will be found in the ***Targeted Solutions*** section below.

Basically, this is what differentiates **TOTAL SECURITY FOR BUSINESS** from the **ADVANCED** platform. However, these solutions are also offered separately and are discussed in more detail in the ***Targeted Solutions*** section below.

Kaspersky Lab®' Targeted Solutions – In the case of an existing infrastructure that already encompasses a myriad of different systems providing some form of security in the network, it may be required to introduce a specific solution to perform a particular task. For this purpose Kaspersky Lab ® offer a number of separate products.

Also, in the case of the two tiers, **SELECT** and **ADVANCED** described above, Administrators might want to add some email security, or scan for malware on their internet gateways, or protect data in transit to their collaboration servers.

The list below is in alphabetical order:

- ***Kaspersky Anti-Spam for Linux*** ® - With the many different versions of Linux, and the extensive development of third party software, Kaspersky Lab® created a separate module that only filters Spam Email on the Linux-based Email Servers.

- ***Kaspersky Data Leakage Protection for Collaboration®*** – This product, launched in March 2015, adds another level of protection to ***Kaspersky Security for Collaboration*** ®. It checks all traffic flowing to and from the collaboration server to detect credit card numbers, passwords, identity numbers, and other criteria that have been configured by the System Administrators. There are also custom dictionaries that can be installed.

- ***Kaspersky Data Leakage Protection for Mail Server*** ® - This product, which was also launched in March 2015, does the same task as its Collaboration counterpart except that it checks for incoming and outgoing mail for possible transferral of confidential information.

- *Kaspersky Security for Collaboration* ® – What exactly is **Collaboration**? Let's take an example to try and explain this. Let's say that a new aircraft is being designed and developers all over the world are involved in this project.

It's time to build the wings and one set of engineers creates a diagram outlining the basic shape of the wing. This diagram is stored in the **Collaboration Server's** database – for example, on Microsoft SharePoint. Next the Electrical Engineers decide that they now need to insert all the electrical cabling into the wing. Whilst they are busy with this the Hydraulic Engineers need to insert all their systems, and as the two sets of engineers are busy populating the diagram stored in the database it is refreshed constantly, so that both systems can be designed simultaneously.

I hope you can understand from my example how useful this type of system can be. The big problem is, (and I hope you had picked this up with my explanation) is that, when dealing with these types of systems, not everyone involved with the project are necessarily in the same office on the same network, and protected by all the company's internal security structures. There are some cases (quite frequently in fact) whereby participants a connecting remotely using a myriad of different connections all with varying security levels. With this in mind it is important to be able to secure the information that is being transmitted between the **Collaboration Server** and the client so that it cannot be tampered with in any way, or stolen whilst in transit.

Kaspersky Security for Collaboration ® offers protection for both the client and the server, and it can also be an add-on to the **SELECT** and **ADVANCED** levels of security as described above.

- *Kaspersky Security for File Server* ® - As the need for storage increases in a network we find that an increased number of file servers are required and added to the network. This cluster of file servers are named *"The Server Farm"* and *Kaspersky Security for File Server* ® protects all the file servers in the farm.

- *Kaspersky Security for Internet Gateway* ® – Data traffic flows through these servers into and out from the internal network but they do not necessarily check for any malware in that traffic. This product adds that additional layer of security to these servers by scanning the traffic flow for any malware. *It is important to note that this product does NOT replace the Internet Gateway; it merely scans the traffic for malware. Although there are some hardware vendors that actually integrate Kaspersky Lab ® AV engine on the hardware level (called SafeStream) in some of their gateway lines, for example, ZyXEL does so in the UTM Firewalls.*

- *Kaspersky Security for Mail Server* ® - Although each endpoint that has a Kaspersky Lab® product installed has its own protection built into the email client, it is an extra measure to scan the emails at the server level *before* they arrive at the endpoint. In addition, with Microsoft Exchange ® **Anti-Spam** is also available on the email server, so these unwanted mails can be blocked thereby reducing unnecessary traffic on the network. This product also supports the Lotus Notes **Domino** ® platform.

- *Kaspersky Security for Mobile* ® - There are two major components that comprise this solution – the *Mobile Device Management Console* that manages the actual mobile devices themselves assisting with Anti-Theft tools, policy and profile configurations, and central console management. The other component is the actual mobile security application that installs on the mobile devices and provides for the anti-malware, anti-phishing and anti-spam protection on the mobile device. In addition to that it creates "containers" that ensure that corporate applications and data are separated from the personal information on the device and encrypted correctly. Thus, if the device is lost or stolen, or if the employee terminates their employment with the business, all corporate data can be deleted without affecting the personal data. There are also mechanisms to prevent *"Jail Breaking"* on some devices.

The solutions supports Android®, Windows Phone®, and iOS® platforms.

- *Kaspersky Security for Storage* ® – There are specialised data storage servers that use the **NetApp** ® and **EMC Celerra**® platforms and require malware protection that does not hamper their performance. *Kaspersky Security for Storage* ® has been designed specifically for these types of servers offering maximum protection whilst still allowing the computers to deliver optimal performance.
- *Kaspersky Security for Virtualization*® - The world of Virtualization has become exceptionally popular and with this has come the need for protection on these *Virtual Machines* (abbreviated *VM's*). Kaspersky Lab® have produced a product range to meets these requirements and they are able to operate in the following three modes of operation:
  - *Agentless* – In this mode the Anti-Malware protection that runs on the *VM* does not have an agent running in the background.

To briefly explain, when a Kaspersky Lab ®' product runs on an endpoint there is a special *Network Agent* that is installed and runs in the background. Through this agent the *Security Centre* can identify and communicate securely with the endpoint.

Now, in the *Agentless* state, there is no direct *Network Agent* that runs on each **VM.** Instead, the agent runs between the **Hypervisor** and the *Security Centre* and it is the **Hypervisor** itself that manages all of its *VM's.*

The benefits of running the **Anti-Malware** in this mode, is that there is very little resource usage on the **VM.** The downside, however, is that *only* the *Kaspersky Anti-Malware* is functional; there are no other features available.

The platform that Kaspersky Lab® supports with this mode of operation is **VMWare**® with **VShield**® running as its **Hypervisor.**

○ *Light Agent* – In this mode there is a *Light Network Agent* that runs on the *VM,* allowing *some* communication with the *Security Centre.* This means that, although more resources are used on the *VM,* there are more features available, and in this mode all the **Endpoint Controls** are available as well as the **Anti-Malware.**

The supported platforms with this mode of operation are again **VMWare**® (with no need for **VShield**®), **Microsoft Hyper-V**® and **Citrix XEN**®.

○ *Full Agent* – In this mode several more features are available. As well as the **Anti-Malware** and **Endpoint Controls** the tools that make up the *Kaspersky Systems Management*® are able to operate on *VM's* in this mode. Obviously, the downside is that the resource usage on the *VM* is quite substantial.

Please Note that *Encryption* offered by Kaspersky Lab® will **NOT** run on any *VM.*

The platforms that support this mode of operation are **VMWare**®, **Microsoft Hyper-V**®, **Citrix XEN**®, **Virtual PC**®, **Virtual Box**®, and **Parallels**®.

Kaspersky For Virtualization® is offered in three products: *Kaspersky For Virtualization*®, *Server*, *Kaspersky For Virtualization*®, *Desktop*, and *Kaspersky For Virtualization*®, *Core*.

I'm sure that you understand the difference between *Server* and *Desktop*, but *Core*?

Some companies would determine a specific number of *VM's* that they run pretty much on a static quantity; it is thus easy to purchase a definite number of licenses for these. But **Service Providers** are different in that they sell or hire out these *VM's* to the public based on demand and this means that the quantities fluctuate. So in this case it is not easy to purchase licenses per *VM*; instead we have to look at another method to calculate costs.

The heart of any computer is the **Central Processing Unit** or **CPU.** This is the brain behind everything and the **CPU's** that are used today have more than one *core.* To explain this every single software program is written in code, one line at a time. A **CPU** that has one *core* will tackle each line of code as it is presented to it. As the need for faster computing has increased the modern **CPU's** are *Multi-Cored*; in other words, they have more than one **core.** So a **Dual Core CPU** will have two **cores**; a **Quad Core CPU** will have four **cores.** So when software is presented to a *Multi-Core CPU* each **core** processes a line of code.

A single **core** in a **CPU** is capable of managing approximately eight *VM's* and *Kaspersky For Virtualization* ®, *Core* then provides licenses for each **core** of the **CPU**, regardless of how many *VM's* are run on that server.

- *Kaspersky Systems Management* ® – This is an extremely useful suite of tools that adds to the security of the network as well as ease of management. Some of these features are offered as separate third party products but this would result in multiple management consoles, additional server resources, increased costs, and potential problems with compatibility. The entire

Kaspersky Systems Management ® suite is managed by ***Kaspersky Security Centre*** ® and contains the following tools:

- ○ **Vulnerability Assessment** – The system can check the entire network to determine where the weak spots are for security.
- ○ **Patch Management** – Almost all third party commercial products that are installed and run on the network can be updated via the ***Kaspersky Security Center*** ®. The updates are downloaded, ensured that they are genuine by checking the digital certificates, and stored locally on the server. Tasks are prioritized according to the most important updates to be applied to the endpoints first.
- ○ **Hardware/Software Inventories** – The system scans all endpoints on the network and records all hardware and software on those computers. Any changes to either the hardware or the software can send alerts to the System Administrator who will be able to act accordingly.
- ○ **License Management** – Combined with the **Inventory Management** the system maintains records of all licenses purchased against licenses used in the network.
- ○ **Operating System Deployment** – It is possible to deploy pre-defined images from the ***Security Centre*** to remote endpoints, and "***Wake-on-LAN***" technology is supported.
- ○ **Software Distribution** – In addition to OS deployment additional software can be deployed remotely to the endpoints. Advanced Scheduling allows the software to be deployed and installed during off-peak times so that normal working conditions are not affected.

Small Office Security - There is a vast majority of small businesses that contain less than 50 computers and one of the major problems is that these small companies cannot afford to employ a full-time technician to administer their small networks.

In several cases this responsibility falls upon one of the existing staff members who perhaps has little IT experience. An endpoint security platform is desired that is easy to deploy and administer whilst offering a high rate of security for the network.

It is for this reason why Kaspersky Lab ® developed the ***Kaspersky Small Office Security*** ® package for Microsoft Windows ®, Apple MAC ® and Android ® platforms. Using a centrally managed friendly console the following features can be deployed to the small network:

- **Anti-Malware** – Award winning Anti-Malware protection on all computers against known and unknown malware with Cloud assisted security and Automatic Exploit Prevention.
- **Financial Data Security** – These features offer you a *"Safe Money"* facility as well as *Virtual* and *Secure Keyboard.* Your passwords are also remembered and protected. These features are all described above in **Personal Security.**
- **Internet Protection** – Hidden Browser Exploits are blocked on all protected computers and suspicious downloads are identified and blocked. The system can also identify *phishing* websites that will attempt to steal data.
- **User Access Control** – Website access, including social networking and other leisure sites can be controlled as well as Instant Messaging applications. Gaming can also be blocked or regulated.

- **Data Protection** – Backup facilities are available and automated and can directed to disc, file servers, or online data storage. File and folder encryption for all users is available and *File Shredder* (as explained above) is included.
- **Web-based console** for managing the installed security applications across the network – in essence, it is very similar to Kaspersky Security Center as it is designed to assist the management of security software, but it is much easier and simpler, since it was specifically designed to address the needs of small businesses. Which not necessarily need to deploy a dedicated server and can even outsource the management tasks to a more experienced IT professionals.

To give you an idea of the difference between Kaspersky Small Office Security, Kaspersky Total Security – Multi-Device (the flagship of the consumer line) and Kaspersky Endpoint Security for Business, please look at this table:

	KASPERSKY TOTAL SECURITY — MULTI-DEVICE	KASPERSKY SMALL OFFICE SECURITY	KASPERSKY ENDPOINT SECURITY FOR BUSINESS
Server support	No	Yes	Yes
License packs, maximum	5 maximum	50 maximum	No maximum
Remote management console	No	Yes	Yes
1 license covers platforms	Mobile OR Desktop	Mobile AND Desktop AND Windows Server	Mobile AND Desktop AND Server – Windows, Linux, MAC

Requires a level of IT expertise to use	No	No	Yes
Includes Mail Server security	No	No	Yes

c. Office Packages – Nearly every computer in existence today has somesort of Office package installed which includes a Word Processor, Spreadsheet, and Email Client. It is basically one of the first base packages that almost everyone needs in order to do anything productive on the computer.

There are various Office packages on the market, namely (in alphabetical order) Corel's ***WordPerfect Suite*** ®, ***Lotus SmartSuite***®, ***Microsoft Office*** ®, and ***Open Office*** ®, which is an Office package designed with Unix.

I personally am experienced with ***Microsoft Office*** ®, so I am going to describe the components that make up this package, but similar components can be quite easily found in the other Office brands.

Microsoft® offers several different combinations of these separate modules in various offerings. Now, I'm not going to go into any detail as to the different packages that are available for ***Microsoft Office*** ® for the simple reason that there are too many to mention here. What I am doing however is to describe each available module in the ***Microsoft Office*** ® family. I have listed them below in alphabetical order. There are also several miscellaneous tools that augment the Microsoft Office® family, but I'm not going to mention them here.

Right! On with the modules!

Access ® -   This is quite a nice powerful database package which works in conjunction with its big brother, SQL. It is extremely flexible in that you can create databases for just about anything, and it is fully programmable for those big projects.

Excel® -   I use this software very often, and have even done a bit of programming in *Excel®*. It is your Spreadsheet software and is extremely powerful in what you can do with it. The tables you see in this book were all designed using this software. It also allows you to create graphs, and other useful ways to represent data.

FrontPage® -   Your Web Page designing software, *FrontPage®* takes all the mysticism out of creating your own web sites. Originally, web sites had to be created straight from source code which is beyond most people and thus Web Site Design became the territory of programmers. But with the invention of *FrontPage®* and other similar software almost anybody is able to create these sites quickly and easily.

Outlook -   Aha! The lifeblood of my computer! This is your email client, and your **Customer Relations Management** console (take a look at Chapters 13 and 17). My whole professional life revolves around this package and it is a definite upgrade to *Outlook Express®* which is shipped with your Microsoft® Operating System. There are other CRM packages that are admittedly more powerful than *Outlook®*, but for my needs it is perfect.

PowerPoint® -   If you need to design a presentation (see also Chapter 12) then you need a package like this to create your slides. It contains features like animation and sound that can give you a truly professional finish to your project.

Project -   If you are a Project Manager, then you will live in a package such as this one. Many projects become quite involved with deadlines to meet, staff and contractors to hire and schedule, materials to be ordered, and budgets to be carefully adhered to, in order to successfully complete a project, sometimes costing in the excess of millions of Rands (or Dollars).

Publisher - There is a designer in all of us, and this application will assist you in creating anything from birthday cards to complete magazines. Applications such as this one are used by most magazine and newspaper companies to design professional publications. This book no doubt, in its final formatting process, was developed using such a package.

Visio - One of my favourite programs, Visio allows me to create technical drawings for just about anything. The diagrams in this book were all designed using *Visio*. Of course there are several more powerful **CAD** (**Computer Aided Design**) packages such as *AutoCAD* that allow Engineers and Architects the ability to design drawings for their client, but personally I find *Visio* quite easy to use.

Word - This is your Word Processor, or, put another way, an electric typewriter on steroids. There are some incredible things that can be done with this package. For example, this entire book was written in *MS Word*, and I'll probably write the next one using the same software.

d. Games – These things are the stuff that influences the entire hardware industry as people need more and more powerful computers to run these types of software. They have created billion-Dollar industries and continue to do so, and will carry on far into the future.

So why are games so popular? Well, for one they offer us mere mortals an escape route from the real world whereby we can fantasize that we are the big, burly warrior, resplendent in his tough armour and toting a whopping monster-busting shotgun.

They are however the bane of the poor technician when an aspirant gamer brings his favourite computer into the shop and starts shouting the odds because the new game he has just purchased doesn't run properly. Then the poor technician has to explain that the customer needs to upgrade his machine.

This sad story has happened many, many times before, and will continue unabated.

There are a few items here that the gamer is going to love owning to make their gaming experience bigger and badder. Let's take a look.

Joysticks - Keyboards and mice just don't do it for the serious gamer. No, you need a joystick, and it's got to have more buttons and levers than the space shuttle. And if the gamer is into driving games, than a steering wheel complete with pedals is the way to go.

RAM - You can have the video cards, you can have the sound cards, but if you don't have enough RAM then nothing is going to help. The gamer needs at least 2 GB of RAM loaded into his computer in order for the game to run properly.

Sound - Ok, you've got cool graphics, but you gotta have the sound blasting all around you. This is the next must for the serious gamer, and the louder the better. There are some really good quality sound cards on the market, but they need to be coupled with a good set of surround sound speakers. For those times when it's two o'clock in the morning and you don't want to wake the neighbours up, the gamer also needs to invest in a good pair of headphones.

Video Cards - Games are all about playability and graphics. The better the graphics, the more realistic the game becomes. But the average computer just isn't powerful enough to handle the amount of code that needs to be processed at lightning-fast speeds so it needs a little help in the form of **Graphic Accelerators**. These specialized video cards have their own built-in processor that assists the main system processor in handling all the code that pertains to displaying the graphical images on the computer screen.

e. Printers – These peripherals are essential add-ons to computers. Yes, the obvious thing they can do is print documents, but these can assist the user to print out their work reports, information for their children' projects, and even shopping lists. There are various types of printers on the market, and I'm going to briefly look at each kind so that you can become a little more familiar of where they are normally used.

Dot Matrix - These were the first printers that were developed for computers, and are still in existence today. Why? Well, they are **impact** printers which mean that there are pins inside the print head that strike in certain combinations onto the paper it is printing on (and between it and the paper is the ink ribbon, which provides the ink for the impression), and this leads to some interesting applications. In the accounting world invoices are extremely important and there are always two (and sometimes three) copies that are required: one for the customer and one for the company. We use what is commonly known as **NCR (No**

Carbon required) paper which means that if an impact happens on the front page it imprints an exact duplicated image onto the back page. Using the contact of the pins in the print head we can thus create two images; the first begin the front page with the normal printer ink and then the second (or back page) with the imprint.

Another good application is the printing of accounts for debtors. Admittedly, dot matrix printers are not the best when it comes to printing graphics, and they are extremely noisy, but they are probably the best workhorse printer in existence and their economy in terms of ink usage is unparalleled. They are also used in pharmacies to print labels to place on medicine bottles.

Incidentally, dot matrix printers are not very good with colours, because the ink is placed onto a ribbon that is strung between two spools and passes through the print head. A maximum of two colours can be applied to this ribbon, and normally a red colour occupies the top row of the ribbon whilst the bottom row contains black.

Inkjet - In today's society the **inkjet** printer is possibly the most popular because of many reasons:

i. They are able to reproduce colour with incredible resolution, so photographic printing is possible.

ii. These printers are extremely affordable

iii. Inkjet printers have a small **footprint**. What is meant by this is the amount of space a printer takes up on a desk or table.

iv. These peripherals are able to print directly onto CD's, thereby making them extremely versatile.

However, as a disadvantage, inkjet printers are slower than laser printers (discussed shortly). Also, they are not economical when considering ink usage. Lastly, the hard copies that are produced are not waterproof. In other words, if water splashes on to the paper, the ink will run.

Bubble Jet -   **Bubble Jet** printers, which are patented by Canon, are very similar to inkjet printers in capabilities. Their printing mechanism differs however, giving them a higher resolution than inkjet printers.

With inkjet printers the print head consists of sometimes up to forty eight individual jets which spray ink much in the same way you would spry ink with a toothbrush. The net result is thousands of tiny dots appearing very close together. A downside of this is edges and lines have a fuzzy edge to them.

Bubble Jet printers form tiny bubbles from the jets that burst and overlap each other when they land on the paper. Although there are some slightly fuzzy edges there is a definite increase in resolution making them more viable in photographic printing.

The downside of bubble jet printers is that they use more ink than inkjet printers. Their hard copies are also not waterproof.

Laser -   The business printer of choice! These printers are fast, efficient, economical, and capable of very large printing quantities. Up until a few years ago colour laser printers were extremely expensive, but nowadays the prices are reducing dramatically and now they are more affordable Admittedly, the initial costs are much higher than inkjet printers, and there are higher maintenance costs involved, including the costs of the replacement toners and the toner drums, but the overall printing costs per page are much less than inkjet printers.

Without going into too much detail concerning the mechanics behind the printer, their resolution is much sharper than both the inkjet and the bubble jet printers. There is a downside, however. The temperatures of the **curing** or **fusing** rollers can reach heats of up to 120^0 Celsius, which means that the inked image is burnt into the paper. This means that, if you decide to print on transparencies for Overhead Projectors, you cannot use normal plastic ones because they will melt and could cause possible damage to the inside mechanisms. Also, you are not able to print onto CD's and DVD's because of the problem with the heat – they will melt!

A good point to note which this heating process is that the images become waterproof, and will not run or smear it they come into contact with liquids.

Last point – they do have a larger footprint than inkjet and bubble jet printers.

Multifunction - These are combination devices, and are now becoming the preferred choice in small businesses today because of their versatility and initial costs. Both inkjet or laser models are available, and basically these are combination fax/ scanner/ printer machines. Instead of having a separate scanner, separate fax machine, and separate printer, these three functionalities have been built into one device, which means that the overall cost of the unit works out cheaper than purchasing all three devices separately, and they take up less space in an office. On another note, the multifunction device uses less mains power, and only uses one plug point.

Plotter - I mentioned earlier in this chapter about **CAD**, or **Computer Aided Design** software. This software allows engineers and architects to create technical drawings. Some of these drawings are large. As an example, have you ever seen blueprints to a building, either in real or on movies? Take a look at the size. Now how do you think they are printed?

Ok, background information here. In the stationery world there are specifications given to the standard sizes of paper. The following formula might assist you in understanding these sizes.

1 x A0 = 2 x A1 = 4 x A2 = 8 x A3 = 16 x A4 = 32 x A5 = 64 x A6

The largest laser and inkjet printers available are A3, whilst dot matrix printers can be up to 132 columns, which equates to the A3 standard. Bigger than this will not be economically viable to manufacture.

Plotters cater for the larger sizes by using different coloured pens with extremely fine nibs as the "print heads" and they scoot around the print area drawing the various lines and objects as is necessary to recreate the entire drawing on paper.

A variation of the plotter is the **router**, which uses knife blades instead of pens are print heads, and are used to cut out various shapes on many different types of material including paper, plastic, Perspex, wood, and metal. Sign Writers sometimes user routers to cut out the shapes they are going to use on plastic or Perspex to paint onto signs, etc.

Thermal -   These printers have for the most part taken over the market from **Receipt Printers**, which are effectively miniature dot matrix printers used for printing receipts (or, as known in some countries, cash slips) at tills in shops and at ATM's (**Automated Teller Machines**). Thermal printers apply small amounts of heat to certain areas of specially prepared paper, exposing images wherever heat is introduced.

A disadvantage of using thermal paper is, when it is exposed to any other sort of heat, including sunlight, the entire sheet turns black effectively muddling the intended image from view.

Wax -   These are fairly large, expensive printers primarily used in the magazine industry. They are also known as **Thermal Wax Printers**.

They melt dots of wax-based ink which adheres to almost any surface including paper, complex synthetics, and film. The result is a high-resolution colour image with a shiny look, and a smooth feel to it. Take a look at most of your magazines on the shelves. If they have a shiny, glossy look to them, then chances are they were printed with these types of printers.

f. Miscellaneous - There are several other devices that can be added to a normal computer to enhance its functionality and capabilities. I have listed some of these are listed in alphabetical order, but there are far more that can be added. This is just to give you an inkling of what is out there and what is available.

Biometrics Readers - In the world of security the ability to recognize people based upon their unique features has become extremely important of late.

It is a known scientific fact that a fingerprint (or footprint) is unique amongst people, as is the retina at the back of the eye. Based upon this knowledge **Fingerprint Readers** and **Retina Scanners** have been developed to assist companies in increasing their security. Also included are **Face Recognition** systems.

CCTV –   Big Brother is watching you!!! And in the increasing need to monitor activities in businesses (and in homes for that matter) **Closed Circuit Television** has now moved into the computer environment, turning the computer into what is known in the Security World as a **DVR (Digital Video Recorder)**, allowing the internal hard drive to store the recorded images much in the same way the original VCR video tapes of the past did, but at a fraction of the cost.

Digital Cameras – The world of photography is not even safe anymore from the onslaught of computers and technology, and digital cameras are now fast replacing the traditional models as the preferred medium with which to record images. Most cameras are also capable of recording video footage, and have even invaded the Mobile Phone world!

Digital Tablets – Architects and Engineers covet their drawing boards and these allow them to create their drawings and diagrams which are part of their profession. With the addition of **CAD (Computer Aided Design)** software these professionals now have a way of creating these drawings onto computer. Some of them still feel the need to physically "draw" the diagrams and digital tablets are a way of allowing them to perform these activities.

These tablets are also used primarily for artists who wish to create drawings on the computer, and some handwriting gurus also find the need for these devices.

Microphones - Ah, there are many needs for the humble microphone indeed, from recording your voice in a dictation-type manner, to speaking to somebody halfway across the world through the Internet, to using them in a Call Centre environment, the microphone is designed in many different fashions as are extremely reasonably priced. This is a definite add-on product to include with new computer purchases.

Scanners -

These devices allow you to copy almost any document (image, picture, whatever) into the computer by scanning it, digitizing the information, and importing it into the computer to be manipulated as either pictures or, with the benefit of **Optical Character Recognition** technology, as text, alleviating the need to reproduce vast amounts of written or typed documents. Another type of common scanner is the **Barcode Scanner**, which scans the barcodes of items to be purchased in a supermarket to identify their retail prices.

Till Drawers –

Coupled with Barcode Scanners (explained above) the traditional cash till is now being replaced with computer which can do the same job.

TV Cards -

So ok, you don't need a television anymore! Just buy a card that fits into your computer and you can watch TV right there on your computer! And, with digital technology, you have much more features that are available to you.

Webcams -

Using communication technology through the Internet you can now have a conversation with anyone in the world at any time, ad you can view them as well. These video cameras allow us to see each other whilst we are conversing, thus making teleconferencing a feasible solution to participating in remote business meetings.

CONCLUSION

In order to make yourself some decent commission and establish a good reputation in your field you need to start practicing Value Added Reselling.

You need to question your customers and clients more to find out what their needs are and then act on them. Even though at the time your client might not have the money to purchase that new graphics card at the time, they eventually will because they have shown you a definite interest in the product. If necessary take down the client's details and see if you can source another model that will fit their budget. Or make a note somewhere of their interest and when you have a special running on that item that the client is interested in, contact them. You might gain another sale!

SUMMARY – CHAPTER 6.

In order to provide clients with an added service and to generate additional revenues for your company you need to take into consideration additional accessories to sell a client when they purchase their computer.

We call this term **Value Added Reselling** and it is what makes the difference between an average IT Company and a superb IT Company.

EXAMPLES OF ADD-ONS

We look at different possible additional options that a client can explore when they purchase their computer.

a. Internet - One of the most popular add-on products on offer today; access to the Internet has become part of normal everyday life for most people, and there are various packages available that will connect people in a matter of a few hours. There are various options available which include:

Bandwidth -   This term refers to the speeds you will experience when you are connected to the Internet, and you could equate this to the lanes on a highway, and the maximum speed you are allowed to travel on that highway.

Connection type - There are two kinds that allow you to connect to the Internet, namely **Physical** and **Wireless**.

Physical -   These different standards refer to physical cabled connections to the Internet ranging from copper cables to Fibre Optic cables. Copper cables uses two data transmission types, being **analogue** and **digital**, whilst Fibre Optic cables only uses **digital** transmissions

ADSL -   This acronym stands for **Asymmetrical Digital Subscriber Line** uses copper lines, much like the Analogue situation, above. Downstream data flow is normally much large than that of the upstream flow, making it more ideal for home users.

Analogue -   A **Modem** (**Mod**ulator/ **Dem**odulator) is a device that converts analogue signals from the copper cables to digital ones to be used in computers. These modems use normal telephone networks for connection.

Broadband - This term is an abbreviation of **Broadband Internet Access** and is basically a high data rate Internet access system which is compared with normal dial-up modems used in Analogue connections.

DSL - **Digital Subscriber Line** (formerly known as **Digital Subscriber Loop**) provides digital data transmission over the wires on a local telephone network. DSL does not convert at all, but rather maintains the original digital coding which means that both voice and data can coincide on the copper phone lines. DSL offers **ADSL** and **SDSL**.

ISDN - The **Integrated Services Digital Network** is a telephone network that operates in much the same way as Analogue networks in that a dial up connection is performed to connect to a particular exchange and then either voice or data is transmitted.

There are three kinds of service-related interfaces that are offered, namely:

Basic Rate Interface (BRI), **Primary Rate Interface (PRI)**, and **Broadband – ISDN (B-ISDN)**.

Leased Line - A **Leased Line** is a direct communications connection between two places. There are no "dial-up" requirements as this connection is permanent, and can be used for both telephone and data services.

SDSL - **Symmetrical Digital Subscriber Line** is similar to ADSL (explained above) but the major difference is the fact that the upstream and downstream data volumes are the same, meaning that it becomes more attractive to the business sector, as both services are required.

Wireless - These standards define the different types of wireless connections that are available to allow computer to attach to the Internet without having to use physical cables.

Bluetooth - This wireless protocol was designed to exchange data over short between fixed and mobile devices, such as cellphones and laptops, and was originally designed to replace the cumbersome RS232 serial data cables.

EDGE - **Enhanced Data rates for GSM Evolution** is a backward-compatible digital mobile phone technology that offers improved data transmission rates and is offered as an extension to the standard **GSM.** It is considered to be a 3G technology, and using various compressions and encoding techniques it almost triples the potential of GSM/GPRS networks.

GPRS - **GSM** mobile phones use the **GPRS** (**General Packet Radio Service**) system to transmit data. The **GPRS** core network is the centralized part of the **GPRS** system and also provides support for **3G** and **WCDMA** based networks.

GSM - The **Global System for Mobile Communications** standard is the most popular standard used globally, and an estimated over 80% of the global market uses this standard, allowing for communications between different Mobile Phone Operators. Furthermore, the signals are all digital in nature giving a better clarity of speech, and allowing the simultaneous of data transfer.

HSDPA - **High-Speed Downlink Packet Access** is basically an enhanced **3G** communications protocol giving the user higher data transfer speeds with greater volumes. Current uses support download speeds of up to 14.4 Mbps.

3G - This is the **Third Generation** of telecommunications standards and general technology for mobile networking. 3G networks allow network operators to offer customers a wider range of more advanced services while achieving greater network capacity through improved spectral efficiency.

3GPP - **3GPP** stands for **3rd Generation Partnership Project** and is a collaboration between groups of telecommunications associations, to create a third generation (**3G**) cell phone system specification that meets with the **ITU**'s (**International Telecommunication Union**) requirements.

4G - This is the **Fourth Generation** of telecommunications standards and general technology for mobile networking and where it adds to **3G** is it offers broadband Internet access to **Laptops** with **wireless modems**, **Smartphones**, and other mobile devices incorporating **Mobile Web Access, High Definition Mobile** and 3D **Television,** and **Cloud Computing.**

WCDMA -   This **Wideband Code Division Multiple Access** basically is an air interface found in 3G networks, and is used to communicate with other systems.

Domain and website hosting - Base **Domains** are hosted by clusters of servers in several countries throughout the world that the Internet is based on. Secondary Servers connect to these to give use Second Level Domains and we as users connect to these Second Level Servers.

You can also own your own domain and have it hosted anywhere in the world by **Internet Service Providers.**

You can then design **websites** that are hosted by ISP's and are accessed when your domain is looked for.

Emails and aliases – Email addresses are normally hosted by ISP's (in which case their domain is used as the email extension) although you can have your own email server on your site, meaning that your email address will have your domain as your email extension. You can also have aliases which are alternative email addresses based on your domain name.

b. Anti-Virus– This is an almost compulsory additional purchase a client must make when they purchase any type of computer such as PC, laptop, Smartphone or tablet. As an example, we look at the Kaspersky Lab ® family of products, which have added Cloud-based protection of the ***Kaspersky Security Network*** ®

Personal Security -

This family of products are designed for single computers (such as home users) and consists of *Kaspersky Anti-Virus 2015, Kaspersky Internet Security 2015, and Kaspersky Total Security Multi-Device 2015.* The following table illustrates the features of these packages.

	Kaspersky Anti-Virus 2015	Kaspersky Internet Security - Multi-Device 2015	Kaspersky Total Security - Multi-Device 2015
	Essential Protection	Premium Protection	Ultimate Protection
Proactive Defense	XXX	XXX	XXX
Antivirus	XXX	XXX	XXX
Tweaking of computer security settings	X	XX	XXX
Personal data protection	X	XX	XXX
Parental control		XXX	XXX
Application Control and Safe Run		XXX	XXX
Firewall		XXX	XXX
Dangerous website blocker		XXX	XXX
Anti-spam		XXX	XXX
Network security management		X	XXX
Password Manager			XXX
Data backup and recovery			XXX
Protection for Android devices		XXX	XXX
Protection for iOS		X	XXX
Protection for MAC		XX	XXX
Protection for Windows Phone		XXX	XXX
Public Wi-Fi protection		XXX	XXX
Webcam Protection		XXX	XXX

Business Security –

Kaspersky Endpoint Security for Business ®, which focuses on the *amount* of security required by the business sector, is completely configured and administered by *Kaspersky Security Centre*®. There are four tiers of protection as depicted in the below diagram.

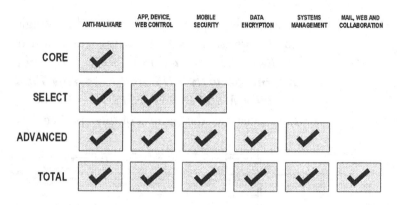

	ANTI-MALWARE	APP, DEVICE, WEB CONTROL	MOBILE SECURITY	DATA ENCRYPTION	SYSTEMS MANAGEMENT	MAIL, WEB AND COLLABORATION
CORE	✔					
SELECT	✔	✔	✔			
ADVANCED	✔	✔	✔	✔	✔	
TOTAL	✔	✔	✔	✔	✔	✔

Kaspersky Lab® Targeted Solutions – As well as the complete suite of protection Kaspersky Lab® have also developed a range of solutions focussed on different areas of protection and these can be used in any environment (listed in alphabetical order):

- *Kaspersky Anti-Spam for Linux* ® - This is an Anti-Spam filter for Linux-based Mail Servers.
- *Kaspersky Data Leakage Protection for Collaboration*® - This product is an add-on to *Kaspersky Security for Collaboration* ® and assists in preventing the transmitting of personal information.
- *Kaspersky Data Leakage Protection for Mail Server* ® - This product is an add-on to *Kaspersky Security for Mail Server* ® and assists in preventing the transmitting of personal information.
- *Kaspersky Security for Collaboration* ® - This is used with **Microsoft SharePoint** ® it protects the data flowing to and from the database.
- *Kaspersky Security for File Server* ® - This product protects all file servers.
- *Kaspersky Security for Internet Gateway* ® - It scans traffic for malware flowing through the gateway. It does *not* replace the actual gateway itself.
- *Kaspersky Security for Mail Server* ® - If the platform is **Microsoft Exchange** ® then the Anti-

Spam component is also included. Support for **Lotus Notes Domino** ® is included.

- *Kaspersky Security for Mobile*® - Two components make up this solution – *Mobile Device Management* and *Endpoint Protection Platform.* The product supports Android®, Windows Phone®, and iOS® platforms.

- *Kaspersky Security for Storage* ® - **EMC Celerra**® and **NetApp** ® platforms are both supported with this product than concentrates on offering maximum protection whilst minimising performance damping.

- *Kaspersky Security for Virtualization* ® - Kaspersky Lab® have created three products that will run in three different modes of operation:

  - *Agentless* – This uses the least resources on a *VM* and provides only **Anti-Malware** on the *VM.* **VMWare** ® with **VShield** ® is supported in this mode of operation.

  - *Light Agent* – A *Light Network Agent* runs on the *VM,* allowing *some* communication with the *Security Centre.* More resources are used on the *VM* but **Anti-Malware** and **Endpoint Controls** become available. **VMWare** ® (with no need for **VShield** ®), **Microsoft Hyper-V** ® and **Citrix XEN** ® are supported platforms for this mode of operation.

  - *Full Agent* – Using a substantial amount of resources on the *VM* this mode of operation offers **Anti-Malware, Endpoint Controls,** and the components of *Kaspersky Systems Management*®. However, **Encryption** is **NOT** available. **VMWare**®, **Microsoft Hyper-V**®, **Citrix XEN**®, **Virtual PC**®, **Virtual Box**®, and **Parallels** ® are supported platforms.

There are three products available: *Kaspersky For Virtualization*®, *Server*, *Kaspersky For Virtualization*®,

Desktop, and **Kaspersky For Virtualization®, Core.** The first two license the number of **VM's** whilst **Kaspersky For Virtualization®, Core** licenses the number of **cores** in the **CPU**, of which eight **VM's** can operate per **core.**

- **Kaspersky Systems Management®** - A suite of tools to assist with the management and protection of the network. These tools include:
  - **Vulnerability Assessment**
  - **Patch Management**
  - **Hardware/Software Inventories**
  - **License Management**
  - **Operating System Deployment**
  - **Software Distribution**

Kaspersky Small Office Security® - This package is designed for up to 50 computers with support for Microsoft Windows® and Android® platforms. Designed for ease of use by persons with limited technical knowledge, it contains the following features:

- **Anti-Malware**
- **Financial Data Security**
- **Internet Protection**
- **User Access Control**
- **Data Protection**

c. Office Packages – In order for anybody to perform anything constructive on a computer they will need some sort of Office Package. We look at, as an example, the **Microsoft Office®** package. The following are modules that combine to form the **Microsoft Office®** package.

Access® -   This is quite a nice powerful database package which works in conjunction with its big brother, SQL. It is extremely flexible in that you can create databases for just about anything, and it is fully programmable for those big projects.

Excel ® – This is a spreadsheet application and has become a mainstay in business applications to create ways to represent data that is easily readable and understandable to audiences.

FrontPage ® – Many people require the need to design their own websites and this package offers an easy method of doing so to those who do not have the expertise to perform this task.

Outlook – This acts as your complete email client and Customer Relations Management Package.

PowerPoint ® – Powerful business presentations can be designed using this package.

Project ® – Project Managers require the use of these packages to map out the complexities of large scale business projects.

Publisher ® – In order to create professional pamphlets, brochures, and magazines a good design application is required. *Publisher* ® is an easy to use application that is extremely powerful in its functionality.

Visio ® – A Layman's version of a **Computer Aided Design** package, *Visio* ® allows almost anyone to create good quality technical drawings.

Word ® – This is your word processing package, allowing you to create professional typed documents.

d. Games – These have become a driving force behind the development of the computer industry. In the search to provide the perfect gaming environment, there are certain accessories that can be added, namely:

Joysticks –   **Joysticks** and other similar devices augment that handling and controlling of games from a users' perspective and there are several types that are commercially available.

RAM –   The amount of **RAM** a gamer requires to properly run games is more so than that required for business use, and typically 2GB or more is now required to run many games.

Sound –   Surround Sound has become the norm when paying the latest games and a good sound card with corresponding speakers is now much sought after by gamers.

Video Cards – As the graphics of games increase thereby making them as realistic as possible, so to are **Graphics Accelerators** required to be added to computers, which effectively have auxiliary processors on the cards to assist the main processor in dealing with the amount of code that needs to be manipulated in order to draw the images onto the screen.

e. Printers – These are essential peripherals to computers in order to create hard copies and information stored in the computers. Types of printers are:

Dot Matrix –   This was the first type of printer that was designed which uses combinations of pins in the print heads to impact with the printing paper (through an **ink ribbon**) to imprint characters. They are also known as **Impact Printers** and are used in the Accounting Profession to reproduce multiple invoices.

Inkjet –   These are the mainstay of colour printers and spray coloured inks onto paper. They are relatively economical to use, use low power, and have small footprints. The hard copies that are produced are not waterproof.

Bubble Jet –   **Bubble Jet Printers** are similar in operation to **Inkjet Printers** but instead of spraying ink onto paper each jet in the print head create a bubble of ink which "folds" onto the paper, thereby giving a much sharper resolution. The downside is that they tend to use more ink than Inkjet Printers. The hard copies that are produced are not waterproof.

Laser –   These are the business printers of choice because they are fast, quiet, economical, and capable of large printing quantities. They use a powdered ink with is heated onto the paper thereby giving a waterproof hard copy.

Multifunction –   **Multifunction Printers** combine the benefits of **Inkjet** (or **Laser**, depending on the model) **Printers**, **Scanners**, and **Facsimile Machines** into one device saving in power, space, money, and convenience.

Plotter –   Large Scale drawings especially used in the Engineering and Architectural Industries are capable with these devices which use drawing pens as the printing heads to draw onto large pieces of paper.

Router -   These are types of plotters that use knife blades instead of drawing pens to precision cut through certain material. An interesting application of these "printers" would be in the creation of Jigsaw Puzzles for the Hobby Industry.

Adrian Noble

Thermal -   **Thermal printers** apply small amounts of heat to certain areas of specially prepared paper, exposing images wherever heat is introduced. They are normally found as receipt printers at **Point Of Sale Terminals** to issue customers with proofs of purchase.

Wax -   These are fairly large, expensive printers primarily used in the magazine industry. They are also known as **Thermal Wax Printers** which work by melting dots of wax-based ink to adhere to almost any surface. The result is a glossy, high resolution hard copy.

f. Miscellaneous – These are additional add-ons that can be considered.

Biometrics Readers -   **Fingerprint Readers** and **Retina Scanners** have been developed to assist companies in increasing their security.

CCTV –   **Closed Circuit Television** have now been adapted for use in computer networks transforming normal computers into **Digital Video Recorders**.

Digital Cameras –   These devices have become more affordable and desirable than traditional photography and allow people to store photographs and video footage directly into computers.

Digital Tablets –   These are primarily used for engineers, architects, and artists and allow freehand drawing and writing to be entered into computers quickly.

Microphones – These have become extremely common and allow us to store voice into the computer and also allow us to communicate with other people all over the world.

Scanners - These devices allow you to copy almost any document (image, picture, whatever) into the computer by scanning it, digitizing the information, and importing it into the computer. **Barcode Scanners** have also revolutionized the retail industry by allowing the barcodes of potential purchases to be scanned and identified at the **Point of Sale** Points.

Till Drawers – **Till Drawers** are normally now combined with **Barcode Scanners** to transform computers into **Point of Sale** units.

TV Cards – Engineers have given us the technology to view television directly on a computer with many functions that are not available in normal television sets.

Webcams – Combined with microphones **Webcams** allow to physically view the people we are communicating with remotely.

CHAPTER 7.
TIME MANAGEMENT

This is an extremely important aspect of the sales person's life. Without this facet nobody can hope to focus their day and so achieve greatness in the sales world.

There are nine hours in the average work day (eight hours if you honour an hour for lunch) and if you hope to succeed you need to structure your working day in order to utilize these hours to the maximum.

However, you, as a sales person, will often find that nine hours is just not enough time to get everything done, and invariably you will find yourself working in the evenings and on weekends just to get everything up to date.

In this section we analyse how we can use these hours to our benefit, and, if necessary, what work we can leave to complete after normal working hours.

Before we go any further there is a rule here that you should remember because many Sales Managers remember this rule, and they use this rule when deciding whether you are being productive or not.

A Salesman's work is never finished!!!

Now what do we mean by this? No sales person should ever say that they have no work to do. Ever!!! If you are not actively marketing and selling to people, you should then be either preparing quotes, proposals, reports, or presentations, or should be preparing lists of new people to contact. The day a Sales Manager walks past a Sales Person's desk and find them twiddling their thumbs, or playing games, or searching the Internet for things that are not work-related, is the day they probably will be fired!

You must remember that your job is unlike anybody else's with respect to the fact that you determine your own salary, and because of this you must be productive at all times. It is a known fact that sales is difficult – hell, anybody will tell you that, and you can pick up any Sales book off the shelf of any bookshop and you will find this same statement- **sales is difficult**! Of course it is, because if it were easy then more people will be doing this kind of job because, whether you like it or not, it is also one of the most rewarding jobs to be in, especially from a financial perspective. But it takes a hell of a lot of determination and dedication to get it done properly.

So the next time you decide that you would like to play a game, or search the Internet, think to yourself, "How much money am I stealing from myself by playing this game?"

Right, lecture over; now let's get back in here.

THE AVERAGE WORK DAY

The average working day starts at 08h00 and ends at 17h00. This is normal for almost everybody, and so we will look at these hours in a little more detail and try to structure our work day to coincide with everybody else's.

There is something you need to bear in mind before we continue along this little journey. These suggestions are merely guidelines and should not be taken into absolute account, because there will be times that you will have to override these ideas for various reasons ranging from preparing quotations, proposals and reports, urgent or large meetings and presentations, to power outages. These structures are merely for the ideal working day, and if you need to alter the mix then by all means go ahead.

Right, so now the day is basically structured into two parts: **Marketing and Non-Marketing.**

Alright, let's just think about this for a minute here. Most people arrive at work at 08h00 (or just before). What's the first thing they do? Probably greet everybody and head straight for the coffee machine. The next step is they probably head for their desk and switch on their computer, unpack the goodies they have brought with them to work (lunch, notes, etc) and then start slipping through their diaries to see what is in store for the day. One or two quick phone calls are probably made internally to greet somebody else in the office, and then the average person starts to set their mind into work mode.

Don't worry; this is quite normal and probably even happens to you.

The bottom line is here, nobody gets any serious work done before 09h00, and, if they are those unfortunates, some companies schedule general staff meetings first thing in the morning, which means that they have to now focus between 08h00 and 09h00 and **then** only start their day's routines.

So where does this leave you? You basically have an hour whereby you cannot even hope to contact anybody to sell them anything, or setup a meeting, or whatever. You have what is known as a **non-marketing hour**.

Right, let's carry on here. After 09h00 most people are now in work mode and are performing their tasks (hopefully) and this normally continues until lunchtime, which normally occurs between the hours of 12h00 until 14h00. Some people take a tea break between 09h00 and 12h00 (normally this happens at about 10h00) but these breaks are often only fifteen minutes so the person is generally in the office and hence is contactable.

So lunchtime happens between these hours, and in most companies occurs for one hour (sixty minutes). During this time most people leave the office to either grab a bit to eat, or to run some personal errands. Hell, some people even go shopping, but the bottom line is here you have another two **non-marketing hours** here.

So, the people get back from lunch and start their afternoon. With the exclusion of an afternoon tea break (in some cases) generally productive work is done between 14h00 and 16h00. Right, we have one hour left of work.

In this last hour people are starting to shut down their work day. They are finishing their paperwork (or some other task) and are starting to prepare to pack up and go home. This is the last **non-marketing hour** of the day.

Now, let's add up these hours.

08h00 – 09h00 – non-marketing hour
09h00 – 12h00 – marketing hours
12h00 – 14h00 – non-marketing hours
14h00 – 16h00 – marketing hours
16h00 – 17h00 – non-marketing hours

So if we total this then that means that out of every day we have a sum of:

5 marketing hours
4 non-marketing hours

Just remember, this is the **average working day**. Some people work longer or shorter than these hours, or they work completely opposite to these hours, but this is the standard accepted by the general populace. If you happen to be working with situations that differ from these, then you need to find out what their "normal" work day consists of with regards to times before you can apply your time to suit their schedules.

Right, so what do we mean by **marketing** and **non-marketing hours**? Let's look at these, shall we?

Marketing Hours

These hours should be spent contacting the people. These are the hours whereby you should be scheduling meetings, or participating in those meetings, with your prospective clients.

In the case of cold calling, you should be on the telephone trying to get hold of the correct people to setup meetings.

In the case of actual meetings, you should be at the prospect's office engaging them in a sales discussion.

In the case of presentations, you should be starting your presentation to your prospective clients.

Let's look at some rough figures here to get an indication of the quantities of marketing that can be performed during this time.

In the case of cold calling; the average telephone cold call consists of approximately five minutes (sometimes more, sometimes less; we are working on averages here). Within those five minutes you should be able to wade through the receptionist in order to get to the right person to speak to. You should be able to introduce yourself and state your case. You should be able to schedule a meeting, and you should be able to say your farewells.

After your phone call, normally ten minutes are spent in consolidating the information you have just received from your new prospect, and/or scheduling the meeting in your diary, and preparing yourself for the next phone call.

So given this then, at least one client can be contacted and consolidated in about fifteen minutes. You have five marketing hours, or three hundred minutes to perform this task. This means that it is feasible to contact approximately twenty people in a working day, which equates to about a hundred people in a working week (Monday to Friday). Success and failure statistics will be covered in the chapter on Sales Analysis (Chapter 16), so don't worry about this now.

In the case of actual meetings, the average meeting takes approximately thirty minutes to an hour (sometimes more, sometimes less, but again we are assuming averages here). Travelling times generally take about an hour between meetings. For this scenario, let's look at the first marketing segment of the day – 09h00 to 12h00. If you travel to the client and arrive there at 09h00 you then can have a meeting (assume it to be from 09h00 until 10h00). You then take an hour to travel to your next meeting (10h00 – 11h00) and your second meeting can start at

11h00 and finish at 12h00. You now have two hours to get to your next meeting which can start at 14h00 and finish at 15h00. Now, if you are clever, you can schedule another meeting close by and run that from 15h00 until 16h00 (give or take a few minutes).

This in effect means that you have been able to perform four meetings in a working day, or twenty meetings in a working week (Monday to Friday).

Lastly then, let's look at presentations. The average sales presentation takes about twenty minutes, and the question-and-answer session thereafter can take anything up to about thirty minutes. But you also need some time to prepare your presentation. So let's look at these segments again.

You can travel and setup your first presentation before 09h00, and then you can run your presentation from 09h00 until 10h00. Then, you can shut down and move to your next presentation and setup by 11h00, and run this until 12h00. Right, so that now gives you two hours before your next presentation, which can begin at 14h00 until 15h00. Unfortunately you will not have time to run another presentation, so in an average working day you should be able to host three presentations, or fifteen in a working week (Monday to Friday).

I'll reiterate again here – these times and figures are ideals only, and should not be taken as hard and fast rules; they are merely guidelines to illustrate ideal situations.

To summarise then, the following is possible:

Cold Calling – 20 people a day = 100 people a week
Meetings – 4 meetings a day = 20 meetings a week
Presentations – 3 presentations a day = 15 presentations a week

NON-MARKETING HOURS

So everybody takes a break at work for lunch and/or personal affairs. It is natural human behaviour, but during these times you can use these periods productively.

In some rare occasions you might be able to get in a bit of active marketing but generally most people will be unavailable and hence you will be sitting with these hours ticking by. So what can we do during these hours?

There are actually many tasks that can be performed during this time.

Firstly, you need to prepare lists of people to contact. This takes time to prepare. Also, as a sales person you need to structure your Sales Reports (see Chapter 16) to hand in to your Sales Manager. You can spend this time organizing your quotations. There are several things that need to be done and can easily be scheduled to be tackled during these periods.

Also, and this forms part of every serious organization, there are always sales meetings that occur. Some companies structure them once a week; some businesses schedule them once a day. In any case, your Sales Manager should schedule them to happen during these on-marketing periods.

So what about your lunch break? Some sales people take them; some don't. Myself personally, I eat on the run, so to speak. I normally sit at my desk and while I am working I am munching on something. In the event that I need to go out to pay accounts, then I do so, but I try to be a quick as possible so that I can get back to work. After all, these hours are productive, and every minute counts.

For those of you who like to actually take your lunch hour, then do so, but if you are going to a restaurant for a meal, try to couple it with a business lunch. That way you are having a meeting as well as having a meal. And the best thing is that you can write it off as a business expense, so it doesn't cost you anything.

AFTER HOURS WORK

Like I said earlier, being in sales is not easy, and you will often find that there are not enough hours in the normal work day to get everything done. So unfortunately you have to put in a bit of overtime to get everything done.

The hours outside of normal office hours can be treated as **non-marketing** hours, but there is a difference here. You no longer have the inconvenience of the hustle and bustle of the office to distract you, so your concentration levels will be much higher. In addition, you are generally more relaxed because you are in comfortable surroundings, you are wearing comfortable clothing, and you can choose how long to work.

A quick digression here. Somehow, either through the company or on your own steam, get yourself a laptop. If not, then at the very least install a desktop computer in your home and use a flash drive to transfer work to and from your computer. The prices of laptops nowadays make it a viable option to get your hands on one, and hook in a wireless Internet connection. Without this piece of equipment your work performance will be severely hampered, trust me. The machine does not have to be the most powerful system in the world, but it should be able to handle your mail client, some word processing, and some spreadsheet work. Maybe throw in a bit of presentation design, and the ability to access the Internet. Most computers today can cope with this workload.

There are certain tasks that I like to leave for these hours (and normally I put in a few hours work every weekend). During my profession as a Product Manager I was expected to, amongst other things, design presentations and create budget reports, and also put together proposals for the other sales people in the company who were less experienced than me. Take a look at my sample proposal (pages 243 to 266) and you will see just how much work is involved in these. The budget reports frequently were approximately thirty pages in size with vital information. These sorts of things I used to leave until the weekend when I could sit quietly and correlate my thoughts properly in order to get the work done.

When I was not performing these tasks I worked on something else. I use *Microsoft Outlook* ® (as discussed in Chapter 13) as my diary and CRM facility, and generally during a normal work day I receive emails and new contacts that I actually don't have time to sort. So I leave this sort of work for the weekend. I also have my **Outlook** setup so that it can store emails in my **Outbox** until I have reconnected to the Internet, so I sit and prepare emails (meeting requests, additional information, "Hello, I haven't heard from you in a while…" mails, and send them out. As soon as I am back in the office and connected to the network my **Outlook** automatically sends these emails out on my behalf without me having to worry about them, and I can concentrate on my work for the day.

I also sometimes prepare lists of people to contact for the coming week. This frees up those non-marketing hours for quotes, proposals, etc and this work is boring in any case. I prefer to do this sort of thing on the weekend, and I know that I can then set small targets for myself for the coming week because I know that the people on the list I prepare must all be contacted by Friday in that coming week. If not, then I know I am behind on my schedule.

5 – 3 – 2 – 1 STRATEGY

In Chapter 5 I discussed briefly this strategy. I'm going to take another look at it here.

Please remember, **this is a guideline only, and should not be taken literally!** It is an ideal model that we would all like to follow, but sometimes life doesn't allow us that luxury.

Ok, so how does this work?

Well, the 5 equals "5 meetings a day".

The 3 equals "3 new clients"

2 equates to "2 old clients"

And the 1 equals (1 order").

So let's put this together. Each day, you should try to have five meetings. Of those five meetings three should be new clients (thus increasing your client base), two should be former clients (thus maintaining your relations with your old clients), and you should bring back at least one order to the office, no matter how big or small.

Now think about this – there are twenty working days in a month on average (Monday to Friday). If you receive an order each day that becomes twenty orders a month!!! How does that shake up your spinal cord?

Of course, to put this strategy in place it means that you will have to do your non-marketing work outside of normal office hours, and spend the entire day marketing, but if you can achieve this then you will definitely be on your way to greatness!

CONCLUSION

You need to structure your time effectively to be as productive as possible, so that you can maximise your sales.

Understandably, this does take a lot of discipline and you will at times be tempted to goof off, but there is something here you must remember: if you don't contact that person then somebody else will and you will lose out on vital money in your back pocket! And to win the prospect back will take even more work. Why give yourself more work to do?

So bear this in mind the next time you decide not to work.

SUMMARY – CHAPTER 7.

In order to succeed at sales a sales person needs to strategize their work time effectively otherwise they will find that the time will disappear without any real productivity being done. If not checked this will escalate dramatically over the days that follow, and eventually the sales person will discover that their sales performance has lagged for the month.

The Average Work Day – In most cases the average work day is from 08h00 and 17h00 and it is during these hours that you will be able to contact people in order to setup or conduct meetings, or perform follow ups. Presentations are also performed during these hours.

During the normal work day, various tasks can be performed at different times. These are based upon basic human nature. Such examples are:

- 08h00 – 09h00 – **non-marketing hour** – most people are just arriving at their workplace and they are normally concentrating on planning their schedule for the day. They should not be contacted at these times for business.
- 09h00-12h00 – **marketing hours** – during these hours clients and prospects can be contacted for business – related activities.
- 12h00 – 14h00 – **non-marketing hours** – these are the lunch hours and many workers are not available during these times.
- 14h00 – 16h00 – **marketing hours** - during these hours clients and prospects can be contacted for business – related activities.
- 16h00 – 17h00 – **non-marketing hours** – at this time most people are concentrating on their administrative work, and also preparing to pack up for the day and leave work. Very little marketing can be conducted at this time.

Marketing Hours - During those hours that you are able to market to prospective clients and activities such as cold calling, presentations, and conducting actual meetings are feasible.

If we look at time concerning these activities the following is possible:

Cold Calling – 20 people a day = 100 people a week
Meetings – 4 meetings a day = 20 meetings a week
Presentations – 3 presentations a day = 15 presentations a week

Non-Marketing Hours - Whilst people are not available to contact you can concentrate on administrative duties such as preparing lists of people to contact, or preparing quotes and proposals, or finalizing your sales reports for your manager. In addition you can also schedule your lunch time to coincide with these hours. If you can, try to schedule a business lunch.

After Hours Work - The types of activities that can be performed in the evenings and on the weekends (including Public and Religious holidays) are similar to those performed during non-marketing hours. In addition, you can setup emails etc, and update your CRM applications.

5 – 3 – 2 – 1 Strategy - This strategy, if followed as closely as possible, will lead to a success in sales.

The strategy is as follows:
The 5 equals "5 meetings a day".
The 3 equals "3 new clients"
2 equates to "2 old clients"
And the 1 equals (1 order").

Chapter 8.
Marketing Triangles and Selling Aspects

Many years ago I was involved with a company which was owned by an extremely clever businessman. As part of my training he taught me the Marketing Triangle and I would like to take this opportunity to present it to you. You might find a use for it somewhere in your career.

Basically, there are always three elements that comprise a business, namely **Product**, **Marketing**, and **Administration**. Let's look at each aspect in a little more detail.

Product – In order to have a business you need to have a **Product** or **Service** to sell. In our industry that **product** could be anything from computers, cabling, network equipment, or holistic solutions. **Services** can include labour, training, Internet Service Providing, or the provision of Engineers or Technicians to a client's site (also known as **Labour Broking**). You must have a product to sell otherwise you have no means to make a profit.

Marketing – People must be aware that your product and business exists so you need to advertise your product and your business. It's not enough just to build a shop in a shopping mall. You might catch shoppers walking past, but in order to be a success you cannot rely just on this type of buyer; you need to make more people aware of your existence.

Administration – Right you have your product, and you have your marketing in place, but you need a background to your business. You need somebody (or some people) who work in the wings concentrating on processing orders and managing the company's finances. These people are also responsible for paying your salary and your commission. This element is extremely important to ensure the success of the business.

These three basic elements work hand in hand together to ensure a business thrives, and many failures occur as a result of the owners neglecting one or some of these elements.

As a sales person, how can you adopt these concepts to your career? Well, product is necessary because without it you will have nothing to sell! You also need to know that product in order to sell it. Later on in this chapter I will discuss **Product Knowledge** in a bit more detail.

Marketing is also very important, and as a sales person you need to ensure that as many people are aware of your product as possible. There is an entire chapter devoted to marketing and advertising. Without proper marketing you will never hope to make any sales.

Where you become involved in the **Administration** side of things in ensuring that your quotations and proposals are designed correctly, and that, once they are accepted, the orders are processed properly. You also need to ensure that your client affects payment for those goods and services they have received otherwise you will lose out on your commission. Another role you play in this realm is the production of your Sales Reports, which are discussed in another chapter.

PRODUCT KNOWLEDGE

You cannot sell what you don't know! This might seem an obvious statement but I have come across so many sales people that tout their products and when questioned further, they flounder, with many ums and ahs, leaving you with an impression of disgust and distrust because that person knows nothing about the product they are selling.

When you start your career in a new company your very first task is to get to know the products that you will be selling. If you are more technically minded then you probably would like to get into the mechanics of the products, but at the very least you need to have at least a working knowledge of the product in order to get by and to handle some of the more technical questions that will be thrown at you by the consumer.

When I am introduced to a new product range I always take at least a day or two to get to know the product better. If I have the opportunity I play around a little with the merchandise to see first-hand what it does and what it can do. I also gather as much information as I can about its benefits and advantages, and then

I start strategizing as to where I can promote those benefits to prospective buyers.

When you actually sell your products to a buyer, concentrate on what you have learnt about the products and use that information to impart to your client. If necessary, try to take a trained technician along with you to your meeting so that they can assist you in dealing with any technical questions that might be asked. In some cases you might even need to take your Sales Manager with you to assist in making the deal, especially if there are questions that you do not have the authority to answer, such as when dealing with profitability. However this might not always be possible and you need to prepare yourself for the onslaught of questions that will be thrown at you.

So how do you deal with this?

I have come across so many Sales People that, when they don't know the answer to the questions that have been posed to them, they attempt to lie their way out of the confrontation.

In my very first position as a Computer Salesman (and I'm now talking about fifteen years ago) we had an altercation with our Technical Department, and in this they were very correct with their protests.

They accused us of "selling the client a Volkswagen Beetle and telling them it could fly!" Now what they meant by this is Sales People tend to embellish the benefits of various products, and lead the prospective buyer to believe that it can produce various kinds of miracles. When the deal is sealed and the time comes for the technicians to implement the solutions into the clients' sites, the users become extremely irate when the system does not do what the client wanted, because the sales person sold an incorrect solution in the first place just to get the sale.

In order to save yourself these embarrassments adopt the following policy always:

> *"I don't know but I can find out for you and get back to you!"*

If a buyer asks you a question and you don't know the answer, be honest and frank with them and tell them that you do not know the answer to their question, and then offer to find out and let them know in due course. And make sure that you do follow up on this and do the necessary research. The prospect will respect you more for your honesty, and it will give you time to confer with your Technical Department to find out the correct solution for your client's needs.

Never be too hasty to make the sale until you are absolutely sure that what you are offering is what the client wants and needs. A hasty sale now might end up a lost sale if you have sold an incorrect solution, and might also lead to a sense of distrust between you and your client which will hamper future sales with that company.

There is another little saying that I learnt whilst I was involved with Industrial Engineering, and I think it is time that I impart this to you now.

"Do it right the first time!"

Whatever you do, whatever you endeavour to do, take the time to make sure that the job is done correctly the first time around. My son, who is nine years old, has a chore of washing dishes in the house. When he started this chore about a year ago, his attempts were not very good. He would only half-wash the dishes, leaving grease and grime on them. Inevitably he would have to repeat the process all over again, and it has taken me a year to teach him this little idiom. If you take a little more time and make sure that all your "i's" are dotted and your "t's" are crossed, then you will not have comebacks and you can be proud of yourself of having done a job well. Too, your technicians and your client will also be happy with you because they will not have wasted time in having to redo the job.

When you sell a solution make absolutely sure that it will fit in with what the buyer wants. If not, then spend more time gathering information from the person and then discuss it with your Technical Department and make certain that you will not sell a "flying Beetle".

BE PREPARED FOR MEETINGS

When you schedule a meeting with a prospective client you are committing yourself in many different ways. Firstly, you are committing your time in leaving the office and travelling to the buyer's premises. Secondly, you are spending money in travelling costs to get to those premises. Thirdly, you are committing the reputation of the company you work for. Lastly, you are committing your own ability to make a sale.

Knowing all this then, a meeting with a client is an important affair indeed, and one that should not be taken lightly! Many sales people schedule meetings just to get out of the office and to show the boss on their Sales Reports that there has been some sort of activity. I have seen this so many times in the past. But it must be understood that adopting this type of attitude will only hurt you in the long run.

In my past employment my former boss always spoke of this story which irked her to no end.

She had a young lady employed as a Sales Lady in the company who used to spend many hours out of the office visiting clients. However, at the end of each month when Management perused her Sales Reports it was ascertained that she was not closing that many sales. The bosses erroneously assumed that she was having a problem with her closing abilities, and decided that they needed to send her on a few Sales training courses to see if they could correct her problems.

After doing so they again perused her Sales Reports over a few subsequent months and discovered that things had not changed very much: she was getting out and seeing the people, but she was not closing sales. So they investigated further.

What was discovered was that this lady was practicing the art of "Comfort Visits" and was apparently very good at it.

Now what this meant was that she was constantly visiting her clients that were her friends, and perhaps having a cup of coffee and gossiping about arbitrary things that were definitely not work related. Needless to say she was very shortly thereafter fired from that position.

Your job is to make sales for your company and this is what you should be concentrating on every day of your life. I have mentioned before that Sales is an extremely difficult job: it takes discipline and dedication to make it work. It takes a lot of guts to go out and meet new people and deal with their objections and rejections, but that is what you are contracted to do, so you must do it well.

When you schedule a meeting you need to do it with a purpose in mind. Eventually, if you have done your job well, you will gain a sale out of your efforts. You need to ensure that at the end of your meeting you have achieved something.

When dealing with corporate companies you will need to visit the prospective client a good many times before you will be able to make the sale, so with every visit you need to have a definite plan as to what will be discussed during the meeting and what you will hope to achieve at the end of the time. After all, it is costing you in both petrol (gas for our American friends) and time in committing to that meeting.

This then brings me to the whole point of this discussion. You need to prepare yourself for that meeting. Never arrive at a client if you are not sure as to what will be discussed, and make sure that you have all the necessary knowledge to deal with any questions that may arise during the event. If not, your prospect will get the impression that you do not know what is being discussed and they will resent their time that you have wasted.

I will give you an example of this by a case history from my own personal experience.

Recently I was working for a company who deals with the South African Government. Now in this country there is a company whose sole job is to collect all the requisitions from the

Governmental Departments and then procure the goods and/or services from the various suppliers around the country.

In order to have the chance to secure some of those contracts I needed to become familiar with the Account Managers at the Purchasing Company. I had setup a meeting with one of the senior managers. I had just started with this company so there was a lot of information I did not know.

Ok, so I went to my meeting and met with this gentleman, and he might as well have been speaking Chinese to me, because he was asking questions on topics that I absolutely knew nothing about, and it was clear within the first fifteen minutes that he got the impression that I knew nothing about what I was selling.

He was very much correct in his assumption, and I left that meeting felling extremely embarrassed. Needless to say I have never been able to schedule another meeting with him again!

I maintained from that experience that if my Sales Manager was attending that meeting with me, I probably would have been fired on the spot because I forgot the cardinal rule – **always be prepared for your meetings!**

Make sure that you have the necessary product knowledge to guide the meeting. If needed, take appropriate documentation with you to support your sales pitch. And ensure that you follow up on that meeting.

DRESS CODES

In the chapter on Cold Calling (Chapter 5) I mentioned this aspect a little and here I'm going to expand on that idea a little more.

You are a representative of your company, and unfortunately people tend to judge you within the first thirty seconds of meeting you. The very first impression they have of you is generally how they will label you in the future, so you need to ensure that that first impression is the best one that you can make so that the client is more pleasantly disposed towards you in the future.

One of the first impressions that people get is that of your physical appearance and thus you need to look as professional as possible. In the one company I worked for we had a salesman who insisted in coming to work in jeans and T-shirt, and we were dealing mainly with corporate clients. He would go off to his meetings dressed like this, and invariably his sales performance was not very good.

You need to dress according to the client you will be meeting with, because the Rule of Magnetism works in human nature as well. This rule, taken from Physical Science, states that:

"Like attracts like, and unlike repels each other!"

And in human relations, this rule is quite true. If you are meeting with a banker, for example, you will find them dressed in a formal suit, complete with tie and blazer. For ladies similar attire is also apparent. If you are meeting with a farmer, you will find them dressed in some sort of safari suit, probably with a hat and **veldskoen** (this is a term adopted by South Africans which refers to a particular type of leather or hide-based shoe that is extremely useful when working out in the fields).

Bearing this in mind, you need to dress accordingly, remembering that it is always better to be overdressed than underdressed. It would be permissible to meet with a farmer dressed in a collar and tie, but wearing a T-shirt, shorts, and sandals might not be appropriate.

Also, due to the climate of South Africa, a new dress code seems to have been readily adopted in all provinces. This code includes neat slacks (trousers, pants, etc), good shoes, and golf shirts, possibly with the company's emblem on the pocket. Generally speaking, this type of dress is accepted in any circle, and is a code that I have adopted for my own use.

Being a male I have mainly concentrated on dress codes for males, but with the ladies I must admit that I'm not the expert when discussing dress codes. I can say however that the ladies should also dress professionally without revealing too much, if you know what I mean. It does give the wrong impression, especially when the client is also a lady.

If you tend to match dress codes with the people you will be meeting with, then they unconsciously find that they can relate to you better because you look like them. Keep this in mind.

CONCLUSION

In order to be successful in your sales you need to be prepared. You must know your products, and know them well. When committing yourself to meetings you must ensure that you know what you will be talking about, and where you would like that meeting to go.

Make sure that you are presentable when you meet with your prospects because the last thing you want is to lose a multi-million Dollar sale because you had a spot of egg on your tie.

If you don't know something, don't lie because it will always bite you in the back. Just be truthful and admit to the client that you don't know but make sure you find out for the client!

Nuff said!

SUMMARY – CHAPTER 8.

Basically, there are always three elements that comprise a business, namely **Product**, **Marketing**, and **Administration**.

Product – In order to have a business you need to have a **Product** or **Service** to sell. You must have a product to sell otherwise you have no means to make a profit.

Marketing – People must be aware that your product and business exists so you need to advertise your product and your business, and you need to make more people aware of your existence.

Administration – You need an administrative background to your business. You need somebody (or some people) who work in the wings concentrating on processing orders and managing the company's finances.

Product Knowledge

You cannot sell what you don't know! When you start your career in a new company your very first task is to get to know the products that you will be selling.

When you actually sell your products to a buyer, concentrate on what you have learnt about the products and use that information to impart to your client.

If a buyer asks you a question and you don't know the answer, be honest and frank with them and tell them that you do not know the answer to their question, and then offer to find out and let them know in due course. And make sure that you do follow up on this and do the necessary research.

When you sell a solution make absolutely sure that it will fit in with what the buyer wants. If not, then spend more time gathering information from the person and then discuss it with your Technical Department to ensure the solution will meet their needs.

BE PREPARED FOR MEETINGS

When you schedule a meeting you need to do it with a purpose in mind. Eventually, if you have done your job well, you will gain a sale out of your efforts. You need to ensure that at the end of your meeting you have achieved something.

When dealing with corporate companies you will need to visit the prospective client a good many times before you will be able to make the sale, so with every visit you need to have a definite plan as to what will be discussed during the meeting and what you will hope to achieve at the end of the time.

Never arrive at a client for a meeting if you are not sure as to what will be discussed, and make sure that you have all the necessary knowledge to deal with any questions that may arise during the event. If not, your prospect will get the impression that you do not know what is being discussed and they will resent their time that you have wasted.

Make sure that you have the necessary product knowledge to guide the meeting. If needed, take appropriate documentation or people with you to support your sales pitch. And ensure that you follow up on that meeting.

DRESS CODES

You are a representative of your company, and unfortunately people tend to judge you within the first thirty seconds of meeting you. The very first impression they have of you is generally how they will label you in the future, so you need to ensure that that first impression is the best one that you can make so that the client is more pleasantly disposed towards you in the future.

You need to dress according to the client you will be meeting with, because the Rule of Magnetism works in human nature as well. This rule, taken from Physical Science, states that:

> *"Like attracts like, and unlike repels each other!"*

This means that you should dress according to your client, but remember that it is always better to be overdressed than underdressed.

If you tend to match dress codes with the people you will be meeting with, then they unconsciously find that they can relate to you better because you look like them. Keep this in mind.

CHAPTER 9.
CLIENT SITE ANALYSIS

One of the major problems we face in the IT industry is the lack of standardization within clients' sites. In so many cases your company is forced to adopt a client's site (and hence their network infrastructure) and adapt it to the standards of your company.

In extremely rare cases you might be lucky enough to be able to build the entire network from scratch (and this only if you are involved in the construction of the actual building where the network will be eventually housed), but even so you will most definitely have to work with your client's existing computer hardware and software.

Once you have adopted such a site you will often find such anomalies as incorrect or shoddy cabling, old, outdated computers, very little or improper security policies, and outdated software. In addition you will often find problems with their software licensing and this could in time lead to legal software audits which, if not checked, could lead to the eventual financial downfall of your hard-earned client because of the legalities surrounding this.

This chapter has been consolidated to assist the Sales Engineer in performing these site evaluations and helps in identifying various anomalies in an attempt to standardize the site.

Such standardization in any IT company should be adhered to as soon as possible because not only does it help to reduce eventual technical support requests (thereby allowing the engineers to concentrate on new sites instead of existing ones) – it also lends to the professionalism of the IT company.

A quick definition here before we continue. The term **Transparent (Technological) Solution** will be discussed in this manual, so we need to briefly outline exactly what this means. Basically this means a solution provided to a client that will operate in the background with minimal interference and will be maintained completely in the background, without the knowledge of the users.

Oh, and you will notice that I have just used a term of **Sales Engineer** instead of **Sales Person**. The term **Sales Engineer** is given to a Sales Person who has some good technical background behind them, and uses these technical abilities in order to further enhance their sales.

OK, I hope this helps you. Let's carry on.

There is an ever-increasing need to move businesses towards new technology that is being offered in the marketplace and because of this proper transparent solution implementation is often overlooked due to the following reasons:

Budget constraints – Money is probably one of the biggest deciding factors when deciding on quality IT solutions and because of this many companies are forced to either purchase sub-standard equipment, or utilize the services of under-qualified personnel in order to achieve an acceptable solution. Bearing in mind that almost all businesses in today's society cannot operate adequately without the use of modern technology, we are finding a definite increase in the priority of IT-related budgets in order to cater for these needs. Carefully planned projects will, in most cases, should be able to offer sufficient flexibility to cater for such budgets.

Time constraints – A major factor when deploying IT solutions within a company is time. Many companies cannot afford the necessary downtime associated with these implementations and this then often lead to the introduction of temporary solutions which sometimes affects the overall productivity and efficiency of the business. We often find that incorrect Project Management is the culprit when faced with these sorts of dilemmas.

Personnel constraints – Many companies in the beginning settle for solutions that actually do not sufficiently meets their needs due to various reasons, one of which is the lack of funds. In order to counteract the problems that these existing problems invariably give, part of the budget allocated to IT is forced to accommodate various technical personnel to repair and maintain these types of solutions, either permanently on site, contractually on site, or required as the need arises. Obviously, the need for human intervention will always be required, but correctly deployed transparent solutions will reduce the number of anomalies encountered within a company's IT infrastructure, and consequently reduce the number of required technical personnel. Given this factor it becomes an important selling perspective to educate your potential client on selecting the correct solution. Although they initially will be spending more capital on the proper solution, in the long term they will benefit from decreased requirements of technical personnel.

A good illustration of this is to glean information from your client as to their current expenses with regards to how often they require technicians. Calculate these costs over a twelve month period and add these to how much they spent on their current solution (taking into account natural inflation). Then estimate the costs of your proposed solution and divide this amount over the same period. You should see a marked difference in overall costs, and this then can assist you in convincing the client that your solution will be a better option.

Training constraints – As the level of technology increases, so the level of complexity and flexibility of available solutions increase. This new technology will always mean that the End User personnel will need to be properly trained to be able to use the new solutions. To minimize this requirement proper deployment of transparent solutions will ensure that the average user will require minimal training – most of the evolving solution should take place at the level of the trained IT personnel, and this means the average user should not be aware (or vaguely aware) that these changes are taking place.

The goal then of a transparent solution is to design an infrastructure that is as seamless as possible, that never fails, never give errors or problems, and should be totally user friendly to the average end user. Obviously no solution currently in existence can ever match this ideal, but we are ever nearing this goal.

SITE EVALUATIONS

In nearly all clients you encounter will have existing installed bases (in other words, existing computers and networks). These existing bases will need to be investigated and interrogated in order to identify problem areas before any future projects can be implemented. These evaluations then become extremely important and it is because of this that we concentrate heavily on this in this chapter.

Initial site evaluations are generally conducted in three phases:

1. **The initial visit** – This is the **site analysis**
2. **The proposal** – This is based on the analysis and deals with subsequent repairs and alterations (where necessary)
3. **The project** – This is the actual implementation of the solution

The procedure discussed below focuses on a typical commercial client, but can be easily adapted to cater for any site evaluation.

The initial site visit is discussed in detail below, and an outline of the proposal based upon this visit is also covered.

Part 3, which deals with the actual project, is beyond the scope of this book. However, there are a few points that I have included in this section that need to be considered as part of the project.

INITIAL SITE VISIT -

The initial site inspection is by far the most important step in this exercise because the clients' first expectations of the sales representative will probably involve a fair amount of distrust and apprehension.

Think about this for a second. A client has spent a great deal of time and money in having his/her IT infrastructure implemented in the first place. Probably the main reason why you are being invited to perform the analysis in the first place is because the current solution is not meeting their needs and they are hesitant about placing their trust (and hard earned profits) into another IT company that might not deliver satisfactory results.

I'm going to digress briefly at this stage and quickly analyze the differences between **Sales** and **Technical**. A Sales Person's job is to sell a client a solution. Yes, a fair amount of product knowledge is required in order to be successful, but generally the extent of the knowledge is sufficient to be able to answer any questions that arise from the client. A Sales Person's greatest tool is his or her mouth (and brain of course). Some Sales People have quite a good technical ability but their main focus not to get the thing to work. Their job is to make sure that the "thing" will work for the client.

A Technician (or **Engineer** as I like to call them) greatest ability is to understand how the "thing" works and to get it to work. They, generally speaking, are not very good in conversing with the client at all and hence should not be focussed in selling the product or service to the client. They must simply make it work.

In the situation of these site inspections, unless the Sales Representative has an extremely good technical ability, it is strongly advisable to ensure that an Engineer accompanies you during your visit, to assist you in identifying all the problems. Remember, it is the Engineer who eventually will need to make sure the solution works, if the client accepts your proposal, and hence they need to tell you what they will need in order for this to happen.

The following areas should be addressed at this first visit:

Basic Network infrastructure – An understanding of the basic infrastructure needs to be obtained and wherever possible rough sketches of the physical layout should be recorded for later reference. These should include the location of each computer in the company, the location of the servers and any other involved network equipment such as switches, routers, cabinets, and other, similar devices.

Computer hardware – The number of computers, and hence the number of users, should also be recorded. Basic information of the CPU, RAM, and hard drives should be recorded if at all possible, as this information forms part of the proposal. Any other network devices and peripherals, such as printers, should also be recorded, as well as their configurations within the network. A useful tool in this case is to download and use a software computer interrogator which tells you everything from the hardware to what software has been installed on each computer in a matter of minutes. If you can obtain and use one this will definitely help because later on, when it comes time to starting working on the project to standardize the network, drivers for each device (sound card, graphics card, etc) can be easier to identify without having to physically open each computer in order to recognize these items.

Cabling anomalies –

Existing cable should be inspected for any defects or incorrect installations. Also worth noting at this point is an inspection of the existing cable trays for future expansion purposes. Wherever possible Digital Cameras are invaluable in recording such anomalies as the site can be inspected remotely by cabling personnel, and informed decisions can be made off-site. Many are a site I have visited in the past that have shown extreme anomalies, and even in the Reception Area!!! Some of these have also been other IT companies!!! These anomalies, such as loose cabling hanging from the ceilings, to mazes of cables lying under tables and behind computers, can lead to a multitude of problems ranging from people inadvertently kicking cables when they walk past, to rats eating at cables in the ceilings. Furthermore, untidy cabling in the Reception Area especially leads to a very poor perception of the company when visitors arrive. So take a look at note all of these problems.

Critical application software –

Any application software that is important to the overall functioning of the client's business should be recorded. Proper licensing is a vital component of any installed base because audits are carried out on a regular basis on random to different companies. If one of your clients happens to be involved the fines involved can be crippling to any business. This aspect of the audit is a very important part of the process.

Expansion probabilities – It is important at this stage to discuss any future expansion needs the client requires. Normally, a client's installed base is evaluated on a yearly basis, so any futures expansion probabilities should be based on these time factors. Obviously, information pertaining to these factors will influence the eventual outcome of the solution.

Budget constraints – Without a proper indication of the client's budget, a proposal and project plan cannot be accurately generated. However, and this should be noted, many projects requiring major overhauling of the existing infrastructure would require vast sums of money so you will often find that several companies will request these proposals so that they can include them into their budgets for the following year.

If this is indeed the case, mention in your proposal current pricing as well as inflated pricing if they were to accept the solution a year later than anticipated. This will allow your prospective client to accurately budget for the solution, and would also help you to receive the contract when it is accepted because you very kindly have performed most of the background work for your prospect.

User problems – Each individual user (in the case of corporate clients, randomly selected samples of users) should be addressed with any problems they are facing locally. These should be noted and mentioned in the proposal. In some cases, a simple questionnaire cold be drafted and emailed to each user (or printed and hand delivered if there are problems with the email system, or those users who do not have access to emails).

These valuable sources of information can direct the technicians in assisting you to select the correct types of solutions to solve these various issues.

THE PROPOSAL -

Based on the information obtained from the initial site visit an accurate proposal based on the client's needs can be prepared and presented to the client. Costs involved in each of the stages are included in the proposal so that the client is aware of the effects this will produce on the budget.

In another chapter we will analyze a proposal in greater detail and expand on the information covered here.

This proposal should contain the following sections:

List of existing installed base - This information, obtained from the initial site visit, serves as an important background for any future upgrades or alterations. Where applicable, incompatible hardware will need to be replaced and it is in this section that such replacements are justified.

Formal hardware and software audit - Each computer in the network is interrogated. A complete list of the computers' hardware as well as serial numbers is recorded. This list includes, but is not restricted to printers, network devices and other peripheral devices attached to the network. Furthermore, a formal software audit is also performed to ensure complete legality within the client's business. Such information is consolidated and any anomalies are recorded. Often the costs involved in legalizing software far outweigh the client's budget. In these cases it is advisable to forward the software audit to the end of the proposed project, whereby acceptable arrangements can be made with the respective software dealers in accordance with the client's financial position. These lists are consolidated and stored, and will be discussed in more detail later. Lastly, each computer should be sealed against unauthorized access. This protects the client against any controversies arising in the future with regards to damaged or missing hardware.

Server audit – Although generally integrated with the formal hardware and software audit, the server interrogation is by far the most important interrogation of the entire infrastructure. Apart from the usual hardware and software audits, security policies, server roles, naming conventions, and other software configurations should be recorded and analyzed. General server performance benchmarks should also be recorded and hence subsequent suggestions regarding increasing the servers' performances can be discussed.

Physical topology – In your initial examination you should have identified and recorded the cabling anomalies that currently exist in your prospective client's company. Part of your proposal should include a brief description of these findings and options are discussed here with respect to rectifying these problems.

Cable labelling – Although overlooked by many IT companies, correct cable labelling is a vital part to any network cable infrastructure. Not only does it dramatically reduce fault tracing in the future, but it also serves as an indication of future expansion requirements – as more network points are needed, the need for additional network devices increase. Correct labelling eliminates the common mistake of leaving redundant cables plugged into the appropriate network devices.

Many IT companies have adopted a numerical policy when labelling, and thus point 1 corresponds to place 1 on the network device. This policy however creates confusion when applied to corporate networks. The Industrial Sector has adopted a better policy, which could quite easily be extended through to the IT industry. This policy is better explained by way of example:

Consider the following scenario – a 24-port switch is connected in the Server Room and a network point from the reception area is to be connected to this switch on port number 19. The Industrial method of labelling uses a "to-from" strategy on both ends of the cable, with an acceptable naming convention. Once a naming convention has been adhered to it becomes quite easy to identify all required labels. In this example the following convention is used:

SR – Server Room
SW1 – Switch 1
: 19 – Port 19
REC – Reception Area
: 1 – Point 1

Thus the label attached to the cable connected to the switch will read as follows:

REC: 1 – SRSW1: 19

And the label attached to the cable connected to the network point will read as follows:

SRSW1: 19 – REC: 1

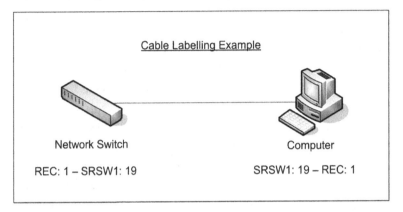

Cable Labelling Example

Network Switch

REC: 1 – SRSW1: 19

Computer

SRSW1: 19 – REC: 1

Network diagrams – Earlier on in this chapter it was suggested that sketches should be drawn during the initial visit to the client. These sketches, combined with actual cable tracings performed during the project implementation, and the cable labels discussed above, will serve as blueprints for formal network diagrams to be designed. These diagrams facilitate fault finding as well as future expansion possibilities. As part of your proposal you could include some of these diagrams. Not only does it help your client to visualize his/her infrastructure, it helps you later on to plan your project more accurately. In some cases, printed versions of these diagrams can be discussed and edited between you and your client, which will help the client to see exactly what the finished product will look like.

There is a side-line here. The actual **project** is not the scope of this book but the following six points, which also form part of the proposal, should be included in the project implementation.

CD/DVD/Memory Stick Storage – This section is of vital importance because the whole client's IT infrastructure is recorded thus. It involves the recording and storage of drivers, network diagrams, installation software, and user information onto CD's, DVD's, or **Memory Sticks** (also known as *Flash Drives*). Two copies are made: one is kept at the client's premises and the other is stored at the IT support company. Thus a complete history of the client's site is recorded for future reference. In addition, Support Personnel need simply to ensure that a copy of the client's CD/DVD/Flash Drive need accompany him/her with each visit, so that support charges are reduced.

Drivers – All software drivers pertaining to each computer in the client's installed base are categorized and recorded and drivers that are not present at the client's site can be obtained from the Internet. A complete list of hardware devices should be obtained during your hardware audit.

Installed base – Again from your audit, the entire installed base should also be recorded, as well as upgrades or alterations performed throughout the duration of the project. Furthermore, records of all software licenses should also be stored. These particular records should also be forwarded to the client's insurance company or lawyer.

Network diagrams – These, once designed and finalized, should also be placed on the CD/DVD/Flash Drive.

Installation software – Although the space required far exceeds the capacity inherent in a single CD, a record of all installation software should be kept along with the necessary license keys. With the introduction of writable DVD's and large storage capacity *Flash Drives* and *External Hard Drives* it is possible to store installation software onto these devices. Whichever media you choose copies of all installation software should be created, and the originals either kept at the client's insurance company or lawyer.

User information – Any miscellaneous information such as each user's account name, IP address (where applicable), and email address should also be stored. Programmed scripts and other developments must be added.

SERVICE LEVEL AGREEMENTS –

Often clients request service level agreements during the first visit. This is not advisable because firstly the infrastructure has not been evaluated and secondly accurate measures or future support has not been established. A period of a few months after the completion of the project should be used to monitor the levels of support before any agreements are entered into.

CONCLUSION

Client Site Evaluations are extremely important because it gives you the basis of identifying what is wrong and what needs to be fixed. Without physically examining a clients' site it is impossible to accurately quote on those problems that need to be resolved.

Also, you want the site to be as standardized as possible for five reasons:

- You want to earn a good reputation.
- You want the client to be satisfied that their infrastructure is working properly.
- You want to use the site as a good reference later on.
- You want to earn some good money from the client.
- You don't want to have to keeping sending Technicians back to repair issues that were not identified properly at the start.

SUMMARY – CHAPTER 9.

Often you will adopt old sites when you work with a new client, and once you have adopted such a site you will often find many anomalies as incorrect or shoddy cabling, old, outdated computers, very little or improper security policies, and outdated software that will need to be corrected and hence you will need to perform site evaluations in an attempt to standardize the site.

Proper transparent solution implementation is often overlooked due constraints such as:

Budget constraints – Money constraints often forces many companies to either purchase substandard equipment, or utilize the services of under-qualified personnel in order to achieve an acceptable solution.

Time constraints – Many companies cannot afford the necessary downtime associated with these implementations and this then often lead to the introduction of temporary solutions which sometimes affects the overall productivity and efficiency of the business.

Personnel constraints – Much of a company's budget is spent on the utilizing of Technical Personnel to repair improperly implemented IT infrastructures and this leads to less of an available financial budget when considering new projects.

Training constraints – As the level of technology increases, so the level of complexity and flexibility of available solutions increases which means that the End User Personnel will need to be properly trained to be able to use the new solutions. This affects budgets when considering new projects.

SITE EVALUATIONS

In nearly all clients you encounter will have existing installed bases (in other words, existing computers and networks) which will need to be investigated and interrogated in order to identify problem areas before any future projects can be implemented.

Initial Site Visit – This is the site analysis and the following areas should be addressed:

Basic Network infrastructure – An understanding of the basic infrastructure needs to be obtained and rough sketches of the physical layout should be recorded. These should include the location of each computer in the company, the location of the servers and any other involved network equipment such as switches, routers, cabinets, and other, similar devices.

Computer hardware – The number of computers, and hence the number of users, should also be recorded. Basic information of the CPU, RAM, and hard drives should be recorded if at all possible, as this information forms part of the proposal. Any other network devices and peripherals, such as printers, should also be recorded, as well as their configurations within the network.

Cabling anomalies – Existing cables should be inspected for any defects or incorrect installations. Also worth noting at this point is an inspection of the existing cable trays for future expansion purposes.

Critical application software – Any application software that is important to the overall functioning of the client's business should be recorded as well as the number of licenses the client has.

Expansion probabilities – It is important at this stage to discuss any future expansion needs the client requires.

Budget constraints – You need to establish an indication of the client's budget.

User problems –	Each individual user should be addressed with any problems they are facing locally.

The Proposal – Based on the information obtained from the initial site visit an accurate proposal based on the client's needs can be prepared and presented to the client. Costs involved in each of the stages are included in the proposal so that the client is aware of the effects this will produce on the budget.

The proposal should contain elements of the following:

List of existing installed base –	This information should have been obtained from the initial site visit.
Formal hardware and software audit –	Each computer in the network is interrogated. A complete list of the computers' hardware as well as serial numbers is recorded. This list includes, but is not restricted to printers, network devices and other peripheral devices attached to the network. Also all software is interrogated and matched to the client's licenses.
Server audit –	Apart from the usual hardware and software audits, security policies, server roles, naming conventions, and other software configurations should be recorded and analyzed. General server performance benchmarks should also be recorded
Physical topology –	Part of your proposal should include a brief description of the findings you experienced during your initial site visit and options are discussed here with respect to rectifying these problems.

Cable labelling – Correct cable labelling is a vital part to any network cable infrastructure and The Industrial method of labelling uses a "to-from" strategy on both ends of the cable, with an acceptable naming convention. This is a preferable method of labelling cables.

Network diagrams – The sketches obtained from the initial site visit, combined with actual cable tracings performed during the project implementation, and the cable labels discussed above, will serve as blueprints for formal network diagrams to be designed.

CD/DVD/Memory Stick Storage – The entire client's infrastructure including drivers, network diagrams, installation software, and user information should be stored.

Drivers – All software drivers pertaining to each computer in the client's installed base are categorized and recorded, and drivers that are not present at the client's site can be obtained from the Internet.

Installed base – Again from your audit, the entire installed base should also be recorded, as well as upgrades or alterations performed throughout the duration of the project.

Network diagrams – These, once designed and finalized, should also be placed on the **CD/DVD/ Memory Stick.**

Installation software – A record of all installation software should be kept along with the necessary license keys.

User information – Any miscellaneous information such as each user's account name, IP address (where applicable), and email address should also be stored. Programmed scripts and other developments must be added.

SERVICE LEVEL AGREEMENTS –

Often clients request service level agreements during the first visit. This is not advisable because firstly the infrastructure has not been evaluated and secondly accurate measures or future support has not been established. A period of a few months after the completion of the project should be used to monitor the levels of support before any agreements are entered into.

CHAPTER 10.
QUOTATIONS AND PROPOSALS

A major part of any sales person's job is the ability to prepare and present quotations and proposals to prospective clients. The reasons for these documents are simple: a client firstly wants to know what they are buying and they want to see if they are able to afford it.

People don't generally like hidden surprises and hence they wish to have some sort of written document to allay their fears as to what exactly they will be purchasing.

It must be noted that a quotation can hold its weight in court if the goods and/or services supplied differ wildly from the presented quotation, and thus the sales person needs to make sure that the quotation is accurately compiled.

Of course there might be mistakes and necessary alterations to the quotation from the time it was compiled to the time the client purchases, but it serves to give a good indication to the prospective client as to what their purchase will entail and how much it will cost them.

In addition these documents also assist the sales person in planning their own Sales Forecasts (see the chapter on "Sales Analysis" – Chapter 16) so that they have some sort of indication of their potential sales for the month.

In this chapter we will examine both the quotation and the proposal and look at different aspects of each, how to create one, and the general differences between the two documents.

Before we get into these sections it must be noted that above all else, a sense of professionalism must be reached because these articles become, to a certain extent, a representation of your company and thus they must have a good appearance, be clear and concise, and they must be accurate.

With this in mind let's then delve into these two types of articles.

QUOTATIONS

By definition a quotation is a document prepared and presented by a company to a prospective client detailing certain items the would-be buyer is interested in, with corresponding monetary values attached. It serves to give the buyer an indication of what they will be purchasing and what the total cost will be.

It is not an assumption that the person will be buying at all. Once a quotation is accepted then normally it is converted to a Buying Order (perhaps with an order number from the buyer) and then, once the goods and/or services are delivered to the client and an invoice is created and presented for payment. That invoice should closely match the quotation and, unless there are certain alterations done to the quotation, the values of the quotation and the invoice should match.

A sample quotation is included on page 250 and I am going to refer to this template throughout this discussion.

Even though your company will have a different design to the sample I have prepared, there are certain aspects that should be common in both documents. We are going to look at each in turn so that we can understand exactly what the purpose of each item is.

Incidentally, at this stage you are probably wondering what the difference between a quotation and a proposal is, so let me try to explain it to you here.

With respect to the Information Technology Industry, let's take a look at the nature of a purchase. It could be as simple as acquiring a computer or a piece of software or it could be as complex as an entire restructuring of a client's network. In any case you need to decide the complexity of the request.

Even though over the last ten years or so most people are becoming comfortable with the jargon we commonly use when referring to computers there are often certain terms that people are not familiar with, and if someone does not understand what they are buying they will not buy it because they do not understand its purpose. It is for this reason that we create and present proposals – they offer a more in-depth explanation of what it involved in the purchase.

Also, when there are several choices to be made, a proposal becomes a better document because the explanations of the different choices can be made clear. Typically if an entire project needs to be implemented then the proposal is the perfect tool to present so that the prospect can understand what will be involved in each step of the project.

Company Address
Line 1
Company Address
Line 2

Quotation

Client:		Date:	15/05/05
Address:		Sales Rep:	Adrian Noble
		Quote #:	101
Tel:		ROE:	
Fax:			
Email:			
Contact Person:			

Item List

Item	Description	Unit Price	Qty	Sub-Total
		Sub-Total		
		VAT 14%		
		Total		

Conditions Of Sale:

1. All items quotes are Excluding VAT.
2. This quotation is valid for 30 days from date hereof and the client warrants that they accept and understand that all quoted prices are subject to and may be varied by exchange rate and supplier price fluctuations without notice.
3. Delivery is within 72 hours from date of order and is subject to stock availablity.
5. All prices are based on COD.
6. E&OE.

To accept this quotation please sign, date, and provide an Order Number here:

Sign:	
Date:	
Order #:	

Thank you for your Business!

Kind Regards
Adrian Noble

Unofficially, there is another reason I use a proposal instead of a quotation. If a client is buying something **really** expensive, even if it is a single item, I normally present a proposal because in my opinion, it looks more professional and the prospective buyer tends to adopt the notion that they are more important because you spent a little extra time in developing the proposal for their benefit.

A quotation can be thrown together in a matter of minutes (I have done several whilst on the telephone with the client and have emailed it to them during my conversation with them) but a proposal takes a lot longer to prepare.

Some proposals I have created in a few hours; some of them have taken me at least a week. In the next section I have presented a sample proposal which I put together for school a good number of years ago. This proposal took me an entire week to design, if I remember correctly.

Right! I hope this helps you understand the differences between the two documents.

Rule of thumb: if you are quoting one or two items with very few alternatives, then you present a quote. If however there are many variables, or there are many items, or there are things in there that you know the client will not understand without some sort of explanation, then you prepare a proposal.

Ok, let's look at the different aspects of the standard quotation document.

Letterhead – This is probably a little obvious but I'll explain it anyway. In order for your client to identify the quotation with the company you work for you must have a letterhead at the top of your quotation. Make sure that you include all the contact details such as address, telephone numbers, fax numbers, email addresses, etc.

Date – Again, a bit of an obvious one here, but make sure that you have a date included.

Client Details – This is an important area to have because you need to personalize your quotation and also have a record of who the quotation was addressed to. Try to include as much detail as possible in this area because it alleviates the need to go searching for those details elsewhere when the client accepts the quotation. By having all these details your Orders Department (if you have one in your company) can quickly capture the information and convert your quotation to a Purchase Order.

Sales Rep - This is also an important field because the quotation needs to be assigned to you as the Sales Rep especially if there is more than one Sales Person in the company you work for, otherwise you will not earn your commission from the deal.

Quotation Number - Now this field is interesting. In order to assist both yourself and your Orders Department in differentiating between quotations, especially if there are more than one quote presented to the same client, the Quotation Number is important and should be unique. Also, it helps you when you prepares your Sales Reports as it gives you an indication of how many quotes you have prepared for that month, and hence indicates your activity levels.

Why I say this field is interesting is for some clients it becomes an almost benchmark for them and seems to sway a person's opinion of how much business your company is doing. Let's assume you have just started with your company and you prepare a quote for a client. Ideally you should obviously number it as "1" as it is your first quotation.

WRONG!!!

If you ever present a prospective buyer with a quote numbered as the first quote they will not buy from you because they will have a preconceived notion that they are the very first customer and thus your company does not have any prior experience in the industry. Trust me; I have experienced this in the past.

So how do we get past this? It's quite simple, really. Add a couple of numbers to the quotation number and start from there.

When I perform this exercise I always add 100 to the digits. Thus my quotes start as "101', "102", etc and the client then will be oblivious to the fact that they are the very first client.

Let's get into the body of the quotation.

The next section lists that actual items that the client will be purchasing, and I will explain each part of this section and briefly explain why we have these different parts.

Item - This numbers each item in the quote and is important for the buyer so that they can identify when an item ends and when the next one starts, especially if you have a lot of descriptions of the various items.

Description - Obviously this describes the item being quoted. You need to make sure that your descriptions are clear and concise because you only have so much space available and you need to get the point across in the least amount of text as possible.

One thing I must make a note of here. Try to avoid abbreviations if possible because although you understand what the abbreviation!! stand for the client might not and thus it may cause some confusion on the part of the buyer.

I'm going to make a small digression here. You as the sales person work for commission and generally your monthly commission is calculated from month to month. Thus when you prepare a quotation for a particular month, and you have included this in your Sales Forecast for that month, ideally you would like the buyer to accept that quotation in that same month so that the sale will be calculated for that month.

With this in mind you need to make sure that your quotations are as clear and understandable as possible so that you minimize the number of questions a client may ask of you regarding that quote.

The same is true of including the client's details at the top of the quote. The more information you have included, the quicker the Orders Department can convert the quote to an order, thereby leading to it being included in your monthly sales.

So try to make sure that your quote can be understood by the client so that they will accept it quickly.

Right! Back on to our discussion.

Unit Price - This is the cost of a single item of that description.

Quantity (Qty) - If more than one item is required this then is the quantity of that item.

Sub-Total - This total will be the multiplication of the Unit Price and the Quantity, and illustrates the total amount payable for those items.

At the bottom of your list of items are three entries will tally up the entire list to give you an overall total. I'm not going to explain each one separately because I think this in itself is self-explanatory. I do however need to explain the field called **VAT**. Some countries will call it **Sales Tax**. In South Africa we call it **Value Added Tax** and it is a value that is placed on everything we purchase by the Government. If you have added this value to your items then there should be no value in this field. If, however, you have omitted these values then the VAT needs to be added and placed in this field. In your **Conditions of Sale** (described below) you need to include whether your items are quote including or excluding VAT.

This VAT field is really important because without it your total in your quote will be incorrect and you could be legally bound to provide those goods at the price you quoted, and if you have forgotten to include the VAT you may be in serious trouble indeed!

Incidentally, South Africa works on a percentage of 14% when calculating VAT.

ROE - This stands for **Rate Of Exchange** and is an extremely important field when dealing with goods that were purchased at a different currency to what they are being sold.

In case you don't understand that, let me put it in a different way. Let's say you purchase goods from Europe in Euro currency and sell them in South Africa with a Rand currency, there will be a percentage to convert the currencies to get a relative value.

This percentage will need to be listed in the quotation at the rate that it was converted at the time of preparing the quotation.

Conditions of Sale - These should be listed at the end of each of your quotations, and should also apply to all your proposals as well.

I mentioned earlier that a quotation can become a legally binding document so these conditions need to be carefully and thoroughly thought out so that they protect you from a legal perspective. Some common entries in these fields are:

• Whether your prices include or exclude tax.
• Upon ordering what are the times of stock delivery.

- Now this one is interesting. You can place in here the time limit of your quote. Given that in the Information Technology industry prices change constantly, and the rates of fluctuations between different currencies is rapid, it is important to place a time limit on your quote so that if a prospective buyer requests another quotation and it occurs after the validity period, it allows you to adjust prices accordingly (if necessary) without being legally bound to the previous quote.
- Another nifty term, **which should appear on any quote that you ever prepare**, is a little thing called **E&OE.** This thing stands for "**Errors and Omissions Excepted**" and what it basically means that if you make any mistakes with your quote, like forget to put the tax in, or forget to multiply the quantity by the Unit Price, then you cannot be held legally responsible.

The final entries in the quote are to simply put your name and a suitable Thank You message. Some quotations like to put an Acceptance area in here whereby if a buyer accepts the quote they can simply sign the document and send it back to you for processing in your Orders Department.

So that's basically the outline of a standard quotation.

Now we get onto the meaty one – the **proposal.**

PROPOSALS

First thing's First!

A Proposal must look and be professional!!!

This is a must because this document is worth a lot of money if it is accepted, and as I said earlier, it reflects directly on your company, so you need to spend some time with it to ensure that the document is written well, is clear, is understandable, and is properly structured. If this is done correctly that you are over halfway there in ensuring you will get the business.

Every scenario is different and thus there is not hard and fast rule as to what to put into a proposal, but I am going to refer to the sample proposal below to illustrate what should be included in each and every case.

One thing to note here: if your Business English is not that great then please enlist the assistance of somebody who can edit and proofread your document before you send it out. There is nothing worse than presenting a document if this nature that is misspelt, has numerous punctuation errors, and bad language usage.

Ok, let's get in there!

Cover page -   Each proposal should have some sort of cover page with your company's logo on it, the nature of the proposal, who it is addressed to, and if you like, who it is from (personally, not as a company). A piece of advice here: if you can try to surf the Internet to obtain a company logo of the company you are proposing. It doesn't take too long and adds just a little more decorum to your proposal.

Letterhead -   Each page of your proposal should contain your company's letterhead because this identifies where the proposal came from, and forms a type of uniformity to the proposal. I normally put this in as a header. For the purpose of this book I have not done this but you should in your proposals.

Footer -   You can place your company's list of Directors and Company Registration

Number in as a footer on each page. Again, this identifies the proposal as coming from your company. For the purposes of this book I have not put in the company's footer.

Page numbers - This seems obvious but so many people forget to include page numbers in their proposal.

Salutation - A salutation with the recipients' details should appear together with an introduction as to the nature of the proposal. It serves to personalize the proposal, and also places the reader's frame of mind into the correct context to concentrate on the rest of the document.

Contents - Each section of the proposal should be dealt with in a separate section, and each section should start on a new page. As a rule of thumb ensure that each different aspect of the project is dealt with in a separate section. So as to give the reader an indication of what is entailed at a glance provide a Table of Contents at the beginning.

Site inspection - If you (or your Engineers) have managed to perform an initial site inspection include this in your proposal. It lets the client know what they current have in their infrastructure and as you go through your proposal making changes to their infrastructure the client can refer back to this section so they have a point of reference.

Proposal details - Right! Now you can get into the proposal proper, discussing each change and upgrade. Prices should be included in each section (either including or excluding tax according to your Conditions of Sale). Try to refer back to your original site inspection so that the client knows physically where each change will be made.

Labour Charges – I try to put these in a separate section because they deal purely with services and not products and can change depending on the amount of time that will be spent in performing each section. These values generally tend to be estimates.

Summary of costs – This is an important part of the proposal because it consolidates all the costs discussed throughout the proposal and assists the prospect in seeing the bottom line financially. Of course this section is the one the Financial Director will be most interested in. You must just make sure that you adequately label this section so that it properly correlates with each section in the article.

Conditions of sale – As per your quotations you must include your Conditions of Sale.

Your name – So that your prospect knows from whom the proposal came from you must include your name at the bottom and sign the document as well.

Once you have prepared your proposal make sure that it is professionally bound. You can pick up suitable Presentation

Folders from any stationery store, and it just gives it that finishing touch.

Wherever possible hand deliver the document to your client. When you have your follow-up meeting to discuss the proposal make sure you take your own copy along with you so that you can make notes as you and your prospect discuss the project plan.

Company Address Line 1
Company Address Line 2
Company Telephone Numbers
Company Website Address

Proposal To School

School
Address 1
Address 2
Address 3
DATE: 29 July 2015
Dear Mr. X
RE: Proposal on Network Rectification

Thank you for allowing [your company] the opportunity of providing you a proposal for your solution. We trust that this proposal meets your needs.

This proposal is divided into two parts. Due to the nature of your environment, a five - phase project has had to be devised. This proposal discusses the first two phases of that project. The following three subsequent phases will be proposed and discussed in due course.

PART 1. CURRENT CONFIGURATION

In a preliminary examination the following configurations have been discovered within your school. This section serves to list and determine those findings and thus forms the base of the remainder of this proposal. Wherever applicable, observations have been formalized into tabular form for easy reference.

This section is divided into four parts.

Sub-section 1a lists the current computer configurations within the school.

Sub-section 1b mentions the current network connectivity devices in existence and the inherent connectivity therein.

Sub-section 1c discusses additional roles and functions of various computers within the schools.

Sub-section 1d deals with additional material that might be of some importance in the future.

Sub-Section 1a. Current Computer Configuration

From a previous evaluation of the school's network, the following computer configurations have been determined. These configurations have been presented in tabular form. The ensuing discussions and recommendations will refer wherever possible to these results.

CLASSROOM						
PC	**CPU**	**RAM**	**HDD**	**Extras**	**Printers**	**OS**
Student 1	Intel i3-2100	2GB	320GB			Win 7 Pro
Student 2	Intel i3-2100	2GB	320GB			Win 7 Pro
Student 3	Intel i3-2100	2GB	320GB			Win 7 Pro
Student 4	Intel i3-2100	2GB	320GB		Canon MP280	Win 7 Pro
Student 5	Intel i3-2100	2GB	320GB			Win 7 Pro
Student 6	Intel i5-2500	4GB	500GB			Win 7 Pro
Student 7	Intel i3-2100	2GB	320GB			Win 7 Pro
Student 8	Intel i3-2100	2GB	320GB			Win 7 Pro
Student 9	Intel i3-2100	2GB	320GB		Canon MP280	Win 7 Pro
Student 10	Intel i3-2100	2GB	320GB			Win 7 Pro
Student 11	Intel i3-2100	2GB	320GB			Win 7 Pro
Student 12	Intel i3-2100	2GB	320GB			Win 7 Pro
Student 13	Intel i5-2500	4GB	500GB		Canon MP280	Win 7 Pro
Student 14	Intel i5-2500	4GB	500GB			Win 7 Pro

LIBRARY						
PC	**CPU**	**RAM**	**HDD**	**Extras**	**Printers**	**OS**
Research 1	Intel i3-2100	2GB	320GB			Win 7 Pro
Research 2	Intel i3-2100	2GB	320GB			Win 7 Pro
Librarian	G630	1GB	80GB	LibWin	Canon MP280	Win XP Pro + SP1
Storeroom	G630	1GB	80GB		Canon MP280	Win XP Pro + SP1

ADMINISTRATION BLOCK						
PC	**CPU**	**RAM**	**HDD**	**Extras**	**Printers**	**OS**
Headmaster	Intel i5-2500	4GB	500GB			Win 7 Pro
Deputy Head	Intel i5-2500	4GB	500GB		Epson Workforce 635	Win 7 Pro
Receptionist	Intel i3-2100	1GB	320GB		Brother HL-2270DW	Win XP Pro + SP1
Accountant	G630	1GB	80GB	Int. ISDN	Canon MP280	Win XP Pro + SP1
Office Staff	Intel i3-2100	1GB	320GB			Win XP Pro + SP1
Receipts	G630	1GB	80GB		Epson LQ310	Win XP Pro + SP1

OTHER COMPUTERS						
PC	**CPU**	**RAM**	**HDD**	**Extras**	**Printers**	**OS**
Sports Admin	G630	1GB	80GB			Win XP Pro + SP1
Nurse's Station	N/A	N/A	N/A		Brother HL-2270DW	N/A

Sub-Section 1b. Current Network Connectivity Devices

The following Network Connectivity Devices were observed within the School:

Classroom – 16-port 10/100 Ethernet Switch – free standing. ADSL Router.

Admin - 8-port 10 Base-T hub – free standing. ADSL Router.

As stated in the above Computer configuration, an additional ISDN Controller device was discovered in the Admin Office. This suggests that three lines are currently being rented from Telkom. This issue will be discussed in detail in Part two of the proposal.

Sub-Section 1c. Additional Roles.

Certain computers within the network are serving additional roles. These roles need to be noted as follows:

Classroom – Three workstations have printers attached to them and these are shared for all workstations in the classroom.

Library – Workstation **Librarian** currently has the **LibWin** package installed. This apparently houses the entire library's database.

Administration – There are a few such instances here. Firstly, Workstations **Accounts** and **Receipts** deals with the accounting package, **Edupac**. Furthermore, Workstation **Accounts** uses an internal ISDN Modem to interact with the Internet Banking facility for the school.

Sub-Section 1d. Additional Material in Existence.

Storeroom - There are several computer monitors, keyboards and mice in existence. These will need to be analyzed in the future for viable spare parts.

Headmaster - Currently in his office is an unused Acer USB A4 scanner, which will probably be attached to the network and used in the future.

PART 2. PROJECT ANALYSIS

In this section the proposal is divided into different project projections. These projections are important to ascertain the current situation with respect to the school's current configuration and situation, as well as to ascertain the eventual growth within the organization. Given the multitude of options available to the school, this section requires careful consideration.

This project is divided into five phases. In this particular proposal Phases one and two are discussed in detail. Phases three to five will be discussed in later proposals.

Phase 1 suggests the installation of a server within the classroom, and standardizing the classroom.

Phase 2 covers the connection of the Library computers into the classroom's network.

Phase 3 recommends the standardization of the Administrative section of the school.

Phase 4 then discusses the options of either using a single server or multiple servers to accommodate the entire network.

Phase 5 deals with the final consolidation of the solution, and also mentions a possible Service Level Agreement.

PHASE 1. SERVER-CLIENT SITUATION IN THE CLASSROOM

According to reports ascertained from various Personnel, there are substantial anomalies within the Computer classroom with respect to computer abuse. This section, first and foremost, addresses these issues and places certain control measures in place that restrict and control such variances so as to increase User performance whilst decreasing Support presence in this area.

In our experiences with this situation we find that the Teaching Personnel find it difficult to maintain both the computers and the lessons at hand, and this often is detrimental to the students. We therefore propose certain controls and regulations that are intrinsic on our part to ensure that affected personnel are free from such burdens.

In this phase there are six sections.

Section P1a discusses the installation of a dedicated server within the classroom.

Section P1b covers the reinstallation of the workstations and the implementation of the students' User Profiles.

Section P1c discusses the repair of the cabling within the classroom.

Section P1d deals with the implementation of printers into the network.

Section P1e lists the quotation for the two requested laptop computers.

Section P1f lists a summary of costs for Phase one.

SECTION P1a. SERVER INCLUSION

In analysis of your current situation it is apparent that the students within the school are wilfully abusing the property offered to them. In our experiences this is common, and thus a suggested migration to a more secure solution will not only benefit the student by preventing a potential stray of focus during lessons, it will also allow the involved Teacher to concentrate more on the lessons at hand than to be concerned about errant behaviour in the classroom.

Adjacent to the classroom is a storeroom which would serve as an ideal area to house a dedicated server which will then control the workstations within the classroom.

One of the workstations can be converted into a server which will then monitor the entire network, but this then would mean that the converted workstation would need to be replaced. The solution in this regard would be to quote on a separate server, asfollows:

School Server
OEM Tower Chassis with 600W PSU
Integrated Motherboard
Intel Core i7 -2600 Processor
16GB RAM
1 TB Hard Drive
Super Multi DVD Writer
Keyboard
Mouse
24" LCD Monitor
650VA Line-Interactive UPS

Total for above system   R 7 900.00

In lieu of the fact that the school is currently involved with the Microsoft ® Schools Agreement, a Server Operating System need not be supplied with the server.

265

In the above server a 650VA UPS has been quoted together with a CD Writer. The writer serves to act as a data backup mechanism for the classroom. The UPS serves to protect the server against power surges or blackouts.

The Internet is rife with external threats and the school will require an Anti-Malware solution for the entire infrastructure as well as a means of preventing students from introducing various forms of malware from devices brought into the school such as Memory Sticks, CD's and DVD's, and Mobile Devices.

Kaspersky Endpoint Security for Business, SELECT, Public Sector has been chosen for a complete Endpoint Protection Solution and is provided with a 1 year subscription and a Media Kit.

According to our analysis (listed in Section 1 above) there is currently a total of twenty six computers within the school. An additional two laptops are being quoted (Section P1d below) and Deputy Head has an additional laptop. This gives a total of twenty nine computers. We therefore are quoting you with thirty licenses.

KES, SELECT, Public Sector, per license	R 194.00

• 1 Year Subscription

A total of 30 licenses are required:

30 x User licenses	R 5 820.00

Additional licenses can be purchased as the need arises during the active subscription.

Server configuration – In configuring the new server, the following tasks will need to be performed:

a) The ADSL Router will be configured and administered on the Server.
b) The server's Operating System will be installed. Windows 2008 Server will be installed onto the new computer.
c) Windows 2008 Server's Intrinsic Internet Content Filter will be enabled and configured.

d) Each student will have a User Account setup on the server. Generally speaking, in an Educational situation the User Accounts normally work by Grade, Class, and then Surname. Thus if a pupil, Jane Smith, was in Grade 1, Class A, then her User Name will be something like: "1ASmith".

e) In addition to the User Accounts, Home Directories will be assigned to each user, and will only be able to be accessed by that particular student and the Teacher. As soon as the student logs onto the network for the first time, this home directory will become activated, and will be the default directory for all work saved.

f) Using Windows 2008 Server's intrinsic Backup facility, a solution will be implemented and stored onto the hard drive. It then can be written to CD via the writer.

g) Policies and Profiles will be generated for each Grade, according to the programs they are allowed to use. Logon Scripts will also be generated; this will ensure that all necessary mapped drives and/or printers will become available.

Installation and configuration of the server is as follows:

1 x Point installation	R 500.00
16x25 EGA Trunking per 3 meter length	R 18.00
25x40 EGA Trunking per 3 meter length	R 30.00
Sundries	R 100.00
Labels	R 15.00
Server Labour	R 1 950.00

Please note that the point installations include cable, connectors, labour, and CAT5 boxes. Trunking, labels and sundries are quoted separately. The Trunking has been quoted per length due to the fact that the total amount of Trunking required has not been determined at this stage. Costs involved will be adjusted accordingly.

SECTION P1b. WORKSTATION REINSTALLATION

In order to ensure that no anomalies exist on the network each of the fourteen workstations will need to be completely reinstalled and reconfigured. Once this has been performed each student will be issued a User Account, and will be required to log onto the network. Individual passwords will be established at this stage, and general user security will be discussed.

During reinstallation all serial numbers will be recorded for each workstation. This documentation will be finalized in Phase five of the project.

All External drives will be disabled on the workstations. This will be performed within the ***Kaspersky Security Center*** ® using the ***Endpoint Controls*** and thus informed Teachers will be able to re-enable the drives if the need arises.

Once the policies have been successfully implemented the students will only be allowed to use certain applications as deemed fit by the School's curriculum and these will also be configured with the ***Endpoint Controls.***

Each workstation will require two hours labour to reinstall and configure, including the installation of certain Microsoft ® patches. These patches offer updated security measures, and are a vital component in ensuring that the workstations are protected against viruses and other Internet security breaches. An additional two hours labour will be required to monitor the successful establishment of the students' User Accounts.

Labour charges for this process follow:

30 x workstation labour @ R350.00 per hour   R   10 500.00

SECTION P1c. RECABLING THE NETWORK WITHIN THE CLASSROOM

Upon examination it was established that the entire network in the classroom will need to be labelled. This involves the tracing of the cables from the workstations to the switch.

In Phase two the computers in the Library will be connected to the network. Currently there is a 16-port switch in operation in the classroom, with two ports free. After the installation of the server one port will be available. If the computers in the Library are to be connected to the network, this switch will need to be replaced by a 24-port switch. This 16-port switch will then be moved to the Administration Block and utilized there. This will be further discussed in Phase three of the project.

A Hub Cabinet will need to be installed in the classroom. This cabinet will house all Network Connectivity Devices within the classroom and serves to both protect the devices from unauthorized tampering, and offers proper ventilation. Due to future expansion of the classroom, a 12U Wall Cabinet has been quoted. This will allow for more switches to be installed at a later stage. The following will then be required:

12U Wall Box	R	940.00
1 x Front Mount Tray	R	90.00
1 x Brush Panel	R	70.00
24-port 10/100 N-Way Switch	R	1 410.00
24-port Populated Patch Panel	R	660.00
2 x Wired Fans with finger guards	R	330.00
24 x Patch leads @ R10.00 each	R	240.00
Labels	R	300.00
1 x 40x100 Trunking per 3 meter length	R	115.00
2 x 25x40 Trunking per 3 meter length	R	72.00
Sundries	R	300.00
Installation labour	R	600.00

If you decide at this stage to include a further 16-port Switch (for future expansion purposes) then the following will also be required:

1 x Brush Panel	R	70.00
16-port 10/100 N-Way Switch	R	960.00

16-port Populated Patch Panel	R	640.00
16 x Patch leads @ R10.00 each	R	160.00
Labels	R	200.00

Please note that the above quotations assume that the installed cables are indeed long enough to be mounted into the cabinet. If not then an entire cable reinstallation will be necessary.

SECTION P1d. PRINTER IMPLEMENTATION

During our discussion it was ascertained that the costs involved for replacement cartridges for the current Inkjet printers were extreme. We thus recommend that a Colour Laser Printer be included into the network

The new laser printer will be network-ready and its Administration Console will be configured and administered on the server.

In doing so, this will allow the current three Inkjet printers to become available for use in other areas of the school.

The following Laser printer is ideal for the classroom. Installation and configuration for the printer is also quoted below:

Samsung CLX-3185FW Multifunction Laser Printer	R	6 000.00

- 1'200dpi
- Up to 17 pages per minute Mono; 4 pages per minute Colour
- Built-In A4 Scanner and Fax

The Print Server will require the installation of a network point and this is quoted below:

1 x Point installations	R	500.00
16x25 EGA Trunking per 3 meter length	R	18.00
25x40 EGA Trunking per 3 meter length	R	30.00
Sundries	R	100.00
Labels	R	15.00
Installation and Configuration of the Print Server	R	250.00

SECTION P1e. SUPPLY OF LAPTOPS

During our meeting a request was for two laptops. These are quoted below:

HP 250 G3 Notebook

Intel i3-4005U Processor
4GB RAM
500GB HDD
Super Multi DVD Writer
Integrated WLAN & Webcam
Integrated Bluetooth
15.6" HD Display
Microsoft Windows 8.1 ® 64-Bit
1 Year International Warranty
Carry Case

Total for above system	R	7 000.00
So for 2 such systems:	R	14 000.00

In connecting the laptops to the existing network, two additional network points will need to be installed in the Administration Block. Due to the fact that Phase three of the project involves the standardization of the Administrative Block, the following point installations will be temporary, and will be installed in such a manner as to be easily incorporated into Phase three. Prices for these temporary points follow:

2 x Point installations @ R500.00 each	R 1 000.00
Sundries	R 50.00
Configuration labour @ R350.00 per laptop	R 700.00

Adrian Noble

SECTION P1f. SUMMARY OF COSTS FOR PHASE 1

SECTION P1a. SERVER INCLUSION

Description	Unit Price	Qty	Sub-Total
School Server	R 7,900.00	1	R 7,900.00
KES Select, Public Sector	R 194.00	30	R 5,820.00
Point installation	R 500.00	1	R 500.00
16x25 EGA Trunking per 3 meter length	R 18.00	1	R 18.00
25x40 EGA Trunking per 3 meter length	R 30.00	1	R 30.00
Sundries	R 100.00	1	R 100.00
Labels	R 15.00	1	R 15.00
Server Labour	R 650.00	3	R 1,950.00

SECTION P1b. WORKSTATION REINSTALLATION

Description	Unit Price	Qty	Sub-Total
Workstation Labour	R 350.00	30	R 10,500.00
12U Wall Box	R 940.00	1	R 940.00
Front Mount Tray	R 90.00	1	R 90.00
Brush Panel	R 70.00	1	R 70.00
24-port 10/100 N-Way Switch	R 1,410.00	1	R 1,410.00
24-port Populated Patch Panel	R 660.00	1	R 660.00
Wired Fans with finger guards	R 165.00	2	R 330.00
Patch leads	R 10.00	24	R 240.00
40x100 Trunking per 3 meter length	R 115.00	1	R 115.00
25x40 Trunking per 3 meter length	R 36.00	2	R 72.00
Sundries	R 300.00	1	R 300.00
Installation labour	R 500.00	1	R 500.00

FURTHER EXPANSION

Description	Unit Price	Qty	Sub-Total
Brush Panel	R 70.00	1	R 70.00
16-port 10/100 N-Way Switch	R 960.00	1	R 960.00
16-port Populated Patch Panel	R 640.00	1	R 640.00
Patch Lead	R 10.00	16	R 160.00
Labels	R 200.00	1	R 200.00

SECTION P1d. PRINTER IMPLEMENTATION

Description	Unit Price	Qty	Sub-Total
Samsung CLX-3185FW Multifunction Laser Printer	R 6,000.00	1	R 6,000.00
Point installation	R 500.00	1	R 500.00
16x25 EGA Trunking per 3 meter length	R 18.00	1	R 18.00
25x40 EGA Trunking per 3 meter length	R 30.00	1	R 30.00
Sundries	R 100.00	1	R 100.00
Labels	R 15.00	1	R 15.00
Installation and Configuration	R 250.00	1	R 250.00

SECTION P1e. SUPPLY OF LAPTOPS

Description	Unit Price	Qty	Sub-Total
HP 250 G3 Notebook	R 7,000.00	2	R 14,000.00
Point Installation	R 500.00	2	R 1,000.00
Sundries	R 50.00	1	R 50.00
Configuration Labour	R 350.00	2	R 700.00

PHASE 2. INCLUSION OF LIBRARY COMPUTERS INTO THE NETWORK

Once the establishment of the classroom has been finalized the rest of the network can be added. The first addition will be the computers within the Library. This phase then discusses the inclusion of these workstations into the network.

Promoting the use of the Library Computers for research is both rewarding and important for the student. The knowledge that help and resources can be gained for assistance in projects and general educational experience outside of the classroom should be rigorously encouraged. This addition to the network becomes an important step to opening facilities that might prove vital to a student's development in the future.

The User Accounts that were established in Phase one of the project are still used here, with the customary User Profiles and Policies. A further Monitoring Policy will need to be implemented at this stage to ensure that students are in actual fact searching for educational information on the Internet, and not utilizing the facilities for their own gain.

Phase two is divided into three sections.

Section P2a discusses the cabling required for the Library computers.

Section P2b deals with the software configurations of the Library computers.

Section P2c lists a summary of costs for Phase two.

SECTION P2a. LIBRARY CABLING

There are three computers in the Library that will need to be cabled to the switch installed in the classroom. These three points are quoted below:

3 x Point installations @ R500.00 per point	R	1 500.00
16x25 EGA Trunking per 3 meter length	R	18.00
25x40 EGA Trunking per 3 meter length	R	30.00
Sundries	R	100.00
Labels	R	50.00

Please note that the point installations include cable, connectors, labour, and CAT5 boxes. Trunking, labels and sundries are quoted separately. The Trunking has been quoted per length due to the fact that the total amount of Trunking required has not been determined at this stage. Costs involved will be adjusted accordingly.

SECTION P2b. SOFTWARE CONFIGURATION

The data currently on the Library computers will be ported over onto the server, and included in the backup solution. Access to the Internet via the ADSL controller will be established and monitored.

Configuration for the three workstations is estimated at one hour per workstation. This is quoted below:

3 x Configuration labour @ R350 per hour	R	1 050.00

A further two hours will be required to configure the server in order to accommodate the security and general access via the workstations. Included in this configuration are certain monitoring facilities that will supervise the content of exposed material to the student. The Intrinsic Content Filter within Windows 2008 Server will be further configured to accommodate the new additions.

Server Configuration Labour	R	650.00

SECTION P2c. SUMMARY OF COSTS FOR PHASE 2

SECTION P2a. LIBRARY CABLING			
Description	**Unit Price**	**Qty**	**Sub-Total**
Point installations	R 500.00	3	R 1,500.00
16x25 EGA Trunking per 3 meter length	R 18.00	1	R 18.00
25x40 EGA Trunking per 3 meter length	R 30.00	1	R 30.00
Sundries	R 100.00	1	R 100.00
Labels	R 50.00	1	R 50.00
SECTION P2b. SOFTWARE CONFIGURATION			
Description	**Unit Price**	**Qty**	**Sub-Total**
Configuration labour	R 350.00	3	R 1,050.00
Server Configuration Labour	R 650.00	1	R 650.00

CONCLUSION TO PART 1 OF THE PROJECT

In the next three phases (included in Part two of the proposal), the Administrative Block will be standardized, either connected to the other network, or remain as a separate network, and the whole solution will be consolidated as a whole.

In Lieu of the fact that the requirements of both Phases one and two needs to be completed before the rest of the project proceeds, this section discusses the remainder of the project for the school and will be detailed in a later proposal, namely Part two.

Phase 3 consists of the standardization of the Administrative Block within the school. It details the configuration of the involved workstations, as well as connecting the Sports Admin Workstation and the Nurse's Station workstation to the Administrative Network. The completion of this phase will ensure that the Administrative network is either receptive to the connection of both networks or the continuing segregation of the two networks. This in itself will thus induce the introduction of a secondary Server within the school.

Phase 4 will introduce the possibility of combining the two networks together, thus providing a holistic solution that

275

will be easily manageable. An alternative will be to implement a Server within the Administrative block as a separate entity. A further alternative is to implement a secondary Server within the Administrative Block, with a direct link to the Primary server housed within the Classroom. All three options will be thus addressed, and their respective merits and demerits exposed.

Regardless of the choice offered within this Phase, full Email facilities will be introduced and implemented during this phase, as well as the possibility of future maintenance of a Website. An Intranet is also possible at this stage.

Phase 5 consolidates the entire network into a whole. In this phase all documentation is consolidated and presented to the school for future reference (including formal Network Diagrams of the entire network). Also present in this phase is the eventual remote access by all permanent Personnel within the school. The impending Microsoft ® Software Audit is also addressed during this phase. Certain standards will also be introduced to ensure that the School will be able to operate smoothly in the distant future, without extreme intervention on [your company's] part. Certain Operational and Procedural manuals will provide alternative support in this regard.

CONDITIONS OF SALE

1. All prices exclude VAT unless otherwise specified.
2. All quoted prices are valid for 10 days, and are subject to change without prior notice, based on suppliers' discretion.
3. Delivery is within 2 weeks unless otherwise specified.
4. Labour charges are billed from the time of departure from the company's offices.
5. Labour charges outside of normal working hours are billed at 1 ½ times normal rate. Sundays and Public/ Religious holidays are billed at 2 times normal rate.

6. Delivery charges are billed at R150.00 ex VAT, unless otherwise specified.
7. All goods remain the property of [your company] until paid for in full.
8. A 10% handling fee will be billed for returned goods and will be credited against your account.
9. All prices quoted are based on COD.
10. The following payments are accepted: Cash, Direct Deposits, and Bank Guaranteed cheques.
11. Although every effort will be made by [Your Company] to protect our clients' data, we cannot guarantee that said information will be safeguarded from damage or loss.
12. All hardware warranties are honoured by suppliers, wherever applicable.
13. E&OE

If you have any queries regarding this proposal please do not hesitate to contact me.

Kind regards

Adrian Noble
Business Development Manager

CONCLUSION

Good quotations and proposals are essential because they become a virtual extension of your company. Think about it: you have spent a lot of time and a lot of hard work in setting up the meeting. You have impressed your prospective client with your knowledge and grace. You have made an impact on them with your experience in performing an initial site evaluation. So why mess it all up and not deliver a first class proposal to them?

Rather spend the time and develop your quotations and proposals properly. This will seriously add to the professionalism and will go a long way in securing the deal.

SUMMARY – CHAPTER 10.

QUOTATIONS

By definition a quotation is a document prepared and presented by a company to a prospective client detailing certain items the would-be buyer is interested in, with corresponding monetary values attached. It serves to give the buyer an indication of what they will be purchasing and what the total cost will be.

These are some of the fields explained a little better.

Letterhead - In order for your client to identify the quotation with the company you work for you must have a letterhead at the top of your quotation.

Date - The date of the quotation.

Client Details - These are the details of the recipient of the quote.

Sales Rep - You as the Sales Representative need to appear on the quotation so that you earn commission on the deal from the company you work for.

Quotation Number - The Quotation Number is important and should be unique because it allows the Orders Department to identify the quote from others they are dealing with at the time and it also serves to assist you when you are drafting your Sales Analysis reports.

Item -   This numbers each item in the quote and is important for the buyer so that they can identify when an item ends and when the next one starts.

Description –   This describes the item being quoted. Try to avoid using abbreviations.

Unit Price –   This is the cost of a single item of that description.

Quantity –   If more than one item is required this then is the quantity of that item.

Sub-Total –   This total will be the multiplication of the Unit Price and the Quantity, and illustrates the total amount payable for those items.

ROE –   This stands for **Rate Of Exchange** and is an extremely important field when dealing with goods that were purchased at a different currency to what they are being sold.

Conditions of Sale - These should be listed at the end of each of your quotations, and should also apply to all your proposals as well.

PROPOSALS

A proposal is a quotation that is in a more expanded form and contains many expanded descriptions of the different options that are available.

Again there are some explanations of the fields that should be included.

Cover page – Each proposal should have some sort of cover page with your company's logo on it, the nature of the proposal, who it is addressed to, and who it is from.

Letterhead – Each page of your proposal should contain your company's letterhead because this identifies where the proposal came from, and forms a type of uniformity to the proposal.

Footer – You can place your company's list of Directors and Company Registration Number in as a footer on each page.

Page numbers – Place page numbers in the proposal.

Salutation – A salutation with the recipients' details should appear together with an introduction as to the nature of the proposal.

Contents – Each section of the proposal should be dealt with in a separate section, and each section should start on a new page.

Site inspection – If you (or your Engineers) have managed to perform an initial site inspection include this in your proposal.

Proposal details – Discuss each change and upgrade. Prices should be included in each section, and try to refer back to your original site inspection so that the client knows physically where each change will be made.

Labour Charges – Try to put these in a separate section because they deal purely with services and not products and can change depending on the amount of time that will be spent in performing each section. These values generally tend to be estimates.

Summary of costs – This is an important part of the proposal because it consolidates all the costs discussed throughout the proposal and assists the prospect in seeing the bottom line financially.

Conditions of sale – As per your quotations you must include your Conditions of Sale.

Your name – So that your prospect knows from whom the proposal came from you must include your name at the bottom and sign the document as well.

CHAPTER 11.
SERVICE LEVEL AGREEMENTS

Ok, so what is this thing? I have mentioned elsewhere in this book that computers are tools that assist in running most businesses and if they fail for any reason it is detrimental to the lifeblood of the company concerned. For this reason many clients do become suspicious of allowing IT companies access to their systems. The client becomes extremely worried that work will be done on the systems, and then the network might not work after the technician has left. In addition, there are many "fly-by-nights", or people who do some freelance work until they find permanent employment, and then the former client is left on their own as the technician who was looking after their computers is no longer available and means that more money and time will need to be spent in enlisting the services of yet another IT company.

You must remember that initially large sums of money could be spent in fixing a badly "damaged" computer network, and those technician that initially start a project become familiar with the site and what is involved. To now change to another IT company means that the first step is an initial site visit, wasting more time and yet more money.

So clients start looking towards legal contracts that protect their investments with respect to the time and money they have spent with a particular IT company. They also (as do most clients) want immediate service if and when they ask for it, and a contract gives the customer piece of mind in knowing that the IT company is legally bound to honour the wishes of that client.

A **Service Level Agreement (SLA)** is such a contract that a customer and an IT company enter into offering various support services. The SLA is extremely flexible as the requirements of each site will invariably differ, but once the contract is signed then both the client and the IT Company is assured of a mutual long-lasting business relationship.

From the IT Company's point of view, it is also an assurance of a constant monthly revenue being generated, which assist in the company's monthly business budget.

Due to the fact that different countries enforce diverse laws I did not think it was a good idea to include a sample of a SLA in this book. What I will do however is cover some various areas of a typical SLA in this chapter so as to give you an idea on their typical content.

WHEN TO ENTER INTO A SERVICE LEVEL AGREEMENT

It was mentioned in Chapter 10 that a Service Level Agreement should only be entered into once a site has been properly repaired and this is correct. Some IT Companies prefer to sign the contract before any work is committed to the site, but in my opinion and personal experiences I feel that this will hamper a long term contract. What do I mean by this?

Many sites have problems with their networks ranging from improperly laid cables to inadequate network security, and a good number of hours will be spent up front in dealing with and rectifying these different anomalies. If a **Set Base Rate Contract** (discussed further below) is entered into based upon the number of hours the Technical Department spends initially, the results will definitely be skewed and the client will end up with a contractual fee that will far surpass their future needs and budget. This will probably lead to frustration and a modification of the contract, which could lead to the development of a slight distrust on the part of the client towards the IT Company because they will feel that the IT Company is not concerned about their needs, but instead is more concerned about how much money they can extract from the client.

Unfortunately we all need money, and the temptation to follow this sort of practice is enticing, but it could damage the Support Company's reputation, not only with the current client, but with others and the word will spread throughout the business community.

What I recommend rather, and I have tested this theory out and many sites in the past, with a good measure of success, is to first repair and standardize the site, on an hourly basis (or a negotiated fixed labour rate) and then monitor the site for one or two months thereafter to see how much support they require on average. Based upon these figures I then start considering the SLA and then approach the client with the offer.

The advantages of this train of thought is that, firstly, the IT Company will gain its initial surge of revenue from the preliminary project, and then can enjoy a constant revenue thereafter over a long period of time.

There have been instances whereby **An Intent to Enter into a Service Level Agreement** has been entered into in the past with various clients which basically means that if the client is satisfied with the work performed during the preliminary project phase they will then agree to enter into the more formal SLA. This initial contract then protects the IT Company in that they will be assured that the client will not consider using another Support Company instead once their site has been successfully repaired.

TYPES OF RATES

Negotiations on different rates structures differ wildly because if the individuality of each site and it is because of this that I cannot give you some black-and-white guidelines as to what to negotiate as a standard. What I can however suggest are three very popular schemes that I have used in the past, each with its own merits and demerits.

Pay As You Go -   In this scheme the client pays up front for a certain number of hours each month as a credit, and then when the technician is on site these hours are deducted until the credit has expired. Then additional labour fees are charged as per normal. It is a good practice to offer a discounted labour fee for contracted clients. To make this a little cleared for you, I'll give you an example here.

An IT company normally charges R600.00 to R700.00 per hour for labour on site. After investigations a client requires an average of five hours of onsite support per month. So the client pays an initial charge of R3'500.00 at the start of each month to the IT Company. Once the credit has been depleted, then normal discounted labour charges are billed until the end of the month when the cycle starts again. You could offer a 10% discount on those additional labour charges, effectively meaning that the "normal" labour charge will be R540.00 – R630.00 per hour.

Various customers will argue with you on this next point.

Their question to you will be something like, "What happens if the five hours are not used up in that month? Will they be carried over to the next month?"

This you have to be careful of, because you want to make sure that you are receiving money from the client on a regular basis. What you could agree on, for example, is to state that any hours left over will be carried to the next month, and the next month only, in addition to their standard five hours. Confused? Ok, example!

Month 1 – five hours are paid for up front. Only three are used, giving the client a balance of two unused hours.

Month 2 – five hours are billed as per normal for credit. The two unused hours from the previous month are carried over thereby giving a total credit of seven available labour hours. The client only uses four hours of labour for that month. These would be deducted as follows: the two carried over hours are used and then two hours from the new credit are used, giving a remainder of three available hours.

Month 3 – The five hours are billed for credit. The three hours are carried over from the previous month, giving a total of eight hours credit. The client does not need support at all for that month, so at the end of the month there is still a balance of eight hours.

Month 4 –The client has paid for their five hours up front. There is a credit of five hours from the previous month, but the three hours that are credited from Month two now expire, and are no longer available for use. The total number of credited hours for this month therefore will be ten.

I hope you were able to understand this concept. It ensures that a client cannot accumulate hours of labour, and will thus use those hours each month for maintenance. From the other side of the coin, it also makes sure that the site is constantly monitored so that if a problem arises it can be dealt with quickly and not left to escalate into a possible disaster.

Retainer Credit - This is fairly similar to the above scheme except that instead of calculating numbers of hours up front, a basic credit fee is paid, and the labour is deducted from this, regardless of the charges.

Take a look again at Chapter 1. There are different Technical Support Levels, which means that Specialists are more expensive than Desktop Technicians. So a client will pay a set credit of say, R8'000.00, and then the fees will be deducted off of this credit regardless of the level of service required. If a Specialist is required, more money will be debited off of the client's account then if a

Desktop Technician is required. Once the credit is finished the client must recharge their account.

You can also place expiry dates onto this type of scheme (as is the case of the above method) thereby ensuring a monthly revenue of R8'000.00 being earned, but this you will need to negotiate with your client on a case by case Scenario.

Set Base Rate – These I normally find useful for corporate clients and schools. It basically is a set rate the client pays the IT Support Company each and every month for the duration of the contract. In return they can request support services of any kind and whenever they like. Due to this the monthly fee with be much higher because you need to take into account the type of technician they will require (it might even be more than one needed) and what time of day they will be needed. If it is over the weekend, for example, you as the IT Company is expected to pay your technician's overtime as per their standard contracts. In order to do this you must make sure that the monthly fee paid by the client is sufficient to cover these needs.

You can see that, if not calculated carefully, it could quite quickly end up that the IT Company will run at a financial loss.

Before partaking in such an endeavour, you must monitor that site beforehand o that you have a clear indication of how much monthly support they will need. In addition, you need to state a clause in the contract to say that if a major project ensues during the contract period, then additional charges will be necessary as your Technical Personnel will be involved almost exclusively for the duration of the project. An example of this could be labour charges will be billed but at a much reduced percentage (say 30%

or even 50%). That way you will be able to cover the costs of paying your staff.

SERVICES OFFERED

There are a myriad of services that can be offered, and each depends on the individual situation. I cannot give you every example of a possible service offering because there are so many, but I have singled out a few more common ones and discussed these below. They should give you insights of how you can tailor make service offerings to your unique clients.

Remote Support - This is an extremely useful service to offer because it means that you can repair **some** problems from your offices without having to travel to the client's site. Note that I have highlighted **some** because not every problem can be solved in this manner.

For those of you who are not familiar with this term, there are certain technological advancements that allow us to access a network from another location and perform various functions on that site without having to physically be there.

The benefit to this is that it saves time and money in that to remotely access a site it will take less than a minute, and you save in fuel costs. Also, if you have a client who has numerous branches throughout the country, for example it become very expensive and time consuming to travel to each and every site to perform some tasks. If that site can be controlled from a remote location it makes it a much more feasible option. Another benefit I have just thought of is that site can be accessed any time of the day (provided the computers are switched on and running) meaning that you can perform routine maintenance, such as scanning the hard drives for errors, running anti-virus scans to ensure the cleanliness of the client's machines, or checking to see that the backups were performed correctly.

Incidentally Kaspersky Lab ®' products can allow schedules to be performed on hard drive scans on a network from the Management Console (called ***Kaspersky Security Center*** ®). Using patented technology Kaspersky Lab ® ensures that the scan is staggered, meaning that only a few computers are scanned at any given time, thereby ensuring the network will not be overloaded with network traffic.

There are disadvantages to this system, however. Firstly, you need to gain the permission from your client to setup this kind of system, because it does leave a security leak whereby hackers can also gain access of they can bypass your passwords in the remote software. Secondly, if you have a hardware failure, such as a failed network card or hard drive, then obviously the computer will not be running and hence you will not be able to access it remotely. But the chances of hardware failing is fairly slim under most circumstances you can perform this task quite easily.

You have an option of either charging the client for this service or build it in as an extra service in your contract.

Hardware Specials -As an extra service you can offer certain discounts on hardware purchased by contract clients. This ensures that they purchase equipment from you because sometimes the client might decide to buy something from another vendor because of price, etc.

In addition, you could also extend the offer to permanent employees of the company (not contractors or temporary staff). This increases your revenue, and instils loyalty in the staff of your client's company. They might even refer your company to other friends they know.

Schools – Schools give us some nice potential for service offerings. In my past I have used several of these to secure the client.

For example, examination time is always stressful for any school, because they cannot afford computers to crash in the middle of an exam. So I have offered a temporary Onsite Technician during these times so that if there is a problem it can be fixed immediately. Also in some cases a temporary backup computer, with all the necessary software installed, has been placed on that site to replace another if it fails during an exam.

I have also used the Remote Support facility successfully, and have also used (and still use) the Staff Specials, but have extended this to students as well (take a look at Chapter 3 for clarification on this).

Backup Equipment - I have mentioned this above, but in other situations it does become an important service offering.

In Mission Critical situations, such as hospitals, the Military, conferences, financial institutions, etc the presence of backup systems, whether temporary or permanent, are of paramount performance because downtime is not a feasible option. In some situations permanent equipment can be bought and installed (or even rented), and in other situations temporary equipment can be stored and replaced almost immediately.

Labour Broking - Your IT Company will need to obtain a license for this, but once achieved, it opens up a wealth of possibility for you. What it basically means is that you are able to recruit Technical Personnel (and as a matter of fact any type of personnel you desire) to be placed on a client's site permanently or semi-permanently for the duration of the SLA.

The contractor remains on your payroll, and you handle all the necessary Human Resources behind such an endeavour, but it assists the client is not having to worry about those issues, and they can claim it as a tax deduction which is a bonus for them.

The only thing you need to worry about is to ensure that your client pays you on time, because if they essentially are providing the money for the Technician's salary, but your company effectively pays it over to the staff member. Late payments can cause some serious labour issues in which your company is responsible.

RESPONSE PRIORITIES

It stands to reason that contract clients should have priority over those clients which have not entered into a contract with your company.

This is important as many of your contract clients will have fairly large or intricate infrastructures and downtime for them could be very serious indeed if not attended to timeously.

As part of the SLA you deliver to the prospect you need to include the average response times of your Technical Personnel, and these times might be negotiated from the client's perspective. You also need to give an indication of the escalation procedures within your Technical Department if various issues are not resolved in time or at all. You need to provide contact names so that if there are complaints the client will know whom to contact in a managerial position to deal with those issues.

This seems to be a bone of contention with many people (not only technicians) because people do not like to issue their personal cellphone numbers out to business clients, just in case they are contacted outside of office hours.

In this case it becomes important to supply the relevant technicians with company cellphones so that contract clients have the opportunity to contact the technician on assigned duty outside of office hours with any problems that may arise.

This also brings me to another point. You need to designate duties to your Technical Personnel so that at least one is available outside of normal office hours. It is normally part of SLA's and gives the client assurance that they are looked after constantly.

SECURITY

The security of the network when it comes to SLA's is even more important because it does affect the times that technicians spend at the site. Now I am not talking about security with regards to hackers, viruses, and other malware, because these measures should already be in place or otherwise seriously considered to be implemented as soon as possible. No, I'm talking about security against the client themselves!

Wow! Heavy statement to make! What do I mean by this?

Many users like to fiddle with their computers, and also like to visit certain unwholesome websites that are generally banned according to company policy, so you need to ensure that security measures are in place to prevent users from damaging or exploiting the company's network infrastructure.

If the users are visiting websites, you need to implement a content filter. If the users are receiving many humour-based emails (which in themselves sometimes are large and take up a lot of bandwidth) you need to tweak the Spam filter to block these out.

The worst culprits of these intrusions are students. Oh yes, I have seen it all, and I was also a student once, and our mission was to eventually find a way to crash the University's servers. Students can be quite vandalistic and vindictive, and can create all sorts of havoc if the network is not properly protected. In this then you need to implement policies and profiles to prevent unauthorized access into others' files, the servers, and, if possible, the local hard drive on the computer.

The next thing you need to enforce is a method to seal the cases of the client's computers to prevent anyone who is not part of your company from opening the machines to tinker inside. Many clients who are contracted to an IT Company do from time to time hire alternative technicians in for small jobs. Also, those clients who are more technically minded like to see if they can repair the machines themselves, and in doing so they replace parts with others that might not be compatible. This also affects the revenue of the Support Company because they lose out on the hardware sales.

When I worked for my first IT Company we used to use the lead seals that are also used on fire extinguishers. We used to remove a screw from the back of the case and then apply the lead seal. If the seal was broken for any reason then there was a formal enquiry to determine if the tampered computer was still covered by the SLA, or if additional charges were billed for work performed on the machine to rectify the tinkering.

You really need to ensure that your client's network is protected as best you can.

LEGALITIES

A Service Level Agreement is a legally binding contract and as such you need to make sure that it follows all the rules of the laws of your country (where applicable) and that your IT Company (and you) are adequately covered so that, if things go sour, you or your IT Company cannot be held legally responsible.

A couple of things to note here:

Most often when a computer fails it is directly as a result from software error. For instance, if a computer is connected to mains power, and there is no voltage regulator attached, and there is a dip or surge in the power as the computer is writing information to the hard drive, it could corrupt some of the files thereby making the computer unstable.

Too, malware (viruses, etc) can also attack a computer if it is not properly updated and damage the software on the machine.

Users like to play and fiddle and for the most part they do not understand what they are fiddling with. In this then they could damage software on the computer. They also love to install additional software that might not be legally licensed and might contain bugs, or errors, that affect the performance of both the Operating System and other applications. You need to safeguard against this.

On rare occasions errors can be pinpointed to be a hardware failure, and nobody can be blamed for this. A good way to prevent hardware failures as much as possible is to provide each computer (and all the networking equipment) with **Uninterruptible Power Supplies** (**UPS**'s) which regulates the voltage from mains power, prevents most surges (except lightning – nothing can fully protect against lightning, although the UPS will do the best that it can in these cases) and provides battery backup whilst the mains power is off.

Furthermore, you need to ensure a clause that although you (or the IT Company) will take every precaution possible to safeguard data, there can be no guarantees that the client's data will be fully secure. The best way for you to prepare for this is to implement regular backup sessions at the client's premises and to further backup each computer before you work on it. In the event of a complete hard drive failure, the data can be retrieved, but it is expensive. With this clause in place you are legally protected if anything does go wrong with the client's data, whether it's their fault or yours.

Lastly on this topic, spend the extra money and time and enlist the help of the company's lawyers to go through the proposed contract to make sure that everything makes sense from a legal perspective before you and the client sign the agreements.

CONCLUSION

Service Level Agreements are brilliant ways to secure clients on a long term basis and it really enhances your commission because you will earn every time the client pays their monthly subscription.

Just be careful when drawing up the contract that legally it holds water and that there are no loopholes in it that can get you into trouble.

Make sure as well that you **really** look after these clients because you want them to renew their contract when it expires.

Summary – Chapter 11.

A **Service Level Agreement (SLA)** is a contract that a customer and an IT company enter into offering various support services. The SLA is extremely flexible as the requirements of each site will invariably differ, but once the contract is signed then both the client and the IT Company is assured of a mutual long-lasting business relationship.

When to Enter into a Service Level Agreement

A Service Level Agreement should only be entered into once a site has been properly repaired. If a Set Base Rate contract, for example, is entered into based upon the number of hours the Technical Department spends initially, the results will definitely be skewed and the client will end up with a contractual fee that will far surpass their future needs and budget.

Types of Rates

Below are three popular themes that can be adapted to establish a SLA.

Pay As You Go – In this scheme the client pays up front for a certain number of hours each month as a credit, and then when the technician is on site these hours are deducted until the credit has expired. Then additional labour fees are charged as per normal, or at a discounted rate.

Retainer Credit – This is fairly similar to the **Pay As You Go** scheme except that instead of calculating numbers of hours up front, a basic credit fee is paid, and the labour is deducted from this, regardless of the charges.

Set Base Rate – It is a set rate the client pays the IT Support Company each and every month for the duration of the contract. In return they can request support services of any kind and whenever they like.

SERVICES OFFERED

The following examples are a few of the types of services that can be offered in a SLA.

Remote Support – This means that you connect to a client's network from a remote location to repair any problems. Of course, there will be some problems that cannot be fixed in this manner, but it does save in time and fuel costs.

Hardware Specials – As an extra service you can offer certain discounts on hardware purchased by contract clients. This ensures that they purchase equipment from you because sometimes the client might decide to buy something from another vendor.

Schools – An example of a possible services offering is:

A temporary Onsite Technician can be provided during the times of examinations so that if there is a problem it can be fixed immediately. Temporary backup computers can also be provided.

Backup Equipment - In Mission Critical situations the presence of backup systems, whether temporary of permanent, are of paramount performance In some situations permanent equipment can be bought and installed, and in other situations temporary equipment can be stored and replaced almost immediately.

Labour Broking –   Your IT Company will need to obtain a license for Labour Broking, which means that you are able to recruit Technical Personnel to be placed on a client's site permanently or semi-permanently for the duration of the SLA, but the personnel will remain on the payroll of your company.

RESPONSE PRIORITIES

Contract clients should have priority over those clients which have not entered into a contract with your company.

As part of the SLA you deliver to the prospect you need to include the average response times of your Technical Personnel, and these times might be negotiated from the client's perspective. You also need to give an indication of the escalation procedures within your Technical Department if various issues re not resolved in time or at all. You need to provide contact names so that if there are complaints the client will know whom to contact in a managerial position to deal with those issues.

SECURITY

As part of the SLA you need to secure the client's network against attacks, both internal and external.

You need to ensure that security measures are in place to prevent users from damaging or exploiting the company's network infrastructure.

If the users are visiting websites, you need to implement a content filter. If the users are receiving emails that are against the Company Policy you need to tweak the Spam filter to block these out.

You need a method to seal the cases of the client's computers to prevent anyone who is not part of your company from opening the machines to tinker inside.

LEGALITIES

A Service Level Agreement is a legally binding contract and as such you need to make sure that it follows all the rules of the laws of your country (where applicable) and that your IT Company (and you) are adequately covered so that, if things go wrong, you or your IT Company cannot be held legally responsible.

Spend the extra money and time and enlist the help of the company's lawyers to go through the proposed contract to make sure that everything makes sense from a legal perspective before you and the client sign the agreements.

CHAPTER 12.
PRESENTATIONS AND
CONVENTIONS

This seems to be a swear word for many people. The thought of standing up in front of a crowd of people and talking to them breaks even the bravest of us out in a cold sweat, and you start contemplating chewing your finger nails again.

It's strange, but it seems that many people can sell, and sell well, but when it comes to presenting in front of a crowd we are immediately transported back to our school days, standing in front of the class having to blurt out orals on all sorts of subjects in front of hostile crowds; and we panic.

Admittedly some have the "gift of the gab" – the gift of begin able to face hordes and tout their goods. But somewhere along the way of your career you unfortunately have to do the dirty deed.

I admit that I am a good public speaker. I used to be a lecturer for three years, and I was good at orals in school, and I have found in the companies I have worked for that whenever a presentation was due I normally was the one tasked with the job.

It doesn't mean I like it!

I also experience the nausea, and the cold sweats, and the panic attacks, worrying that I'm going to forget what I am supposed to say. I also stand five minutes before I need to start, muttering under my breath and asking myself why I put myself through these tortures. I also ask myself why I couldn't wake up that morning with a terrible dire illness so that I could avoid the inevitable. But once I'm a few minutes into the presentation it all seems to flow as it should.

And I find that after each presentation, whether it's five minutes or forty five minutes (yes, I have run presentations that long) I am always physically drained. Maybe it's the adrenalin flowing through my blood stream from nervousness (probably is) but I'm always glad when the job's done.

I cannot stand up there and talk for you, but I can give you some pointers to help you along your own torture (some of you are probably saying, "How can he say that, because I absolutely **love** presentations?") and hopefully you'll get it right!

I have also included a section on conventions and exhibitions in this chapter because you will also be presenting at these events, but on a much smaller scale.

So let's get our teeth into this chapter.

THE REASON FOR PRESENTATIONS

What is the whole purpose for having presentations in the first place? When you visit a company and present your products and services to the relevant people, such as the Directors, you are imparting information to a single company, to a single client.

Presentations are methods to inform a group of people from different companies about your products and services. Think about this: a meeting at a company takes about an hour and a half to two hours: half an hour or an hour to travel to the client and then approximately an hour for the meeting. And there is a chance that you might not make the sale from your efforts.

A presentation probably will take anything up to three hours, and sometimes even longer. However, the major difference is that you are targeting a number of companies. Let's assume you are presenting to a group of a hundred people. In another chapter later on in this book I discuss success ratios and generally speaking, in a group of ten people you should obtain at least two people. So in a group of a hundred you will probably gain about twenty clients.

Given that you have spent three hours for the effort, it is well worth your while to perform presentations wherever possible because, if you were to visit each of those hundred clients, at two hours per company, you would then be spending a total of two hundred hours in visiting each company, and then you cannot be assured that you will gain business from each and every business.

Although to some people presentations become a daunting affair, logistically it becomes a necessary part of your sales strategy, and hence is an aspect that you need to master.

PRESENTATION DESIGN

A well designed presentation is paramount to a good performance. There will be situations when you will not have the benefits of props and presentations running in the background but for the sake of this discussion we are going to assume that you have the opportunity of running a proper presentation.

The reasons for designing and using presentations in the first place are:

- It gives you keywords and cues to work off of so that you can remember the order of events as they occur.
- It gives an impression of being more professional, especially when considering the reputation of the company you work for.
- In another chapter of the book I discuss the benefits of visual aids in advertising. The same is true of presentations. A good presentation should have many visual cues because that is what the audience will remember the most. We will discuss this further shortly.

There are several commercial presentation packages available and any one will serve the same purpose. I normally use ***Microsoft's PowerPoint*** ® to do the job, as it is an extremely powerful package with many features.

I'm not going to go through a ***PowerPoint*** ® tutorial with you, because that is beyond the scope of this book, but I'm going to mention some of the features that you can use throughout this chapter.

A good presentation should flow logically from one point into another, and this is important because you need to make sure that your audience can fully understand the information that is being imparted to them.

When designing these documents, there are a number of things to remember, namely:

Colour Schemes – Psychologists have proven that people respond differently to different colours, for instance, blue tends to calm people down whilst red seems to provoke the rage and excitement in people. Clashing colours (such as using orange and green together) can sometimes give people a headache as their eyes and brain try to focus on the colours. Here is an interesting one that you probably didn't think of. In ***PowerPoint*** ® you have the ability to view the slide show in monochrome (i.e. black and white). Why am I emphasizing this? Have you ever thought about those people suffering from Colour Blindness? If you have difficulty in viewing the slide show in monochrome then you run the risk of losing the interest of these sufferers in your audience because they will not be able to discern your work.

Text – I have sat through so many presentations, and almost every time the designer (and presenter) makes this same mistake. What is the reason for the slide show in the first place? It gives the audience a point of reference; something to look at **whilst they listen to you**.

"Whilst they listen to you!" Here is your key phrase. So many designers stick so much text onto their slides, or they like to prove their mastery of the English language by shoving a sentence of such exquisitely High English that the audience have to read that sentence a few times before they actually understand what it means.

It's a lovely tactic that lawyers use every day so that they can confuse the common layman. So why would you want to confuse your audience? You want them to listen to what you have to say, otherwise why even bother saying anything at all? Rather just type everything up and hand these out to your audience, and then you won't have to waste their time and yours by coming together to view a presentation.

Now that I have admonished you, let me explain what you **should** do here.

You must use small sentences with normal, plain, everyday English. You must make sure that the sentence can be read in less than two seconds so that you can regain the listener's attention as quickly as possible. You must also use the least possible text on your slides because the person will not be listening to what you are saying whilst they are reading.

Animations – Here we are going exactly the opposite. Animations grab people's attention and gives them something to focus on whilst they are listening. The Motion Picture Industry started in the late 1800's because the designers realized that they could hold the attention of the audience longer if they had moving pictures, and then later on they combined these moving pictures with some narration from a person off in the wings, and it was found that there was a marked improvement of audience response and memory retention. PowerPoint® has many different animation features that you can employ in your own slide shows.

Length –

You need to be careful on the length of your slide show because you need to remember that people can only absorb so much information before their brains shut off to external stimuli whilst they are assimilating the information they have received. In my experiences slide shows that are longer than thirty slides generally do not work. In calculating the length of your presentation versus the length of the slide show, you need to be aware of this fact. I will discuss this shortly.

Memory –

Have you ever played the Memory Game, whereby there is a bunch of different objects that are shown to you, one at a time, and then you have to remember as many as you can? Ever played it? I bet you remember perhaps the first two items, and the last two items, and everything in between you forgot about? Do you agree? Well, you need to take this into consideration when putting together your slide show for your presentation.

Given that the audience is trying to listen to you whilst attempting to read a list of features on a slide you have put up on the screen, chances are that in a list of five features they will remember the first one and the last one and then forget about the rest. Similarly, showing three or four slides of pure information in succession will mean that most people will remember the first and last slide and forget about the rest. You need to stagger your slides so that you have at most two slides with information and then one of pictures and animation: give your audience time to absorb the information slides. You then must have some sort of summary at the end of the presentation so that, if people have forgotten some of the information, they will remember it when you bring up the summary.

Slide Size –   Some persons do not see as well as others, especially when they are sitting at the back of the audience hall. You need to ensure that the pictures and text you display in your slide show can be easily seen and read even from the back of the hall you will be using for your event. This also ties in with colour schemes because for those with poor eyesight, certain colours and combinations of colours become difficult to discern.

I think, after going through these points, that you have discovered that designing presentations is almost an art, and I therefore suggest that if you have somebody creative around you, ask for their assistance in putting these documents together. At the very least, test it out on a few people before committing yourself to using it in a proper event.

There is something else I would just like to add at this point. In my personal experiences I have discovered that I cannot use somebody else's presentation and introduce it to an audience, primarily because I do not know what the original speaker was planning when they used their own creation. I always prefer to design my own for various reasons. Firstly, I know exactly what I have put into the document, so I know what slide will be coming next. Secondly, when I use timings (discussed below) I know exactly when the next slide will appear. Lastly, I would have taken into consideration the auditorium I will be using, and thus I will have compensated for those who sit at the back of the hall.

This is just my personal opinion; some of you might think differently on this.

READING FROM NOTES VS OFF THE CUFF

Many people find that they cannot speak in public without the necessity of a prepared speech. Have you ever studied politicians on television whilst they deliver some sort of speech to the crowds? Nearly always they are reading from some printed material in order to impart their message to the crowds. Compare this to the times when they are campaigning for their local elections? During these times the politicians are not using any sort of printed materials. Instead they speak "off the cuff", or also known as "impromptu speech". They speak their minds, and they speak of what they know. More often than not these prepared speeches are consolidated by their assistants, and the politicians only get to look through the printed material moments before they are required to impart the information to the crowds.

You may be tempted when public speaking to make use of notes whilst you are selling your products and many of you do require this as some sort of assistant to guide you through your presentation. However, your audience needs to sense that you are talking to them; that each of them feel that they are the only one in the room, and I have seen too many Public Speakers bury their noses in their notes and only glance up at their audience periodically.

In my opinion this is wrong because the crowd needs to gain the impression that you are talking directly to them; that you are truly interested in their reactions to your various statements; that you are really interested in them as potential clients.

It is for these reasons that I never use any sort of notes when I deliver presentations, and you can too, if you follow some basic pointers. Of course it will take time for you to adapt your style of presenting from that of using notes to that of speaking impromptu, but believe me you will receive a much better response from your audience once you manage to get this right.

Product Knowledge – There is a whole section elsewhere in this book that is devoted to this topic. You cannot sell what you don't know, and you cannot hope to deliver an entire presentation on a topic you know absolutely nothing about. If you try, then your audience will get the impression that you are talking like a robot, with absolutely no feeling or conviction in your words. They will perceive that you are not versed in your subject, and they will not be convinced about what you are selling.

Think about this one for a second: when a musician performs at a concert they sing their songs with feeling and conviction; they put a tremendous amount of enthusiasm and effort in their performance so that their audience gains as much entertainment out of the event as possible. Too, I have never seen a musician ever use any sorts of notes in their concerts. Why? Because they not only know their material (many of them have written the songs themselves) but they practice, and practice, and practice some more until the entire performance runs like a well-oiled engine. Should you not put as much effort into your performances?

Let's go a little further with this idea. How many albums (records, CD's, DVD's, or whatever) do these musicians sell? How many people participate in their concerts? How many crowds have turned away from such an event feeling unfulfilled? Musicians, as far as I am concerned, are probably some of the world's best sales people. If you can repeat their base enthusiasm and their commitment, then you will most truly win in your career!

Design your own Presentation – I mentioned earlier that to use someone else's presentation will definitely affect your performance during your delivery because unless you study the presentation *ad nauseum*, you will probably forget forthcoming slides and then be forced to pause whilst you re-orientate yourself.

I always maintain that creating your own presentation is still the best practice because you will know exactly what will become the content of the slide show.

When adding text you must bear in mind about what I talked about earlier. I normally place very short, simple sentences in the slides with keywords that I pick up on and that guide me to the next part of the presentation.

These keywords become my "notes" as I work through my speech, and a cursory glance at the slide is generally enough to give me my next keyword to carry on going.

Learn Your Presentation –   I'm going back to the earlier example of the musicians here. Do you realize how much they practice their songs? I'm sure you have seen excerpts on television of their rehearsals before their performances. Too, have you ever seen, either live or on television, how many times they repeat their tracks before the producer is satisfied with the results when recording their songs in the studio?

Similarly, have you ever been to the theatre, or experienced working in a production? Sometimes the actors spend up to six weeks in rehearsals before the actual play is released to the public.

The point I'm making here is the more you rehearse your speech (whether you have physically written it down, or memorized keywords to work around), the less you will have to rely on written notes or keywords to get you through and the more confident you will feel.

PRACTICING

So many people, in books and in person, have always said to me, "You must practice your speech in front of a mirror!" Me, personally, uh, uh! Can't do it!

I have tried this method before, and I find that I felt silly, and I cannot take the exercise seriously. Similarly, practicing in front of another person, whether it's my family, a friend or a work colleague, I feel the same way. I'm not saying that these methods do not work; for many presenters they believe that these rehearsals are the perfect mechanism to ensure that their project will run smoothly.

No, the method that works for me is to schedule as many of the Sales Department as possible, with some from the Technical Department, and if I can, my Director, and run the whole presentation from start to finish. Before I start I supply each participant with some paper, etc, and ask them to comment as I go through my speech.

Normally you would run your presentation without interruption (although some of the audience will still interrupt you during your live performance) but in these instances I urge these interruptions because the criticism is what tells you what is not working. If there are no interruptions throughout the entire rehearsal then you can assume that the project is successful. Nevertheless, I still receive some handwritten notes afterwards that suggests otherwise and it then gives me an indication of what I should keep and what I need to change.

The reason why I choose this approach is because it is the closest I am going to get to a "live" environment and thus it puts me in the correct mood to test my work.

PowerPoint ® has the ability to allow timings in the slides, so that certain animations of text or change of slide will occur after a predetermined length of time. Personally, I don't use them very often because I find that when I am speaking impromptu sometimes I tend to embellish a little on a particular point if I see a positive response from the audience. But, there are some who enjoy these features and will prefer to use them. My advice then to those is to ensure that, if you cannot count silently whilst speaking, to at least have access to some sort of timepiece that you can glance at so that you will know when the next feature will arrive.

At the very least have a stopwatch on your lectern that you can glance at, but make sure that you do not make it obvious that you are timing your talking. What I would rather recommend is try to have a clock mounted at the back of the hall that you can see from where you are standing so that the audience will not notice you glancing at the back of the hall for the timing of the feature changes.

Earlier I mentioned the detriment of having too many slides in your show, and this becomes part of your practice. Remember that I suggested you should keep your slide show to not more than thirty slides (or thereabouts; one or two more will not make much of a difference) but part of your practice must be to ensure that your entire speech will fit in with the time allotted to you. Going over the time by one or two minutes will not be a major train smash, but if you feel that you are heading for five minutes or longer, then you need to adjust either the amount that you talk, or you need to reduce the number of slides in your show. Don't forget that every time a keyword is shown it is going to give you an excuse to talk, so by reducing the number of keywords it will effectively reduce the amount you will talk.

As a rule of thumb benchmark, generally speaking each keyword will probably emit about a minutes' worth of speech (sometimes it can be two minutes, so work on these two figures) and thus if you only have thirty minutes in which to present your product, you cannot have more than fifteen keywords. Some of those will induce a minute's worth of talking; some of them are going to induce two minutes worth. But combined with the in - between slides (pictures, animations, etc) you will be surprised to notice that the thirty minutes will go by quicker that you'd expect.

Some of the hardest presentations I have done is to be able to slam a delivery in ten minutes flat, and then have only five minutes for questions and answers (I will discuss questions and answers below), because with some products, there is just so much information to impart that you are hard pressed to decide what to leave out! When you have these types of situations, and you have a basket of products to choose from, try to select the one that has the least amount of information. If you are not able to do this, then mention the major points and apologize beforehand to your audience for the scant information, but suggest that they schedule meetings with you at a later stage so that you can discuss the products further.

VOICE INFLECTIONS

When I was in junior school I was involved in the school choir for a few years and at that time we had a brilliant Music Teacher who sadly is no longer with us. She taught us to project our voices in such a way that the school choir could basically perform anywhere, anytime, without the use of microphones. Luckily I have carried this little gift with me into adulthood, and even now, it is an unconscious process, and I am very grateful for the training I received. Just don't ever ask me to sing now, 'cause I really suck. Even after a few beers, and a Karaoke machine, I still can't do the job. My Music Teacher would be turning in her grave if she was to hear me now.

Anyway, back to our discussion (sorry for digressing- had to get that out). I cannot even suggest you now go out and find the nearest Music Teacher to teach you how to project your voice, because that's going to take a couple of years, but what I can suggest is the following:

First thing's first! Get hold of an auditorium and start talking. Ask somebody to sit at the back and see if they can hear you. Now I don't mean they can just hear you; I mean can they hear you **clearly**. If they can't then you know that you need to employ the assistance of a microphone to help you along. I'll talk a little more about microphones shortly.

Secondly, you need to make sure that you talk clearly, and don't mumble. There are many people that seem to have this problem, and I generally put it down to nerves. Have you noticed that many musicians have this same problem? They start singing but they don't say their words properly so you end up not hearing the words but instead listen to the melody, and then the whole meaning of the song is lost. Again, this I'm going to battle to impart to you because it's difficult to explain to you in writing. You kinda like need to plug in with a Speech and Drama Teacher who can show you how it is done. And this can be accomplished in a few lessons, so it is feasible for you to pursue.

The next little thing that tends to throw people a wobbly! Many, many sales people talk too fast! It's in their nature, and generally is reactant to the person's state of mind at the time. When people are excited or anxious, they talk faster. When people are calm, their speech slows down. When delivering speeches, this practice is a definite no-no because you are going to lose your audience's attention. If you are culprit of this, you need to learn to slow your speech down. Not an easy thing, but the only way you are going to do this is by using a tape recorder. This is something that you cannot sit in your bedroom and try out because you will be conscious of the exercise and you are going to definitely cheat!

No, the best way of doing this is in the field. Most cell phones now have an audio recording function, so what I suggest is while you are on the phone with a client (land line or whatever) hit the Record button on your cell phone and register the conversation. Another way is during your next meeting. Follow the same practice. Then, when you get home, sit back and listen to yourself, and see if you are a culprit of this problem. If you are, then you need to get hold of a friend, family member or colleague and practice talking to them and get them to assist you in slowing down by signalling in some way when you start to speed up! Again, this is one you're going to have to practice.

Microphones, the marvel of inventions! They allow you to reach the farthest corners of the universe but they need some practice in order to work for you, and not against you. It's a common practice amongst singers to "eat the microphone" but then they have the benefits of background instrumentals to help them along. You don't!

If a microphone is held too close to the mouth, then certain sounds create an explosive "pop" in the loudspeakers that can be irritating, and for those listeners with sensitive ears, can actually be quite painful. Before using these devices in a live environment, you need to practice with it to determine the correct volume and the correct distance to hold the microphone so that you can be clearly heard but without the "pop". This unfortunately takes practice.

The Actual Presentation

The day of your presentation has arrived finally, and all your hours of preparation is about to be put to the test.

So what to do?

Well, you need to make sure that your presentation is loaded onto a laptop, and a reliable one at that. It is no good whatsoever for the laptop you are using to suddenly crash in the middle of your presentation. Test the presentation beforehand to make absolutely sure that it is running properly.

Then you need to get to the venue at least an hour beforehand to make sure that everything is in order. You need to ensure that the viewing screen is available, and that seating arrangements have been properly prepared. If you decide on the clock, you need to make sure that you can see it properly (also, check that it is working and that the batteries have not run out). You need to setup the Overhead Projector and ensure that it runs properly from your laptop. If you have the luxury of a remote, ensure it has fresh batteries. Also, if you are using an infra-red pointer, again ensure that its batteries are also fresh.

If a microphone and speakers are to be used, check that the system is working properly and that any cables you have laid are properly secured. I normally use a roll of packaging tape to secure the cables (the plastic brown tape you use to seal cardboard boxes with) if I have to run them across any of the carpeting.

Find a position for yourself to stand whilst talking that will not obstruct the screen in any way, but you are fairly close to the overhead projector so that your remote (if you are using one) will be in range. Also, you need to test your pointer to make sure it can reach the farthest point of the screen.

Your dress code – try to look as neat as possible, and if you have a blazer, use it, with a tie and collar, of course. Ladies; you should also try to look as professional as possible. Dress like you are worth a million bucks! Something here to remember; under no account should you wear colours that are going to distract the audience. Either keep it plain and simple (black or white) but don't wear "loud" colours.

In some instances you might be able to greet guests at the door. If this is possible, then try to make an effort to greet at least some of them, because this increases your Public Relations. Have a bowl or dish or box or something and try to urge your guests to drop their business cards into this receptacle. Although you will perhaps have some of their contact details from the invitee list, it's always nice to have their full details from their cards.

A few things to note whilst you are delivering your speech.

Firstly, make certain that at the beginning of your presentation you greet your audience and briefly introduce yourself. And don't forget to request that all cell phones are either switched off or placed on Silent, because there is nothing more distracting than having a cell phone ring in the middle of a delivery.

Next, don't fidget! Keep your hands clasped either in front of you, or behind you, or hands at your sides, but don't fidget! It will most certainly distract your audience.

Now remember, you are in control of this presentation, so take control and be bold and speak with conviction, because you know your speech, and you know what you are talking about. Try to visualize each audience member as a big bank note, because, yes, that's exactly what they mean to you. Horrible way to think of it, hey?

Also, you need to maintain eye contact with your audience. Even if you don't actually look at each of them in the eye (some people find that they lose their nerve if they actually look at their audience) then pretend you are looking at them, from left to centre to right. Look at their hairstyles or their ears, if need be, but make sure that the audience believes that you are actually looking at them.

Oh, something I almost forgot about. Provide each of your audience with some sort of writing material and a pen or pencil, so that they can take notes during your presentation if need be.

Lastly, at the end of your presentation, thank your audience for participating (you could even do this at the beginning) and let them know that your Question-and-Answer period is now available. This is covered below.

Oops! Something else I have forgotten. Make sure you have plenty of business cards, and your technician as well (discussed in the next part).

QUESTION-AND-ANSWER PERIOD

This is where your technician kicks in. Whenever I deliver a presentation I always make sure I have a technician available for this purpose, because your Question-and-Answer sessions can get quite hectic, and normally members of your audience ask you questions that you just cannot answer.

As an added bonus, if anything goes wrong with your laptop during the presentation, you have your very own technician right there with you to fix any problems.

Now you have to be careful to watch the time of these sessions, because, depending on your venue, it might be scheduled for another event thus limiting your available time. Generally speaking, a fifteen minute allotted time should be sufficient, but, if you feel that the answers to some of the questions are going to be too long, then give them your business card (or your technician's, depending on the type of question), take down the person's details (don't forget to give them yours in return) and offer to contact them at another time. In this way you will have scored another meeting, and another potential client!

Don't be afraid of these Q&A sessions because this is perhaps your best gauge to see if your audience is interested in your products.

CONVENTIONS AND EXHIBITIONS

These are interesting times in your career life. Some find them exciting; others find them tedious; still others worry about the expense associated with participating in these events. The bottom line is, if your company can afford it, it becomes the perfect opportunity to showcase your company and your products. However, there are many such events, each one targeting difference audiences, and thus you need to carefully scrutinize the details of each forthcoming event to make sure that your company will be suited for such an event.

There are many different aspects of exhibiting that you need to be aware of in order to participate. Obviously money is an issue, and you need to ensure that you are able to adequately budget for these occasions. I will briefly look at each issue that is necessary to ensure a great success.

Before we get into these, normally these exhibitions span approximately three or four days. Some events run shorter; some run longer, but you need to be aware of the length of the occasion and plan for this time span.

Sponsorship - The costs of these conventions can sometimes be horrific, and many but the biggest IT companies cannot afford to be a part of the show. If your company is in a position of selling or distributing a product range that is manufactured by a third party company then it might be advisable to negotiate the marketing costs with them as a form of sponsorship. Even if the supplier cannot supply the full Marketing Cost, they could at least contribute certain percentages to ease the financial blow.

Stand Design -	The design of your stand, or place where your will be exhibiting, is extremely important because it needs to catch the eye of the passing crowd whilst not to appear gaudy and unprofessional. Many exhibitions offer prizes for the best designed stand. With these pointers in mind it is sometimes beneficial to spend a little extra and enlist the help of a professional designer. In addition, people enjoy visual and auditory effects (as mentioned earlier in the book) so purchasing or hiring a video screen (LCD or similar) and running some product videos with some volume, but not blaring, as this will most certainly put people off.
Handout Marketing Material -	Over and above the costs involved in the design of the stand, the quantity of marketing material that will be handed out to passers-by and interested parties will definitely chew up a good portion of the overall Marketing Budget, and you need to calculate the required quantities over the number of days you will be exhibiting. A nice way to figure this out is to request an average number of guests who will visit the convention. These numbers should be obtainable by the Event Organizers who will have a good, educated estimate of these numbers.

The obvious material, such as brochures and leaflets, should appear in abundance, but people also like gimmicks, and the provision of a few different types of these branded with your company's logo will go a long way to stay in a visitor's memory long after they been to the event.

Some examples I have experienced in the past have been: rubber balls, pens, flash disks and tins of breath mints. At one show one stand were giving away small travelling combination locks for your computer cables. At another event branded sunglasses were being handed out.

The more inventive you can be (whilst obviously watching the costs of the goodies) the more the visitors will remember you.

However, there is something I do need to caution you on. Many schools negotiate with Event Organizers in allowing some of their students to visit the exhibition on a particular day (some call this "Open Day"). It gives the students an opportunity for a School Outing, and the teachers hope that the students will become inspired by what they see to consider Information Technology as a profession when they leave school.

There will be some students that will take these outings seriously, but the majority of them will see this as an opportunity to skip school for the day and gather as many "freebies" and they can.

Trust me; I have seen this time and time again. These students try to collect as many free samples and brochures, and whatever else they can lay their hands on, and most of that marketing material will end up in the dustbin (trash can for our American readers) without even a cursory glance of the contents.

In addition, many students will want to fiddle with your stand, especially the computers, and for some unknown reason the very first thing they beeline for is an opportunity to access the Internet. If the exhibition computer is unable to connect to the Internet, the next best thing they try for are either games or music.

In any case, they will in some way damage those computers, mark my words, and it can range from either deleting some information, to actual physical damage to the machines.

How do we combat this? First step – find out from the Organizers if such a day has been scheduled and when.

Next step – hide as many of your "freebies" as possible and only leave out a few brochures ad pamphlets.

Last step – make sure you have extra staff on hand to act as "security guards" to keep their eye on the computers and the stand.

There is no other way to avoid these stampedes.

Information Sheets - The whole reason for these events is to make contact with potential clients and gain possible business from them. This is why you need plenty of Information Sheets with spaces to capture as much detail as possible about the visitors to your stand. These sheets are then handed out to the Sales Department back at the office after the show has ended so that they can follow up and create new business for the company.

Another extremely important way of doing this is the practice of collecting business cards, and giving yours in return.

There is something very important you must remember in any situation:

"Never give out your business card without receiving one in return!"

Business cards cost money to produce, and so many sales people hand them out willy nilly without collecting one back from the receiver in return. Many, many people will never even look at your business card, and it will become a waste. If you can get one of their cards in return, or at least their contact details, then you will have gained in the situation, because you will have another potential lead to follow up on.

Some visitors don't like to waste time whilst you stand there writing all their contact information down on your Information Sheet, so another way to do this is to run some sort of Lucky Dip Draw.

In one event my company negotiated with the Event Organizers and a Lucky Dip voucher was handed out to each visitor at the entrance to the Exhibition Hall. In order to qualify for the Lucky Dip Draw (I think it was a Home Theatre System that was the prize) the visitor needed to fill in their details and then drop the form in at our company's stand. In this way you get the visitor to fill their information in for you!

Stand Attendance - For anybody, the monotony of manning the stands does take its toll. The staff become tired, their legs get sore, and the repetitive conversations about your products start to grind on the nerves after a couple of hours. For this reason staff should be rotated often (normally every four hours or so). You will need at least one Sales Person and one Technician to man the stand at any stage (obviously more staff will be needed if the stand is larger or if there will be many visitors).

Back at the office you will have to run on a Skeleton Crew, and it is advisable to advertise on your website and in your email signatures that this will be the case whilst the convention is running so that customers are aware that there might be some delays in their requests being processed.

CONCLUSION

The art of presenting is an important one to put in your arsenal because it allows you to sell once to many listeners, and becomes a definite time saver. It also gives you an opportunity to showcase you company.

With regards to conventions and exhibitions they are brilliant for company and brand recognition. The major drawback is that of finances; they cost a hell of a lot of money to participate in.

SUMMARY – CHAPTER 12.

Presentations are important as part of promoting your products and services as they reach a large audience in the shortest possible time and act as a way of advertising and exposure for you and your company. Included in this chapter are Exhibitions and Conventions which serve similar purposes.

THE REASON FOR PRESENTATIONS

Presentations are methods to inform a group of people from different companies about your products and services.

It saves time and money because you are meeting with many people from different companies at one time.

PRESENTATION DESIGN

A well designed presentation is paramount to a good performance.

The reasons for designing and using presentations in the first place are:

- It gives you keywords and cues to work off of so that you can remember the order of events as they occur.
- It gives an impression of being more professional, especially when considering the reputation of the company you work for.
- A good presentation should have many visual cues because that is what the audience will remember the most. We will discuss this further shortly.

When designing these documents, there are a number of things to remember, namely:

Colour Schemes – The colour scheme will instil different moods in people. Clashing colours might be offensive to some viewers and those people that are colour blind might not be able to see certain colours so make sure you test your presentation in a monochrome setting so that all the text and images are visible.

Text – You must use small sentences with normal, plain, everyday English. You must make sure that the sentence can be read in less than two seconds so that you can regain the listener's attention as quickly as possible. You must also use the least possible text on your slides because the person will not be listening to what you are saying whilst they are reading.

Animations – Animations grab people's attention and gives them something to focus on whilst they are listening so use plenty of animation in your presentations.

Length – You need to be careful on the length of your slide show because you need to ensure that people will be able to concentrate and absorb all the information you are imparting. Slide shows of more than thirty slides are not advisable.

Memory – Do not make your information lists too long. You need to stagger your slides so that you have at most two slides with information and then one of pictures and animation to give your audience time to absorb the information slides. You then must have some sort of summary at the end of the presentation so that, if people have forgotten some of the information, they will remember it when you bring up the summary.

Slide Size – You must make sure that the pictures and text you display in your slide show can be easily seen and read even from the back of the hall you will be using for your event.

Test out your presentation on some people as a rehearsal and ask for their honest criticisms.

READING FROM NOTES VS OFF THE CUFF

Your audience needs to sense that you are talking to them; they must feel that they are the only one in the room, and so be careful of reading from too many notes.

Some pointers to avoid this are:

Product Knowledge –	You cannot sell what you don't know, and you cannot hope to deliver an entire presentation on a topic you know absolutely nothing about. You need to learn about the product you are presenting on.
Design your own Presentation –	Create your own presentation so that you know what information will appear next and you will be able to use the points in each slide as keywords as you speak.
Learn Your Presentation –	The more you rehearse your speech (whether you have physically written it down, or memorized keywords to work around), the less you will have to rely on written notes or keywords to get you through and the more confident you will feel.

PRACTICING

You need to practice you presentation in front of some people you know so that you can test whether the format and timing of the presentation is correct. Ask the audience for honest criticism so that you will know where adjustments will need to be made.

PowerPoint® has the ability to allow timings in the slides, so that certain animations of text or change of slide will occur after a predetermined length of time. If you do use timings then have access to some sort of timepiece either with you our mounted on the wall at the back of your auditorium so that you can monitor how much time has passed.

Each keyword displayed on a slide will probably emit about a minutes' worth of speech and other animations will probably take another minute, so base the length of your presentation on the time allocated to you, using these criteria.

VOICE INFLECTIONS

You need to test the strength of your voice so visit an auditorium and start talking. Ask somebody to sit at the back and see if they can clearly hear you. If they can't then you know that you need to employ the assistance of a microphone to assist you.

You also need to make sure that you talk clearly, and don't mumble.

Further, make sure you do not speak too quickly or too slowly.

When using a microphone do not place the microphone too near your mouth, neither too far. Test the performance before you actually use it.

THE ACTUAL PRESENTATION

On the day of the presentation you will need to:

- Ensure that your presentation is loaded onto a reliable laptop.
- Arrive at the venue at least an hour beforehand to make sure that everything is in order such as the sound, audio, and seating arrangements, and make sure you have established your speaking position.
- Make sure that your dress code is formal.

During your presentation:

- Make certain that at the beginning of your presentation you greet your audience and briefly introduce yourself.

- Request that all cell phones are either switched off or placed on silent.
- Don't fidget! Keep your hands clasped either in front of you, or behind you, or hands at your sides.
- Be bold and speak with conviction.
- Maintain eye contact with your audience.
- Provide each of your audience with some sort of writing material.
- At the end of your presentation, thank your audience for participating.

QUESTION-AND-ANSWER PERIOD

Try to have a technician available to assist you with queries you cannot answer.

Be careful of the length of time allocated for these sessions. If there are either too many questions, or questions that will take some time to answer, rather take down the person's details and contact them at a later stage for a meeting.

CONVENTIONS AND EXHIBITIONS

These become the perfect opportunity to showcase your company and your products and are important to participate in if your company has the budget to support it.

Sponsorship –	If your company is in a position of selling or distributing a product range that is manufactured by a third party company try to negotiate the marketing costs with the manufacturer as a form of sponsorship.
Stand Design –	The design and position of your stand is important so try to enlist the help of a professional designer

Handout Marketing Material – Calculate the required quantities of marketing material by the number of days you will be exhibiting against the number of expected guests. Try to use "gimmicks" as well as brochures and leaflets.

Information Sheets – You need Information Sheets with spaces to capture as much detail as possible about the visitors to your stand. These sheets are then handed out to the Sales Department back at the office after the show has ended so that they can follow up and create new business for the company.

"Never give out your business card without receiving one in return!"

Stand Attendance – Staff attending the stands should be rotated often (normally every four hours or so). In addition you will need at least one Sales Person and one Technician to man the stand at any stage

Chapter 13.
Customer Relations
Management

There is an old saying that states:

> *"It takes 30 days to gain a customer; it takes 30 seconds to lose a customer!"*

This statement is very accurate in that it is not enough that a client just buys from you; you need to ensure that the relationship between yourself and your client continues over a long period of time so that they will keep coming back to you for more business, or they will be so impressed with your performance that they will start talking to other people.

Elsewhere in the book I discussed **Word of Mouth** advertising, and this is exactly what this is all about. People talk to each other; it's a natural human trait, and if a client is happy with you then they will speak well about you and your company, thereby giving you potentially more business. If you have performed badly however, then this could cause a major problem in your occupation because people talk, and I have found that people generally enjoy talking badly about others than talking good. This being said it becomes of paramount importance to keep your client content.

This chapter concentrates on some methods that you could employ into your strategy that will give you the edge when it comes to service delivery, and will ensure that you will keep your clients and enjoy their business for a long time to come. It must be noted that this list is by no means inexhaustible, and there are many different tactics that can be used to the same effect.

Due to the fact that part of this chapter deals with the use of diaries, I am going to include some aspects of using your email client as a Customer Relations Management facility. In this particular discussion I am going to refer to Microsoft's Outlook ®, because this is the application that I have been using for a very long time and I am familiar with it. There are several other **Customer Relations Management** (CRM) packages out there that can be used instead, but I'm sure you will pick up the basics here. I'm sure Microsoft ® would not mind me using their package here for this discussion.

So how we are going to do this is firstly I'm going to discuss the different methods I normally use and then I'll discuss the CRM package part of it.

BIRTHDAYS

Everybody loves a birthday. Now I know that some people don't like to be reminded of their birthdays because it tells them how old they are getting, but most of this is for show and secretly those people actually enjoy their birthdays. You can use this to a little advantage.

I'm not sure of other countries but in South Africa a person's Identity Number (Social Security Number in the USA) begins with their birth date, so if you can get hold of this number then you've essentially got their birthday date on hand.

When I was a Product Manager we had numerous resellers (IT companies that sold my products to the End User) who had to complete Application forms in order to register with the company I worked for. These forms had a place for the ID numbers of the

Company's Directors and it was from these numbers that I used to get hold of their birthdays.

There are other methods however that you could employ in order to get this information such as asking the receptionist or one of the secretaries for the information. You could even ask the accountant or, if they have one, the Human Resources Department. Don't lie to them: explain why you would like the information and they will quite cheerfully give it to you.

Depending on your resources a birthday salutation can be as simple as sending either an email or an SMS from a cell phone, to posting them a birthday card, to doing something extravagant for your really important clients.

Examples of these extravagances could be taking them to lunch or dinner, or, if you can organize them, tickets to a local sporting event. Obviously these types of gestures must take into consideration your client's schedule, and always check with your client's spouse before organizing any of these events because they might have organized something by themselves. If your client's spouse has organized a dinner for example, it would be bad form to take your client to lunch. In addition, never offer to take your client for a few drinks after work without first consulting their spouse, as your client will invariably be late in getting home (and perhaps a little inebriated in the process) and thus might spoil the surprise that has been organized by the family.

I had an extremely interesting situation quite a number of years ago. The company I was working for had an extremely prominent client, and our contact person was a lady and a mother. I happened to be in reception when the lady (her name was Lisa) was on her cell phone discussing her daughter's sixth birthday which was the following Tuesday. Well I managed to remember that information and on her daughter's birthday I sent an email on behalf of my company wishing her well.

The response I had was overwhelming. Apparently, according to the receptionist, Lisa was so taken aback by the gesture that she was quite emotional, and forever after that client became one of our company's advocates, and as far as I know (some odd six years down the line) that client has still remained loyal to that Support Company.

One quick side-line here! One of the requirements when my resellers sent in their application forms was to supply a copy of their Company Registration. There is a date on that registration that tells you when their company started. Some Directors remember when their company started but most don't. Hey, add this to your Birthday list and I can tell you that you will not go wrong.

Easter and Christmas (and Thanksgiving for our American friends) –

You can go further here and include major holidays. Many companies already follow this tradition, especially at Christmas, and if you incorporate some sort of gesture during these periods, it will stand you in good stead.

FOLLOW-UPS AND THANK YOU GESTURES

This is quite an important gesture to include in your strategy, especially when a client purchases a piece of equipment that involves electricity or with moving parts, such as a computer, or a car.

You must remember here that most of these purchases involve a great deal of money, and the buyer has probably thought long and hard before they have committed themselves. Too, these purchases have been affected to improve their business or, in the case of a car, transport to and from their workplace, so, if anything does go wrong it will affect them begin able to continue with their work, and thus their overall productivity is jeopardized.

Also, many people do not understand how these devices operate and they are going to be distraught when something goes wrong. You need to make sure that they feel that you are with them every step of the way, even after they have bought the goods from you. After all, part of your company's portfolio is **support**, and this is exactly what you want to be able to give them – a virtual lifeline so that they can feel more secure.

A Thank You letter sent to the client a few days after their purchase, whether it is a simple as an email or a physically posted letter, will remind the client that you are still thinking about them personally, and that they are not just simply a statistic to include in the sales person's commission reports. People like to be remembered and this gesture will give them that impression.

In addition to this, a follow up should be carried out about two weeks after their purchase to make sure that everything is still working properly and to find out if there is something they still don't understand. Normally a two week period should be sufficient time for the client to play around with the system, and often there will be questions asked which is perfect for you because sometimes (not all the time, but sometimes) there is something additional the client does need that was not thought of in the original purchase (and hence not supplied) and then this leads to additional business for you.

The big trick here is to get people to remember you. One of the ways of doing this is by repetition. People and animals learn by repetition in different forms and methods and these follow ups and letters serve to remind the client that you exist, leading to them coming back to you when the time comes for them to effect additional purchases. Why do you think advertisements are repeated so often on television? Why do you think a new song is played over and over on the radio? If it is familiar to us then we can relate to it.

Another way for people to remember us is by making an impression to them, whether it is a good or a bad impression.

A slight digression here, but one that is important.

A customer likes to feel that they are important. They feel that they will be spending their entire life savings with you and therefore they want your undivided attention. You as a sales person is probably used to selling computers on a daily basis, but for a customer they don't buy computers every day, so you must be aware of how they are feeling. They will probably be apprehensive and nervous, and will want to get the best value for their money.

Many shoppers will take quite a long time about deciding if this is what they actually want. Some people will most likely bring another person along with them (their spouse or friend) to help reinforce their decision.

I have also on occasion experienced these shoppers who bring along their own "computer expert" who will most certainly throw technical questions back at you, some of which don't have any merit at all – the "expert" will try to show his or her importance to their friend, the prospective buyer. You as a Sales Person must be as patient as possible in these situations, because the "expert' is the decision maker and if they are satisfied with the product you will then get the sale.

Going a little further with this, you must make that person feel like they are the only person in the place. Try as much as possible to avoid any sort of interruptions, whether it is your cell phone, another colleague, even sometimes your own boss. Offer them something to drink perhaps, especially if it is a hot day and you can see that they are flustered by the heat. By doing so you will ensure that that client will remember you, because you have made a good impression: you have made them feel important.

An interesting anecdote I picked up in a sales book a few years ago (I can't remember which one unfortunately) says:

> *"Make that sale as if it is the last sale you will ever do in your life. Ever!"*

If you can remember this and apply it to each and every sale you do, with all the enthusiasm you can muster, then you will definitely increase your sales turnover.

Now this little section leads us into the next section ...

RENEWALS, UPGRADES AND PERIODIC VISITS

I read somewhere that in order to keep up with technology you will need to purchase a new computer at least every three months (maybe even sooner – my information might be out of date). The point is here if you are a multi-millionaire then this is a possibility, but if you are a normal worker like the rest of us then this becomes a bit of an impossibility. In fact, if you are a multi-millionaire then you probably won't be reading this book because you will already have made your money and either know how to sell (in other words, you know more than what I'm explaining in this book) or you don't want to know how to sell. In any case, you're a worker like the rest of us ants and so you need to understand the average person.

As I said before, one should buy a new system every three months, but one can't because of financial restrictions. However, if a client performs an upgrade once a year, then this becomes acceptable especially when you consider that companies' financial budgets are created on an annual basis. Many subscription renewals also occur on an annual basis, and thus the system you sold will be ready for a renewal or an upgrade a year from the date of purchase.

This information you need to store somewhere.

In today's society, our everyday lives become hectic with the toil of dealing with various problems, and thus we quickly tend to forget things, especially when they are not important at the time. Many people have a tendency to worry about only those things that are important at that present moment, and if their computer network is chugging away quite merrily then they don't worry about the possibility of it breaking. Of course, when is does present problems, it then becomes a priority and that person will then act on it in order to fix the problem. But, if you and your engineers have done your job well at the start, then quite often there won't be any anomalies. And then these clients forget about you.

So you need to remind them that you exist!

One way of doing this is by adopting the policy of **courtesy calls**. These can either be a telephone call, an email, or a physical visit to the client just to make sure that everything is running smoothly and there are no problems. Of course if there are, or if the client needs anything else but hasn't got around to addressing their needs, then these become the perfect opportunities for further sales. But the main reason for these visits is to ensure that your client doesn't forget about you.

In retail sales buyers frequently become quite fickle when money is an issue: they habitually search for the cheapest price and in some cases do not consider the value of what they are purchasing. One year they will buy a computer from you and then the next year they will by another from your opposition because they are cheaper than you, or offer free goodies, or whatever. It then becomes your job to ensure that the client stays with you, no matter what the cost. By contacting the client on a regular basis you are cementing your relationship with that client and then they will remember you in the future. If they do happen to purchase based on price and your products do happen to be more expensive than your opposition's then normally that client will come back to you first explaining the situation, and hence will give you the opportunity to secure the sale, either by reducing your price, or giving them some sort of freebie, or whatever. The main point here is the client should at least consult with you to gain your opinion before they proceed with their decision.

In terms of frequency of these visits or calls, it all depends on the volatility of the client's infrastructure. Those clients who tend to have several problems with their infrastructures (mainly caused by user errors) will need to be visited at least once a month, whilst those who have minimal anomalies will probably appreciate a call every three months or so. Too, it also depends on your client itself. If the person is known to be extremely busy then they will not like to be disturbed until such time as they actually do have a problem. In these cases a simple email should suffice. You might not get an answer, or at the very least a simple, short reply, but that client will appreciate that you are still out there, and still thinking about them as a customer.

Newsletters and Specials

A nice way to keep a client interested is to add them to your mailing list, if your company has an available newsletter in circulation. By doing this you are keeping your clients updated on any new information that is made available pertaining to products and services they have purchased from you. Of course, if the client is not interested they can always unsubscribe, or otherwise request to be removed off of that list.

On another note, try to store information about your clients' purchases if you can. The reason for this is invariably your company will have various specials from time to time. These specials might correlate to some of your clients' prior purchases and hence you might have an opportunity to gain some more sales whilst offering a "courtesy call" that we mentioned above.

Using Outlook ® as a CRM

Ok, now for this discussion I am assuming that you are familiar with *MS Outlook* ®, or have at least used it in the past. I therefore am not going to enter into a discussion of how the entire program works. What I am going to do instead is point out some of the features that it has and can be used as a CRM application.

Where applicable I will suggest where you can use these features for the above discussions.

We are going to explain the Contacts, Tasks, Calendar, and the email Drafts facilities' areas. We are also going to look at how to export information from *Outlook* ®, and how to create Distribution Lists.

Contacts -   This is where you can store all the information about your contacts including addresses, telephone numbers, the company they work for, and what their positions are within their company. A couple of things I would like to make you aware of here. Firstly, I mentioned earlier about birthdays. When you open a contact, you can enter their birthday on the second page. What *Outlook* ® does is schedule it in the Calendar (discussed shortly) so that it becomes an event every year whilst the contact is still stored in your *Outlook* ®. It will then come up as a reminder (discussed shortly) on the day, enabling you to take action on it.

The other field I wanted to make you aware of is the "Categories" field at the bottom right hand corner of your Contact's window. You can use the predetermined categories or you can create your own in the "Master Category List". Basically, you can group contacts by different categories, making them easier to find.

Such categories can include things like geographical areas (such as all the clients you have in your own home town), clients grouped according to products they have purchased. For example, you could create a category called "Kaspersky" and group all the clients that have purchased that product. When you have a special available you can inform all those clients in that category.

Tasks -   This feature allows you to schedule certain tasks with start and stop dates. There is a feature called the "Reminder" that can also be scheduled with a date and time. When that Reminder is due a pop-up window will appear on your desktop informing you of that task to be completed. In this way you can automate the entire process so that you do not have to remember everything that happens. An example of suitable tasks are reminders to complete your sales reports for presentation to your Sales Manager, remembering to pay your accounts, and remembering to download information for a client you will be visiting.

Please note that these Reminders will only work if *Outlook*® is currently running on your computer. The same is true of the Calendar, explained below.

Calendar - This feature is extremely useful. Not only does it store and remember your clients' birthdays, and reminds you (with the user of Reminders, explained above) but it can also store all of your scheduled meetings, and remind you of them when the time comes. By default the calendar will inform you fifteen minutes prior to when the meeting will start, but you can always adjust this reminder time so that you can be reminded an hour before your meeting, for example, giving you enough time to leave your office and travel to your meeting.

Not only can you use the calendar to schedule meetings, but you can use it to remind you when a client's purchases are up for a renewal or upgrade. This automates the necessity of trying to remember when your client bought a computer from you, and when it will be time for them to purchase a new one, or renew their *Kaspersky Anti-Virus* subscription. Of course you can also use the Tasks facility to do this, but the big difference is that scheduled Tasks do not appear in the Calendar, so the only way you can review it is to look at the Tasks Pane. By having these items in the Calendar, you can view at a glance all the items scheduled for your day. The choice between the two facilities is entirely up to you.

Furthermore, scheduling meetings are a cinch, as you can select your contact in the Contacts window, right click on it and select either "New Appointment with Client (if you already have a meeting scheduled and would like to put it in the Calendar), or, if you would like to schedule a meeting with your client, you can select "New Meeting Request With Client" which will send them an email requesting the meeting and will await their response. In the meantime it records the information in your Calendar. You can also invite others to the same meeting by adding their email address in the "To" field.

Drafts -   Birthdays, Thank You messages, and literally any other email you wish can be save as a Draft and called up at any time to be edited and sent. Think about it here – if you find yourself typing up a Birthday message, that basically has very similar text, then you can save yourself some time by creating the email and then saving it. It will save itself into the "Drafts" folder and then you can use it as a template. Simply go to this folder, select the email, right click on it and select "Forward". It will keep the original and make a copy, and then all you need to do is put the names and addresses it, make sure the colour of the font is the same (forwarded emails generally take on a different font to the rest of the email) and then send it!

I often use this facility – it save me a lot of time!

Exporting   Most often people use this feature (found in the
and   "File Menu") to back up their email to a **Personal**
Importing -   **Folder File** (.pst file) but I have found another useful feature that can be incorporated into your CRM strategy. You can export your entire list of contacts to an *Excel* ® spreadsheet, meaning that you can use this information in other software, like specialist bulk emailing applications. You can also import information in a similar way.

The big thing to remember here when importing contacts' information into *Outlook* ® is to make sure the fields are the same. What I mean by this is when you perform an export to a spreadsheet, you will see a lot of field headings (trust me, there are a lot). When you import in, you need to make sure those headings exist, in order, so that *Outlook* ® can identify where to put everything.

A hint here: perform an initial Export to an *Excel* ®
Spreadsheet. Then use this spreadsheet as a template for the
other information you want to import back into *Outlook* ®. Just
insert the information you need into the relevant fields in the
template, and then import it in. It should do the job if you have
got everything entered correctly.

Distribution Lists - When sending emails to many contacts
you can create **Distribution Lists** that
can contain several members. This is done
by selecting it from the "Actions" menu.
Once you have created your list and
put your Members in from your list of
contacts, you can assign it to a Category
(for easy storage). When you send your
email simply add the Distribution List to
the BCC field in the mail (make sure it's
the BCC field) and the mail will be sent
to all those members.

Conclusion

Customer Relations Management (CRM) is a vital part of sales
because people like to be remembered from time to time and it
goes a long way to building a long lasting relationship between
them and you.

Once you have established these kinds of clients price no
longer becomes a factor when they decide to purchase anything
from you because they will know that you will look after their
best interests.

I have given you some examples that you can use to cement
your relationships with your clients but there are several more. Do
some research on the Internet or go in search of some books on the
subject, but definitely add this practice to your everyday sales life.

SUMMARY. CHAPTER 13.

"It takes 30 days to gain a customer; it takes 30 seconds to lose a customer!"

It is not enough that a client just buys from you; you need to ensure that the relationship between yourself and your client continues over a long period of time so that they will keep coming back to you for more business, or they will be so impressed with your performance that they will start talking to other people.

The following are some methods to do this:

BIRTHDAYS

Wishing your clients a "Happy Birthday" is a sure fire way to securing long term relationships with them, because it shows them that you care enough to remember their birthday.

The salutation can be as simple as sending an email, to sending them a physical card, to organizing an event for them such as a luncheon or a sporting event.

You can also use this technique during other holidays such as Christmas and Thanksgiving.

FOLLOW-UPS AND THANK YOU GESTURES

A Thank You letter should be sent to the client a few days after their purchase, whether it is a simple as an email or a physically posted letter which will remind the client that you are still thinking about them and were thankful for their business.

In addition to this, a follow up should be carried out about two weeks after their purchase to make sure that everything is still in order and if additional assistance is required.

Renewals, Upgrades and Periodic Visits

Many subscription renewals occur on an annual basis, and generally speaking a computer system would be due for an upgrade a year from the date of purchase under normal average circumstances. In order to affect these you need to store the information somewhere and then remind the client when their renewals and upgrades are due.

In addition you need to perform periodic courtesy calls to make sure that the client remembers you and thus solidifying your relationship so that if there is anything else needed they will most probably contact you. The frequency of these calls is dependent upon each individual client.

Newsletters and Specials

A nice way to keep a client interested is to add them to your mailing list, if your company has an available newsletter in circulation add your clients to them. In this way they will be reminded of your company and they will be aware of any special s you currently have running especially if these special concerns items they have already purchased from you.

Using Outlook ® as a CRM

Using **MS Outlook** ® as an example it can be used as a CRM application. For example:

Contacts –   This is where you can store all the information about your contacts, and their birthdays can also stored and **Outlook** ® will automatically notify you of these events allowing you to take appropriate action. The Categories Field allows you to group your contact in various different ways.

Tasks – This feature allows you to schedule certain tasks with start and stop dates. There is a feature called the "Reminder" that can also be scheduled with a date and time.

Calendar – It can store all of your scheduled meetings, and remind you of them when the time comes. By default the calendar will inform you fifteen minutes prior to when the meeting will start. It can also store birthdays and other up and coming events such as clients' upgrades or renewal dates.

Drafts – Standard email templates can be created and saved in the Draft folder. They then can be edited and sent at any time.

Exporting and Importing – Contacts can be imported and exported meaning that you can transfer this information between other popular applications.

Distribution Lists – When sending emails to many contacts you can create **Distribution Lists** that can contain several members. This means that when you need to send bulk emails out you can send it to a list instead of sending it to each recipient individually.

Chapter 14.
Client Complaints

No matter how good your sales ability is, or how good your product is, or the reputation of the company you work for, you will always receive client complaints about yourself, your product/s, or the company you represent.

Most sales people pale at the thought of having to deal with irate clients but it must be understood that this is all part of the natural sales cycle and these complaints need to be managed efficiently and quickly.

Many experts have voiced the old adage:

"It takes thirty days to make a customer! It takes thirty seconds to lose one!!!"

And this is an extremely important point to consider.

As discussed in other chapters in the book, **Word of Mouth** advertising is probably the most important and effective form of advertising, and a valid complaint could (and in most cases would) be advertised with a negative effect on your business.

OK, so how do we resolve client complaints? The following chapter will cover some of the different aspects of these resolutions.

LISTEN WITH EMPATHY

As discussed in previous manuals, the ability to **listen** to what a customer wants is an extremely important aspect of sales. With complaints there is no difference here – most clients will want to vent off a bit of steam. After all, they have invested time and money in trusting your product and/or service and hence they expect the product and/or service to satisfy their needs. In the event that this is not the case the client has to spend additional time and money in order to voice their dissatisfaction – of course they are going to be angry and quite rightly so! It then becomes your job to nullify the situation and the first step is to listen to their problem or complaint.

Many sales books tout this common statement:

> *"Listen with empathy!"*

But, and I stand to be corrected, numerous sales books I have studied do not actually explain this statement fully.

The dictionary explains **empathy** as:

> *"Empathy – Power of projecting one's personality into (and so fully comprehending) object of contemplation."*

OK, so what does this actually mean? Well, basically what they are saying is (with respect to this particular topic) is that you need to look at the situation from the other person's point of view in order to understand how they are feeling, and hence to be able to adapt and work with this perspective.

Think about it! It's the middle of summer, you're in your lunch hour, and you decide that you need a new tyre for your car. You drive to your local tyre outlet and wait impatiently for them to change your tyre. Once they have finished and you have paid for your goods you look at your watch and reckon that you have just enough time to duck into the nearest fast food store to grab something to eat. On your way there your new tyre suddenly bursts leaving you stranded on the side of the road.

Having to change a tyre in the middle of summer, in your work clothes, with limited time available (provided you have a working spare wheel) would not make anyone's day, notwithstanding the fact that you will lose out on the meal you promised yourself!

How would this make you feel? Would you not like to immediately go back to the tyre place and blast your head off at their incompetence?

So what would you expect from the tyre place? Well, you'd probably want them to come to you and fix the problem, and yes, you would perhaps want to demand that, but after you have calmed down and thought for a few minutes you would realise that that would just not be a feasible idea: you are not the only customer that they deal with, and to justify this might not always be possible. OK, then you want the next best thing – to go back into the store and be treated like the Mayor in the place, and, depending of the type of store, you would probably receive that kind of treatment (hopefully).

But looking at this little example above, your reactions are exactly the same as any other client in a similar situation, and you need to understand this in order to be able to handle the situation properly.

In my past I have had clients bully me with physical violence, swear at me, and even threaten to abuse my family. I even had one such person warn me that they were going to set fire to the company I worked for. Don't worry – in an average sales person's life we experience these threats on an almost daily basis. **Don't take it personally!!!** It is just a natural defensive reaction for some people. Just take it in your stride. The important thing here is:

Let the client vent their anger, swear at you, threaten to boil your kneecaps and rip off your toenails to make stew, and then, when they have calmed down, begin to start resolving the situation.

So how do we do this? Well, again, think like the client. What would you like done given the same situation?

SOLVE THE PROBLEM NOW!!!

An angry person wants action, and immediately! They need some sort of recognition and resolution for their anger and unfortunately you are it!!!

The golden rule here is to solve their problem as quickly as is humanly possible so that they walk away feeling a little better for having voiced their opinions and getting what they want out of the deal.

I have mentioned elsewhere that you must make the customer feel like the most important person in the world when they approach you, but it is doubly so when you are dealing with an irate client.

Understandably, you have a million and one things to accomplish in your working day, and a complaint just confounds the issues you have in the fight against time, but you need to remember that that person can either be your advertising ally or enemy, depending on whether you are able to fix the problem or not.

Ok, so you kinda like need to drop everything that you are doing, turn the phone off, and focus on what your complainant needs to resolve the situation.

As I mentioned before, you will get some real verbal abuse, and admittedly some of it might go against your personal religion, but you have to grit your teeth and stoically accept it because eventually that person will calm down and speak rationally without the need for abusive language, and you can subsequently settle down to the problem at hand.

Under no circumstances should you contradict or interrupt the complainant whilst they are venting!

This is important, because any sort of interruption will make the client feel that psychologically you are superior to them and this will lead to further rage because they will feel that you are looking down on them. No, rather let them rant and rave until their steam has run out, and then you can start attempting to fix the situation.

Give Them a Freebie

In some circumstances you might have the ability and opportunity to offer the customer a gift to appease them whilst their problem is being rectified. Some people will appreciate this gesture, whilst some others will be astute enough to realise what you are trying to accomplish.

Yes, admittedly, this offering of a free whatever will go against your profit, but if you look at the long term consequences of your actions, the slight loss of profit, if it results in the eventual success of the situation, is a small price to pay.

Now, and this I have seen so often, many sales people tend to offer the "freebie" as something that is completely unrelated to the complaint. I feel that this is wrong because the client cannot see the value in what they are getting.

An example of this related "freebie" could be the following:

A client purchases a speed or fishing boat and it has cost them practically all their savings, and some besides. They get home and plan a holiday which includes their boat as the highlight. So they go on their holiday to a lake or whatever, but when they test the boat out properly on the water with some choppy waves, the engine keeps cutting out, but it didn't happen when it was tested back at the showroom.

Obviously the client is going to be extremely furious when they get back home and they will immediately take the boat to you for repair or replacement.

So as a tactic you could offer them some free fishing tackle, or a free tune up as an attempt to give them a "freebie" whilst you fix the problem.

This could work because once the problems have been fixed, the customer can then use their new equipment the next time they go back on holiday, or they can receive a free service when they next come back from their vacation.

These gifts are related to the original purchase and the customer will then become eager again in their investment because now they have received something else they can try out with their asset.

I see no point in offering the client a new wristwatch or sports jacket because these items can be used anywhere and not when they are playing with their boat. No, you need to think about gifts that they can use **only** with their boat.

FOLLOW UP!

Communication is extremely important under these conditions because the client had a poor attitude towards you and your company when they are upset.

Unfortunately you as a sales person do not like negativity and these negative attitudes tend to shy you away. I have done this in the past. The phone call that you need to make to let the client know what is the status of fixing their problem is the last thing you want to do, and you start finding all sorts of excuses to keep putting it off, but unfortunately you have to realise that sometimes there are things you have to do that you don't want to do.

It's like being back at school. You have a school project to do and your teacher has given you two weeks to complete, so you put it off, and put it off, until the weekend before it is due. You then make an excuse why you can't finish it on Friday. Saturday comes along and you tell yourself that you will do the work in the afternoon. Then Saturday evening comes along and you rationalise that you will be able to get it done on Sunday, and you end up spending the entire day finishing the project and skimping out on certain parts just to get the job done. The result? A lower grade from the teacher then you could've earned because you didn't pace yourself over the two weeks and planned your project well.

There is an old adage saying that goes something like:

> *"Never put off until tomorrow something you can do today!"*

This is so true and it also applies to this situation here. The longer you put something off, the more you are going to worry about it, and your imagination is going to think up the worst possible results in your mind causing anguish and fret.

Rather take the bull by the horns, make the phone call to the client, and then you will feel better for it, and you can continue with your day. And you will probably find that the results you were imagining never happened at all!

As far as the client is concerned, they appreciate those contacts more than you think, because they are also stressing about the same thing and want a little reassurance, and you need to take this into consideration the next time you need to keep a client updated.

SOMETIMES THE CUSTOMER IS WRONG!

There are some things to remember here when dealing with customer complaints.

Sometimes the fault is not your own nor your company, nor the device they have. Sometimes the blame lies with the customer.

Like for instance computers. It is not very often that computer hardware fails but software on the other hand fails or many reasons and one of those reasons is because of something the user has done. Either they have deleted something or installed another piece of software that has corrupted the computer or they have let a virus have access to their operating system, but in any event customers don't like to be told they were in the wrong. You are the same, believe me!

Admittedly we have to somehow tell the client that the damage was their doing and there is never any easy way to do this, but it has to be done.

Ok, so how to do it. Well firstly, you need to perform every check and test known to man to prove to the customer that the problem is not the computer (I'm using a computer as an example). Try to get as many unique opinions and reports as you can as proof so that the problem is narrowed down to the point that it is clear that the fault was the customer's and not your own.

Now, here comes the hard part! You need to inform the client. Firstly, never, ever belittle the client, and call them stupid or inept, or insult them in any way. It's business; try not to make it personal.

When you explain where the problem it, ask the customer what they did last when the problem occurred. A customer will always lie or leave out details because they will probably realise that they could have been at fault. But you can never tell a person outright that they are lying about what happened. If you do, or if the person realises that they are at fault they are going to argue with you and probably get angry with you.

Unfortunately you cannot get angry with the client or argue with them either. The best you can do is be firm with them and explain the problem and leave it up to them to decide whether it was their fault or not, but you can never tell them outright that it was their fault. Let them make that choice for themselves.

Yes, that client is going to probably storm out of the store, but give them time and they will calm down and eventually return to effect repairs.

CONCLUSION

Dealing with customer complaints is never an easy job and it is one that we wish we never have to ever deal with in our careers but unfortunately it is a very real part of our lives and something we have to get through.

The best advice I can give is to never lose your temper with the customer and try your best to fix the situation as quickly as possible because you really don't want to lose a client over something silly.

Summary – Chapter 14

You will always receive client complaints about yourself, your product/s, or the company you represent. Dealing with irate clients but it must be understood that this is all part of the natural sales cycle and these complaints need to be managed efficiently and quickly.

Remember:

> *"It takes thirty days to make a customer! It takes thirty seconds to lose one!!!"*

Listen With Empathy

When you listen with empathy it means that you need to look at the situation from the other person's point of view in order to understand how they are feeling, and hence to be able to adapt and work with this perspective.

Many people will be angry with you but let them vent their anger first and then, when they have calmed down, then begin to start resolving the situation.

Solve The Problem NOW!!!

Solve the complainant's problem as quickly as possible so that they walk away feeling a little better.

You need to stop everything that you are doing and focus on what your complainant needs to resolve the situation.

Under no circumstances should you contradict or interrupt the complainant whilst they are venting!

Give Them a Freebie

In some circumstances you might have the ability and opportunity to offer the customer a gift to appease them whilst their problem is being rectified but make sure that the gift is similar to their original purchase.

Follow Up!

Make sure you follow up on the problem and communicate with the client.

> *"Never put off until tomorrow something you can do today!"*

Make sure your follow up is prompt and positive.

Sometimes the Customer is Wrong!

Sometimes the fault is not your own nor your company, nor the device they have. Sometimes the blame lies with the customer.

When you do have to tell the client it is their fault ensure that you can prove it by reports.

Expect the customer to lie about what caused the problem but never contradict them or get angry with them. Rather explain what caused the problem and leave it at that.

CHAPTER 15.
COMPUTER SECURITY

When we talk of crime, we think of people dressed up in dark clothes, balaclavas covering their features, piling out of panel vans and cars, sporting a number of firearms, and robbing a bank or a store. We think of big shoot-outs with hundreds of police cars blocking streets in all directions.

We think of people being taken hostage, hijacking vehicles, murder, and worse, rape.

This has always been the case and is still rife in today's society, much to the mortification of society in general. However, with the advent of computers, and especially with the arrival of the Internet, a new wave of crime has hit the world.

Traditional crime, as described above, is what we are all used to. We see it in movies, we read about it the papers; those unfortunate few actually experience it, and it is what gives us nightmares. In today's society we call this type of crime "Blue Collar Crime". There is another level of crime, and this we call "White Collar Crime".

So what is the difference?

"White Collar Crime", or "Executive Crime" does not involve violence; it does not involve weapons and firearms. What it involves is computers, and is the stealing of information.

We now live in what is known as the "Information Age" and most of our lives are stored as data on computers somewhere in the world. Our jobs, our finances, our very identities are controlled in some way or another by computers, and individuals have learnt ways and methods to manipulate this information for their own benefit. Almost anyone, from sales people to bankers to accountants to clerks to Directors, and in fact, to anyone who has access to a computer and more often, access to the Internet, has the capability of performing White Collar Crime, and this can be just as devastating as stealing someone's car, and is no less punishable.

Unfortunately many people in today's society are not aware of the existence of this type of crime, and those that are do not realize how easy it has become to infiltrate networks of computers in order to extract or damage information for some sort of gain, be it financial or malicious. People assume that "it will never happen to me". They assume that they are not important enough to be attacked.

Wrong!

If a person is able to gain some sort of personal information from you, such as a bank account number, or identity number (in some countries we refer to these as "Social Security Numbers") they have the chance to gain the rest of your most personal information, including your personal finances, and use it to benefit them. Although dramatized in the movies for visual effect, these crimes are very much apparent, and it is no longer a fantasy – it is a reality!

This said, this chapter is devoted to explain the various types of threats that are out there in the technological world, and also details some types of protection that is available to combat these threats. Finally, I have ended this chapter with a "Do's and Don'ts" section that looks at ways of protecting yourself against most of these attacks. Of course this discussion is by no means exhaustive, and also, if you notice, I use the term "**most**" because unless we lock ourselves in a little room on a desert island somewhere, we cannot ever be impervious to the effects of White Collar Crime. But if we become proactive in our approach we can effectively immunize ourselves as much as possible to the hazards of this crime wave.

One thing I have not focused on in this chapter is actual LAN design in order to maximize security because this field is more technical in nature and hence is beyond the scope of this book.

THREATS

The following is a descriptive list of various types of potential threats to your computer and your network. Although the general public refers to all types of threats as **viruses,** this term is actually incorrect because **Viruses** are listed as a class of their own. The term we prefer to adopt as a collective term for all types of threats is **malware**, and I will rather use this term to avoid confusion. I have listed the various malware types in alphabetical order.

Adware – Sometimes developers, especially those that develop software from home or as a means to gain extra income, will approach certain companies to advertise on their behalf for some sort of remuneration. They then build these advertisements into their software before it is released onto the Internet for distribution. In this way the developer is able to recover their costs. Various forms include either the advertisement being automatically played, displayed or downloaded from the Internet after the software package has been installed and in some cases the adverts continue to appear whilst the package is being used. Some types of Adware can also be classified as **Spyware** (discussed below).

Just a little extra to add here. For many people advertising becomes bothersome and irritating, and for many of us we try to ignore or bypass advertising as much as possible. Developers, in knowing this, try to make their advertisements as annoying as possible so that we as users become irritated and attempt to get rid of the annoyances as quickly as possible. Sometimes the users accidentally click on these adverts and hence become involved in the whole concept. But the bottom line is that the advertisement has caught the user's attention, and hence in some way has served its purpose.

Auto-Diallers – In order for a hacker to gain access to your computer in any way he/she will need your computer to be connected to the Internet. Now, with the invention of ADSL and Broadband, this practice is made that much easier because computers are connected to the Internet permanently. There are however many computers and laptops that only connect to the Internet when necessary. So what an Auto-Dialler does is to continually attempt to connect to the Internet so that information can be transferred. An example of this is the extraction of email lists, or the broadcast of emails. Let me give you an example to illustrate this. By its very nature a **Virus** (explained below) will attempt to replicate itself in any way possible. An **Email Virus** will copy itself to email addresses it finds in your Contacts List, create a mail message, and then send it out. To ensure that the email is sent before you are aware of it or are able to stop the transmission an **Auto-Dialler** will be installed at the same time the virus has infected your computer so that as soon as the message has been created the Auto-Dialler will force the computer to automatically connect to the Internet and the message/s will be sent out.

Banners – **Banners** are a form of advertising that is embedded into websites and normally take on the form of some sort of image or multimedia objects using animation, video, or sound to attract as many people as possible. These banners often appear either at the bottom or top of web pages, although some appear anywhere in the page and are usually found in web sites displaying newspaper articles or editorials. **Hackers** have found ways to exploit this relatively simple and very effective form of advertising by modifying the redirection links to web pages of their design that will attempt to perform malicious damage to your computer as soon as the web page loads, or even in some cases attempt to load **Pop-Ups** (see below) to perform damage to your system.

Many Anti-Virus products have facilities whereby the banners are disabled in web browsers.

Hackers – This is a colloquial term that refers to anyone who creates any sort of malware in order to perform some sort of malicious task to your computer, ranging from actual data damage to stealing information. By definition though a **Hacker** is someone who attempts to bypass the securities that have been put in place to protect your computer in order to gain access to it.

Key Loggers – A basic definition of this term is to track or log the keys typed on a keyboard, and normally is performed without the user's knowledge. The recorded history then can help someone identify important information such as User Names and passwords. Types of these **Key**

Loggers include both software and hardware-based types (the hardware versions work at the circuitry level in a computer), remote access versions, and also kinds that take periodic screenshots of your system, thereby recording mouse clicks as well. To combat this Kaspersky Lab ® have built into their software a **Virtual Keyboard**, which is an on-screen keyboard that you can use to enter passwords thereby bypassing any sort of activity at all on your keyboard. Of course Kaspersky Lab ® have also built-in detection facilities to detect against anybody trying to snoop into your computer, such as Remote Desktop Access.

Malware – This is a holistic term that refers to all form of malicious attacks to computers and networks. Many people mistakenly refer to **Malware** as being **Viruses** but, as is discussed below, Viruses are in their own specific class with unique properties. **Malware** is the more correct term to use in generic classification.

Network Attacks – There are so many different kinds of attacks on computer networks that it would be impossible for me to explore each and every possibility in this book. There are however several valuable resources on the marketplace that deal specifically with such issues, and it is strongly recommended that, if you are more interested, run an Internet search for more information.

For this book, however, it (hopefully) will be suffice to say that **Hackers** attempt to penetrate networks on a daily basis, and several of the more common attacks deal with vulnerabilities with the computers' Operating Systems, weak password securities, weak **Network Access Controls** (discussed below), and improper email authentications. Although **Firewalls** (discussed below) and data encryption can be implemented on networks, these types of attacks need to be addressed and hence it would be advisable to enlist the services of Certified Network Security Specialists to analyse a network's weak spots and take appropriate action.

Payload – In order to do some damage to a computer you need some sort of code that will execute to perform various functions. Now in Computer Security we call this code the **Payload** of **Malware**. In order to get that code to the computer various different methods are employed, and are discussed in this section, such as **Viruses, Trojans, Worms,** and others. To explain a little differently I am going to use an example here.

You have some weapons (missiles, fi rearms, or whatever) that you need delivered to your army in another country so that they can fight a war. Let's call these weapons the **Payload.** Now, there are various different ways we can get those weapons to our forces. We can fly them in, or load them into trucks and drive them through. What about loading them onto a boat or submarine, if your army is near water? Another option is to put them into a train. Whatever the method, this would be the **Malware** part of the operation - the transport.

Phishing – This strange term refers to a type of malware that attempts to obtain personal information from bogus emails. Let me give you an example to explain a bit further.

You have often seen in movies the FBI (or other similar organizations) cripple fugitives by accessing their bank accounts and manipulating them in some way as to disable them thereby preventing the fugitive access to cash, identity numbers, etc. Now hackers have realized that by obtaining someone's personal information through a bank they will effectively have access to that person's identity number, bank account number, their password, and hence their financial status. In **Phishing** hackers create false emails that look extremely authentic, complete with the bank's logo and other registered information. They send these out to various people stating that their personal information needs to be updated for some or other reason. Most consumers are not aware that these phishing emails exist and thus most people will innocently complete the requested information and return the email, and give the hacker **all** their information, and access to their personal finances. It is precisely for this reason that banks will **never, ever** send you any sort of email of this nature at all.

In the "Do's and Don'ts" section below we will discuss ways to avoid this.

Pop-Ups – Originally these were purely designed as an advertising gimmick, but potential **Hackers** cottoned on to this idea and realized that some malicious damage can be wrought using this technique. I am getting a little ahead of myself here because some of you probably are not sure as to what these things are, so let me elaborate.

When you access certain websites small auxiliary windows automatically **pops up** (hence the name) informing you of something, and they are usually related to advertising. You need to perform some sort of action (clicking on "OK" or closing the window) before it disappears but the main function is to get you to notice the information it is trying to impart. Now would-be hackers can capitalize on this by attaching code that executes either automatically as the window opens or executes once you have performed some sort of action on the window, thereby effectively infecting your computer.

Many Anti-Virus products protect against this by either disabling pop-ups in the software's settings or scanning the window beforehand to see if there is any attached code and if so, the window will be disabled. In later versions of popular Internet Browsers this feature has also been built in, and you need to be aware of this because in some cases the action of downloading files can be prevented by your settings because some Website Developers use Pop-Ups to action the task of downloading files. It is a simple matter in this case – a notification at the top of your browser window will warn you of this and you can take necessary steps to temporarily disable the blocking feature in order to access the Pop-Up window.

Rootkits – This is a relatively unknown term in the Layman's world, but is quite a damaging type of malware. Only a few Anti-Virus vendors have built protection against these types of attacks into their products, so you need to ensure that the product you use has this facility. Luckily Kaspersky Lab ® has this built into all of their products.

So what exactly is a **Rootkit**? I am going to tell you a story as to how they originated. For obvious reasons I cannot mention any names but it is suffice to say that the company involved is quite a prominent corporation in today's society.

In the late 1980's and early 1990's, with the invention of the CDROM drive, it became possible for people to play ordinary audio (music) CD's in their computer. Then some enterprising individuals developed software that allowed the copying of these CD's onto the computer and onto other CD's. Now, in order to hamper piracy, this company built a small amount of code in each of their music CD's. So when somebody put these CD's into their computer, the code would unobtrusively install itself into the system thereby preventing any sort of copying of the music either onto the hard drive or onto other discs. Although the intentions were honourable, the method was, and still is, illegal. Why?

By accepted International Law, any software may not install itself into any computer without the user's knowledge and hence their permission. This software installed itself without the user's knowledge whatsoever, thus contravening International Regulations. In actual fact there was quite a large court case and invariably the company responsible lost the lawsuit. This very practice led to the invention of **Rootkits** and has evolved into a very dangerous type of malware.

When people visit the Internet, and happen to come across questionable websites, sometimes they expose themselves to these Rootkits. **Hackers** (explained below) develop these applications so that as soon as a user visits their website the code is downloaded and installed into the local computer **without the user even knowing that it is happening at all!** Without some sort of protection these malware can wreak untold havoc with users' computers!

Spam – This is covered in great detail in Chapter 17 so I am not going to go into any specifics here. As a short definition I will say that **Spam** constitutes unsolicited, or unwanted email.

Spyware – By definition, **Spyware** is a type of **malware** that installs onto computers and collects information about the user without their knowledge, and hence in most cases Spyware unobtrusively installs onto the machine and operates in the background so as to not alert the user as to its presence. An example of Spyware is **Key Loggers** (explained above) that install onto public computers so that activities of various users can be monitored.

Although the primary function of Spyware is to collect personal information about users, they can also slow down the functionality of web browsers, change home pages, prevent users from installing additional software, and alter functionality of previously installed applications.

In some instances **Adware** (described above) can be classified as **Spyware** in that there are certain variations of Adware that actually monitor your surfing habits and display advertisements accordingly. For example, let's assume you are interested in model building (planes, boats, trains, etc) and you frequently surf the Internet looking for information on this hobby. The Spyware/ Adware will look at your browsing history and then display specials on various kits and accessories offered from popular vendors based upon your hobby.

There are several products on the market that offer Anti-Spyware, but the more popular Anti-Virus products have this facility built in so that you do not need to purchase an additional product.

Trojans – **Trojans** are, by definition, a type of malware that infiltrates computers, but they have special properties. To explain exactly what these are I am going to give you a bit of history. Most of you should know this story but for the sake of clarification I'm going to briefly explain it again.

In ancient history there was a famous war between the Greeks and Troy, and the invading Greek army was unable to penetrate the city of Troy. So the Greek army built an enormous wooden horse and presented it as a gift to the Trojans by leaving it in front of the city gates. The Queen, Helen, thought it was a peace offering and hence had it brought into the city, where it sat in the central courtyard for the entire day. What the Trojans were unaware of, however, was that the Greeks had hidden a small invading force inside the body of the structure, and when the city finally shut down to sleep in the evening, the invaders exited out of the statue, opened the city gates, and thus the Greek army was able to enter the city.

So how does this relate to computer viruses? There are millions of different applications available on the Internet, the majority of which are designed by amateur software developers who share their projects with the public. These applications we dub "Shareware" and most of the time they are free, although in some instances a small fee is charged. There are so many examples of these applications that I will not even go into the myriad of these types. Some developers, due to various reasons, design code within these applications that will secretly execute once the application is installed into the computer. To make things a little clearer, I'm going to give you an example.

Let's say for example you have downloaded and installed a simple shareware game involving crosswords. Now the developer has built into the game some code that will execute in some way that will end up deleting half of your Operating System! The next time you boot your computer, half of the system is no longer there thus forcing you to reinstall the entire machine! Of course, the hidden code could perform anything from gaining passwords, etc to gathering email addresses. It is not important for this discussion as to what the code does – the important thing is that **something** is executed!

Thus, in computer terms here, the **Trojan** is the actual game itself; it is the wooden horse that carries the **payload** – the invading army, or code that damages the computer in some way.

Although Anti-Virus vendors attempt to detect and identify as many Trojans as possible, thousands of new types are exposed to the Internet on a daily basis, and thus it is up to you as the sales person to educate your clients as to the do's and don'ts of Internet practice. These are covered later in this chapter.

Viruses – Viruses have been in existence since the invention of the Personal Computer in the 1980's, and the name has become a buzzword in modern conversation the world over. Most people use this term to describe almost any attack on a computer but by definition **Viruses** are classed as being of a more specific type. The more correct collective term for computer attacks is **Malware** (as described above).

The explanation of viruses is actually quite simple, and can be defined as **something designed to infiltrate and cause malicious damage**. In medical terms we know this as being a virus that enters a body (animal or human), infiltrates and causes damage to the body, resulting in **disease**, illness, and in some cases, death. Now, we are going to expand a little more on this definition because another important feature of the virus is **to replicate itself**, and is done as quickly as possible, thereby firstly to protect the existence of the species and secondly to inflict as much damage as possible. Of course, in Biology the virus is actually not aware that it is inflicting damage at all: its primary goal is the protection of the species as a whole. But yes, it is a foreign invader and the result of its replication does wreak havoc with the body.

So, in computer terms, the exact same process happens. A **Computer Virus** will penetrate a computer and attempt to duplicate itself as quickly as possible in order to spread as widely as it can. If it can access other computers in the process (such as over a network) it will quite happily do so. However, unlike a biological virus, computer viruses are designed by human beings, and hence there is almost always an ulterior motive behind the creation of the virus in the first place. This motive is normally one of malicious damage and will attempt to corrupt or destroy data stored in the computer. Alternatively, some viruses are designed to copy information and attempt to send the data back to the designer for use in some way.

The **payload** (the actual part of the virus that does the damage) varies so dramatically that I cannot even attempt to explain to you the results – it is purely up to the imagination of the developer as to what they hope to achieve. What I will say though is that almost all of these viruses are restricted to **software** damage. There are only three viruses that I know of that actually damages the physical hardware. I will explain each below but for obvious reasons I will not mention the names of the culprits. Of course there may be many others out there – I only personally know of these three, but it gives you an indication of what these people are capable of creating.

- **Virus 1** – This virus attacks the BIOS (**B**asic **I**nput/ **O**utput **S**ystem) of the computer. To briefly explain the BIOS chip stores the basic information about the computer that instructs the circuitry to behave in certain ways that enables the computer to operate as it is designed to do. Amongst other functions it also tells the computer how to load the Operating System. Now this virus actually clears the code on the physical computer chip, thereby rendering the hardware useless until new code can be programmed into the BIOS chip.

- **Virus 2** – This one fragments the hard drive so dramatically and so quickly that eventually the read/ write heads actually burn out (or rather, the motor that drives the heads burns out) from overuse. We say, in computer terms, that the hard drive has "crashed".

- **Virus 3** – This one was quite interesting. Computer monitors and graphics cards are designed to operate at certain frequencies. If you attempt to increase the frequency past the devices' capabilities you will not be able to view anything on your screen because they are not capable of decoding instructions at those speeds. What this virus actually does is to **force** the hardware to attempt to execute those instructions at frequencies that are way past their capabilities. The net result: either the monitor or the graphics card, or both, physically burn out.

In the Do's and Don'ts section I will discuss ways to protect and to prevent damage from viruses.

A final note on this topic! Many people speculate as to the reason for the existence of viruses. Some people ascertain that Anti-Virus Vendors actually hire people to create these viruses for testing purposes and as a way of actually creating revenue for the vendor.

If the virus exists it give a reason for the vendor to create software to protect against attacks, thereby generating business. In other cases, it is assumed that a developer actually creates these invaders on purpose because "they want to see what happens". In other cases viruses are created quite by accident – the developer, having written some code to perform a completely legitimate function, actually creates a virus instead because of errors in their coding.

Whatever the case, the fact is there are on average 200 new strains of virus that enter the Internet on a daily basis, whatever the reason for their creation in the first place, and hence it is vital that you obtain an Anti-Virus product that responds as quickly as possible to meet and counteract these threats before they can do some serious damage.

More about this in the Do's and Don'ts section.

Worms – This is a specialized type of **Virus** that's sole primary concern is self- replication and it uses some sort of network program to send copies of itself to other computers on the network. However, it differs from viruses in that it does not need to attach itself to any other existing program.

Another big difference is that **Worms** will always do some sort of harm to a network, if only to clog the network's bandwidth, whereas **Viruses** will only corrupt files on a targeted computer. Many worms are only concerned with spreading, and do not attempt to corrupt or any way alter the systems they infect. However, there are several Worms that do have **Payloads** (discussed above) that cause additional damage to computers.

PROTECTION

In order to protect yourself from such threats as discussed above it is imperative that you implement some sort of protection for your computers and networks. In this section I have described some of the more popular types of protection available to meet these demands, but of course there are several more types that are accessible in the marketplace. Again I have listed these in alphabetical order.

Anti-Virus – Throughout this book I have discussed the Kaspersky Lab ® family of security products because I have personally worked with them and have come to know and trust them implicitly. Of course there are several other brands of products on the market that are equally as good, but in selecting a product for use on your personal computer or network, you need to bear in mind that it needs to contain protection against the forms of attacks I have discussed above. I am not going to go into detail as to the features of these products because this I have already discussed in Chapter 6. Suffice it is to say that you need to shop carefully when selecting a product, and as a suggestion here take a look at some of the independent testing companies out there (AV Comparatives is one example) to gain an understanding of the rating of the various products on the market before you commit yourself to actually purchasing one. Also, most products allow you a trial basis to test the software, and you could also look into trying some of these out for yourself. Just a note here: if you do test several different brands be sure to uninstall the previous brand before installing the new brand otherwise there may be several conflicts on your computer.

Content Security Filters – These are often software devices but there are hardware versions available. They can be standalone products or can be incorporated as modules into other products such as Anti-Virus products or **Firewalls** (discussed below). Now what these filters do is to limit the internal network as to how much access the clients can have to the Internet in terms of which websites are allowed and prohibited as the case may be. Common to these filters are such categories as **Black Lists** and **White Lists** and these contain lists of websites that are either taboo (Black List) or acceptable (White List). Examples of Black Listed sites are those containing sex, notorious hacker and warez (sites that share pirated software and serial numbers) sites, gaming sites, and now, the infamous Facebook and related sites. Now, there are so many new websites that are developed and launched on a daily basis that local Network Administrators are hard-pressed to list each and every one. Of course most filters contain a keyword feature that scans websites for potential keyword matches but website developers are becoming even more ingenious at hiding the true nature of their creations and thus it is not always an infallible solution. Instead, many popular Content Security Filters report periodically back to some sort of centralized database facility that is housed at the vendor's offices to update their own local databases. Furthermore, the filters report any new potentially damaging website back to the central database so that it can be broadcast back to the other currently installed filters. Unfortunately, due to different designs and technology these databases are normally limited as to be brand-specific.

Adrian Noble

Most filters also include facilities whereby local administrators can further configure these lists and add or subtract additional criteria based upon their company's specific needs.

Furthermore, some filters have additional features that can limit the times spent surfing the Internet. This ensures that staff concentrate on their work and limit their personal surfing habits to either their lunchtimes or after normal office hours.

Digital Certificates – I am sure most of you have heard about the famous Mark Shuttleworth from South Africa, who created a company in his garage and sold it eventually for a fortune? Well, his company involved the creation of **Digital Certificates**. Now basically what these consist of are virtual labels of authenticity on websites.

Huh?

Right, let me try to explain. When you purchase an Operating System from Microsoft ® you are presented, amongst other things, a label with all sorts of watermarks and metal linings that contain your serial key for the product. These Labels of Authenticity supplied by Microsoft ® ensure that the product you have purchased is genuine and has not been pirated or tampered with in any way.

Now in websites we have similar concepts. You create a website and you have it indexed in the normal way. Now, you wish to ensure that as many people will visit your website and will **trust** it, so you apply for a **Digital Certificate**. What this entails is shipping your complete website off to a company who specializes in checking every aspect of your project to ensure that there are no errors, is secure, and is legitimate. Once this has been achieved that company issues a Digital Certificate and records your website in a central database. Now the certificate itself contains a specific coded identification number. Many **Content Security Filters** (explained above) actually check for the existence of these certificates and if found, the website is automatically deemed to be trusted without any quibbles. Mark Shuttleworth's company performed this exact function, incidentally. Examples of trusted websites are those that belong to banks.

Others are Governmental websites (not necessarily all, but most are Digitally Signed). If you as a user visit one of these websites you can be sure that it is trusted and there will not be any security issues evolving from these visits.

Firewalls – These are either hardware or software-based devices that are designed to allow authorized communications to occur within networks and between networks whilst blocking any sort of unauthorized access. There are several methods that are employed to prevent access where applicable and often combinations of different methods are used simultaneously.

To put the definition another way, **firewalls** inspect network traffic passing through, and allow or deny the information transfer based upon a predetermined and configured set of rules.

It must be understood that **firewalls** do not, by their very function, detect any sort of malware other than network attacks and hence an Anti-Virus product needs to be installed and configured on the firewall, and it is this module, which scans the network traffic for malware.

**Network
Access
Control –**   Whenever a computer, laptop, or other mobile
device such as a cellphone, Smart Phone, or PDA
attempts to connect to a computer network it
will not be allowed any sort of access unless it
complies with a specific set of rules, including
Anti-Virus, Systems updates, and configuration,
provided an NAC solution is installed onto
that network. As soon as the device connects to
the network it is scanned by the NAC system
and only after it has met the requirements
determined by the NAC (and configured by the
Network Administrator) will it be given access
to the network and its resources.

To give you an example of the protection that NAC offers,
let's assume there is an intruder in your office building who is
attempting to access your network. Now, with wireless technology,
this can be easily achieved even if the intruder is sitting in the
office toilets with a handheld PDA device. As long as he or she
has a signal they can attempt to connect to the internal network.
Without NAC the chances of intrusion are that much easier
because there is nothing there to check if the device **belongs** to
that network at all.

A very useful feature of many NAC solutions is to enforce
standards upon non-compliant devices before admission is
granted.

For instance, ***Kaspersky Endpoint Security for Business***®
is Cisco®-NAC compliant, and when the Cisco® NAC detects a
non-compliant device, it instructs ***Kaspersky Security Center***®
to attempt to deploy a local copy of the Anti-Malware software
onto the intruding device before it meets the network's standards
in terms of Anti-Virus compliancy.

Network Monitors – Network Monitors continuously monitor networks for instances of failure or increased activity. Most often these monitors are physical devices that connect into the network through an Ethernet port on a switch connected into the network.

They are extremely configurable and there are several different activities that can be effectively monitored.

They can detect the failure of network devices, increased activity (in the case of users downloading large fi les on a computer, for instance), and email activity, including email broadcasts.

With this monitoring it is possible to identify network attacks by analysing increased activity in a particular firewall, for instance, and the results can be used to locate potential security risks in a network.

Proxy Servers – A **Proxy Server** serves two main functions. Before we get into those roles, I just want to explain something. By definition a Proxy Server is a separate server that exists between an internal network and the Internet, but there is no reason why the software application can exist on an existing server, thus sharing the roles with another software component of the server family.

The first role that a Proxy Server performs is that of protection. How this operates is that to the outside world (i.e. the Internet, other networks, hackers, etc) the internal network is hidden and the only computer that can be identified from the outside is the Proxy Server itself. In this respect then companies can protect the identities of their internal computers from prying eyes.

The second role the Proxy Server performs is that of **caching**. Right, explanation time! Every time your computer downloads a website it downloads **all** the information associated with it (graphics, code, cookies, scripts, etc). This can slow the entire process down and also lead to increased bandwidth usage resulting in speed losses and cost increases. What a Proxy Server does is to download the web page on behalf of the client and then store portions of that website locally so that when the website is revisited, either by that same user or by another, most of the website has already been stored locally and hence only the portions that have changed need be downloaded; the rest is supplied to the client by the Proxy Server. This dramatically improves performance, reduces bandwidth usage, and decreases costs involved.

Spam Filters –As discussed earlier in this chapter, Spam is covered in great detail in Chapter 17 so I am not going to reinvent the wheel by discussing this again. Rather I am just going to touch on a couple of points here. A **Spam Filter**, as the name suggests, monitors all incoming email and identifies legitimate email from spam based on a predetermined set of rules and keywords. These rules and keywords are normally preconfigured in the software itself or by Network Administrators. Most often **Internet Service Providers** (ISP's) have these in place to block the more common spam email, but there are some problems associated with this practice.

Let me explain.

Let's assume there is a type of email that advertising winning free cash on a virtual lottery. Of course many such emails have been created and broadcast and it has become generally accepted that this constitutes Spam, so the ISP configures this into their Anti-Spam filter. There are however some clients who actually would like to receive those mails for their own personal reasons, and hence the ISP then has to remove that ruling resulting in unsuspecting clients again receiving those unwanted mails.

This then becomes a catch-22 situation because the ISP cannot accurately determine the level of filtration that will suite each and every client. This becomes even more of a challenge when your client base is extremely large. Take the large organizations for example, Google, Excite, Yahoo, etc, who service literally millions of subscribers. In these cases they cannot actually use any sort of Spam Filter because the criteria are just too complex.

The answer? Take a look at the Do's and Don'ts section for solutions.

DO'S AND DON'TS

In this section I have listed some Do's and Don'ts that will serve to protect you against most forms of malicious attacks. Obviously this list is by no means exhaustive and there are many of you readers who will say, "Well, he didn't think of this or include that!" and you will be definitely right in that regard because there will be areas of protection that I have overlooked, but hopefully this section will give you some ideas as to how to protect yourself and to think proactively to prevent damage in the future.

Anti-Virus Products – In this chapter, and in Chapter 6, and throughout this book I have discussed Anti-Virus products because they are vital to the protection of your computer against malicious attacks. I hope I have stressed the importance of these products in this book since these threats are very real indeed! Now there are a few Do's and Don'ts you need to be aware of with your Anti-Virus products.

Subscriptions – When you purchase your preferred product it is normally provided with a subscription. Often the default subscription offered spans the duration of 12 months, although 24 and 36-month subscriptions are available. What these enable the user (or rather, the computer) to do is to obtain Virus List updates and software upgrades and/or patches. The Vendor of the software release updated Virus Lists, which contain the latest detected threats of all the malware that is currently in circuit. As new threats are detected the correct antidotes are coded by the vendor's Technical Departments and inserted into the Virus Lists, which are then released to the public for local download. Also, various software patches, updates and new versions are periodically developed and released in a similar manner for local download to update the user's own version of their software.

In order to gain the advantages of such updates the computer must firstly be connected to the Internet, if not permanently, then at least occasionally so that these updates can be automatically downloaded and installed. This then ensures that the product is always up to date to meet the latest challenges.

When the Subscription Period nears its completion the software will in some way or another warn the user that a renewal is imminent, and if the period expires, the software will no longer continue to obtain any updates from the Internet, thus eventually rendering the product useless. It is imperative that users are aware of this and budget for annual renewals.

Execution - In order for the software to be effective it must be permanently executed in the computer. Normally it runs in the background and does not hamper the overall performance of the computer. There are times however that users actively look for ways of improving their computer's performance, such as when games or intensive graphical-based applications are run, and it is at these times that users attempt to disable their Anti-Malware software in order to eke out a little more performance for their system. In the Personal family of products Kaspersky Lab ® have a built-in Gaming setting with their new 2015 versions, and what happens is that when such a program is executed the Kaspersky Lab ® product (either Anti-Virus or Internet Security) will temporarily reduce its footprint to give the application that extra performance it needs to run correctly. This same setting can also be used for graphical intensive software such as CAD programs and other drawing packages.

In the network versions (Kaspersky Lab ® call it ***Endpoint Security for Business***, covered in Chapter 6) certain policies and profiles can be configured by the System Administrator to prevent users from tampering with their Anti-Malware in any way, thus preventing potential security leaks into the network by a user temporarily disabling their local copy consequently allowing a malware threat to gain access into the network.

Scans -   Although the computer is protected it is advisable to schedule a complete system scan at least once a week to ensure that a threat has not been able to bypass the initial protection screens and infiltrate itself into the internal system. You must remember that, regardless of the speed of your vendor in releasing those updates, they must always be **reactive** in their approach to threats and thus there is always a chance that some might just get through. This being said attempt to schedule the scans for when you will not be busy on the computer, such as weekends or evenings. Of course, in a network scenario, this will have been configured centrally by the System Administrator and hence will essentially be out of your hands, but in a Personal Security scenario you must govern your own schedules.

Backups – No matter what you do with your computer, there is a golden cardinal rule that states:

"Always backup your system!"

Read any computer book, or install any software, or talk to anybody about computers; you will always come across this rule. In business backups are normally performed on a daily basis, and in home situations it is advisable to schedule these for once a week. For those of you in the dark, **backups** are copies of the data stored on your hard drive, and are vital in the event of any sort of malfunction, whether it is software-based or hardware-based, because in many cases the data stored is extremely important, and especially so in business environments. By scheduling regular backups you ensure that if you are unfortunate enough to be attacked by a malware threat, and it does irreparable damage to your system, you are able to restore most of your data quite easily once the threat has been successfully eradicated from your system.

Emailing – I have covered quite a bit of information on this topic in Chapter 17, but there are just a couple of pointers I just want to make here.

Firstly, before you send or receive emails ensure that your Anti-Virus software is active. Next, be careful when sending out emails with attachments. The latest versions of email clients have, by default, certain securities that prevent certain types of attachments from being opened because they might contain malware. Ensure that your attachments are not executable files in any way.

When receiving mail, your Anti-Virus software (if active) will warn you before downloading the mail to your computer. Look through the list of incoming mails to make sure that you identify the recipients and the nature of the message. If you are unsure as to either the recipient or the subject matter, rather delete the mail. And be especially aware of those mails containing attachments.

Hard Copy Disposal – There are times in our lives that force us to print information out (we call printed material **Hard Copies** in the computer world) in order for it to be useful to us. Some of that printed material will on occasion contain some or all of our personal information. Examples of this are receipts from your local ATM when you draw money. Also, bank statements are another example. How about when you apply for a new job, and the forms you have to fill in contain much of your personal information? And don't forget hard copies of your Curriculum Vitae? The bottom line is that we print our personal information frequently, and then what do we do with it? We either store it in our wallets or purses (in the case of ATM slips), in our offices, and in our homes (and if you are anything like me, I throw it in a corner on the kitchen counter). When these papers build up enough, we scrunch it up and toss it in the bin. So ok, the garbage people collect what you throw away once a week and take it to the local dump. Now this is a scary thought: what happens after that rubbish has left you?

In the world today unemployment is a very real factor and it affects quite a large percentage of the global population. Take a stroll around your local town, especially in the evenings. How many homeless people did you identify? Now think about this for a second. How many of those homeless people are educated just like you and me? How many of those people have had at one stage of their lives had decent jobs and due to unfortunate circumstances have been forced out onto the street?

Those homeless people have a few choices to make and when their stomachs are hungry it makes them do some crazy things such as turn to crime to ease their suffering. Of course they can attempt to rob stores but that means they need weapons and other resources that they just don't have access to. But some of them know how to use computers, and they probably know of other people who are very good at using computers. They might even know of a few hackers. So think about this for a second. How can they go about getting hold of some bank accounts to rob, or at least sell the information to hackers for their use? Why not visit the local rubbish dump? There are bound to be plenty of papers with this kind of information that unsuspecting people have thrown away. Hey, why not just visit any ATM, because there normally is a small bin placed in front of the machine whereby people throw the receipts away after they have used the machines.

Do you get my point here? **Anybody can steal your information if you let them!!!** It is even worse if your company follows a similar nonchalant practice.

That's why Paper Shredders were invented. They effectively shred paper into several small strips that, when mixed up in the paper bin, becomes almost impossible to put back together, and thus the information printed on them is effectively lost. Now I'm not saying that you should purchase a paper shredder for use at home, but get into the habit of tearing up such documentation before you throw it away. This minimizes the chance of somebody piecing the bits together to obtain a workable copy. Also, try not to keep documentation of this nature in your purse, handbag, wallet or briefcase, because if you are mugged in the street then you have just handed your identity over to the perpetrators.

Personal Spam Filters – As discussed earlier in this chapter Spam Filters are extremely useful in sifting through the collage of emails you receive on a daily basis to determine the legitimate ones from the junk mails, but ISP's are not always able to enforce accurate **Spam Filters**. It is therefore up to you (or your network administrator) to install and configure one on your local computer.

Most personal Anti-Virus products have one built in, and at a network level specific modules can be installed at a server level that will further assist with filtration. Now the desktop versions (the ones on your personal computer) can be quite easily configured to suit your needs as you see fi t and many of them are quite user friendly. The filter that is supplied with Kaspersky Lab ®'s *Internet Security*, for instance, is almost intelligent in that, once it is trained, it identifies strains in received emails that look like Spam and will react accordingly. How this works from a nontechnical perspective is you load with a few mails in the beginning – 15 or 20 to start with. These test mails should consist of both legitimate mails and Spam mails, and you instruct the software to differentiate between Spam mails and normal mails. Based upon the findings with your examples it will continue to intelligently identify incoming mails in the future, and given time the results will become extremely accurate.

Removable Media – There are various ways of getting information into a computer other than through a network or the Internet. Historically two types of drives were developed and were known as **Floppy Disk Drives** and **Stiffy Disk Drives**. Floppy disks were 5.25" magnetic disks housed in square plastic covers and were able to store a total of 360kb of information. Later on the 3.5" Stiffy disk took over, and was able to contain a maximum of 1.44 Mb of information. In today's society we now use **CD**'s and **DVD**'s to load information into computers, and also **Flash Drives** (also known as **Memory Sticks**) to do the same job. Removable hard drives are also another example.

The result: we have several different ways of getting malware into computers without having to resort to the Internet to do the damage. We as users need to be careful when transferring information from any of these media into our computers because they could have collected some malware from a source and hence can transfer it into your computer.

To combat this your need to ensure that your Anti-Virus software is running as it will scan these media every time they are inserted into your computer for malware.

Software – I think all of us like to get things for free and software is no different. How many times have you surfed the Internet and come across "free software"? You've downloaded them, installed them onto your computer to see how they work, and then ended up with only part of the software working because they are only trial versions and you need to purchase full versions. Then you have turned to Shareware Software for free alternatives only to find that the software doesn't work properly.

Now you need to be extremely careful when you download software because sometimes the software contains bugs and doesn't work properly resulting in damage to your Operating System. Still other software downloads all sorts of advertisements onto your computer. And, in the worst case scenario, the software contains hidden malware that installs onto your computer and infects it. The unfortunate rule of the game is to try to stick to legitimate software that you have purchased. Also, that software– try wherever possible to purchase it from a store in a sealed package so that you know that it hasn't been tampered with in any way. If you have to purchase it online, make sure that the website is secure (because of your credit card details) and check its Digital Certificate's authenticity wherever possible.

Before installing any sort of software, make sure that you have a recent backup of your system before you continue, and ensure that your Anti-Virus is running before continuing, especially on software you have downloaded from the Internet.

On last note here: beware of pirated software. It's one thing to locate a serial key on the Internet and use it on commercial software; it's quite another to use a "crack" piece of software that is supplied which you need to run in order to pirate commercial software. Some of these "cracks" contain some sort of malware.

Strong passwords – How many of you have created passwords for your computers, email accounts, and Internet accounts using your names, the names of your spouses, your children, and your pets? Come on, be honest! Raise your hand! Right, back to the movies! How many times have we seen (or read in novels) about the average Police Detective cracking a password in a matter of minutes because they guessed a birthday, or a spouse's name, or something similar?

Sorry guys, this unfortunately happens in reality every day, in all sorts of environments. Most people battle to remember information especially when they are busy. To some people the mere creation of a password for their computer becomes a mundane task so they choose things that they will easily remember, and these become cinches for hackers to crack, particularly when the hacker has gained some personal information about their victim. Also, there are several applications that randomly "guess" most commonly used passwords, both alphabetical and numeric. So how do we prevent this from happening?

There are some basic rules to adhere to, and due to security reasons Network Administrators have enforced many of these on local networks as well as on websites to ensure that users do not take short cuts on security. After all, if a network is breached because of a simple password hack, an entire company could be at risk and the administrator could be out of a job. From your part it does help if you understand some of the rules and stick to them. Eventually these become habits, and assist with your security.

- **Alphanumeric Passwords** – The first rule to examine is that of using a combination of alphabetical characters and numbers combined together to make up a password. As discussed several applications have been developed that guess either purely numeric passwords or alphabetical passwords but it is seldom that these types of applications are capable of doing both because the combinations involved are just too great. Of course you could combine your pet's name with your birthday but this is just asking for trouble. Try to mix the letters and numbers up together to create a completely random combination.

- **Uppercase and Lowercase** – The standard character set is based upon a standard called ASCII and consists of 255 characters, although there are several more in the extended set. These include Uppercase and Lowercase characters, and special characters such as various punctuation marks and other symbols. In the ASCII world, Uppercase and Lowercase characters have different values, so a lower case "a" would return a different value than Uppercase "A". When entering passwords these come into effect, so combining

Uppercase and Lowercase combinations of letters in your passwords further enhances password security.

- **Punctuation Characters** – Sometimes throwing in a few punctuation characters such as "!" and "." Can dramatically enhance the security level of a password especially when they are included in the middle of passwords. Try to include at least one of these.

- **Password Length** – It stands to reason that the longer your password is the more difficult it is to hack because of the many possible combinations that are likely given the length of the password you select. In fact, certain applications and especially particular websites actually demand a limit on the minimal number of characters/ numbers that you can use. In order to be on the safe side you should not limit your password to less than 6 characters/numbers.

- **Password Rotation** – People are lazy; this is a given scientific fact. Those people that are hard workers only do so through a certain amount of discipline but in general the human being lazy entity. Why do I stress this? Because, given the opportunity (or lack thereof) most people will not ever to bother to change their passwords from time to time. Those that do have disciplined themselves, or else, their local network administrators have enforced a policy that forces password changes after prescribed durations. It is important to change your password from time to time because of a number of reasons of security. Firstly, if there is a hacker out there that has been consistently working at trying to crack your password, chances are that he or she will eventually succeed. If they use software to assist them then the likelihood of this happening will definitely increase. Secondly, if you just happen to enter your password whilst a colleague is standing over your shoulder, there is a possibility that he or she can guess your password based on the keys you depress on your keyboard. That colleague can then gain access to your computer.

- **Unattendance** – In any network scenario there are several users sharing resources for various reasons. Each user has a different agenda and hence they will have different needs to each other. Similarly, people are by their very nature individuals (even twins have different personalities) and because of this users have different preferences on their computers. It is for this reason that **User Profiles** were invented so that when a user logs onto a computer their personal settings are loaded and they can begin working. Part of the profile is to store the user's personal information such as websites they have visited and their documents, as well as other miscellaneous settings.

Although you should be in front of your computer all day every day, there will be times when you will have to leave your computer unattended for a while for such reasons as toilet breaks, lunch breaks, and other emergencies. Many users don't even think about this but during those breaks anyone is able to access your computer. If your profile is loaded, and your account has not been secured, anybody can jump onto your computer and do whatever with it and your profile, together with your personal information, can be affected. I am not saying that people purposefully follow this practice in order to damage your profile, but some will take the chance to "quickly" check-up something on the Internet and could inadvertently do something that damages your profile rendering your data useless.

Let me give you a prime example of this. In a typical university there are thousands of students who have legitimate access to the central network for various reasons. The big problem here is that the university only has a limited number of available computers so the students have to share the same computer at different times of the day. Sometimes hundreds of different profiles are loaded onto a single computer in a week. Now can you imagine you left your profile unsecured whilst you go off to lectures? How many people will be able to play around with your profile in your absence? Scary thought indeed!

Microsoft ® have built a locking feature into the Windows Operating System that allows you to lock your computer whilst you are away, and thus, without the correct password, nobody can access your computer unless they are an administrator or they reboot the computer. Either way your profile will automatically log off thereby protecting your personal data from others. Get into this habit even when you go for quick coffee or toilet breaks and you will be sure that your data is secure.

Websites –   We all love to surf the Internet! Agreed? Of course! And we all do it for different reasons, whether it is for information gathering, entertainment (including adult in some cases), gaming, music, or whatever. The point is that the average user accesses thousands of websites in their lives and not all of them are legitimate, or contain Digital Certificates. There will be times that you will come across unsecured websites and you need to be careful which ones you access. First and foremost, make sure your Anti-Virus is switched on and running properly before you climb into a heavy surfing session! Next thing, when running a search on Google or other popular search engines, try to limit your selections from the first 20 results. Results listed past that might have links to questionable websites. Try not to be side-tracked by the many advertisements you come across in your travels because not only do they interrupt your concentration and leave you immersed in completely different missions, some of them might contain malware. Lastly, if you need to enter any sort of personal information make sure that the website is secured (in the case of account numbers, credit card details, etc) and if unsecured, try not to give any specifics such as your address or telephone number.

Last little bit of advice here: clear out your Internet History every once in a while. This clears up space on your hard drive and prevents any of your personal information to fall into the wrong hands.

CONCLUSION

Unfortunately, given the way that computers have affected and altered our lives, we must be acutely aware that White Collar Crime exists in all walks of life and because of this we need to become more aware of the possibilities of exploitation in our lives, and more specifically, our information.

We need to become more proactive in defending ourselves against as many forms of attack as possible, so that we are not affected by the results of these intrusions.

SUMMARY – CHAPTER 15

"White Collar Crime", or "Executive Crime" involves computers, and is the stealing of information.

This chapter explains the various types of threats available and also details some types of protection that combats these threats. There is also a "Do's and Don'ts" section that looks at ways of protecting yourself against most of these attacks.

THREATS

The following is a descriptive list of various types of potential threats to your computer and your network and are listed in alphabetical order.

Adware – In order to generate extra revenue software developers approach various companies and offer to advertise on their behalf for remuneration. These advertisements are built into software before release. Various forms include either the advertisement being automatically played, displayed or downloaded from the Internet after the software package has been installed and in some cases the adverts continue to appear whilst the package is being used. Some types of Adware can also be classified as **Spyware**.

Auto-Diallers –Auto-Diallers attempt to continually connect your computer to the Internet so that Hackers can gain access to it for various reasons.

Banners – **Banners** are a form of advertising that is embedded into websites and normally take on the form of some sort of image or multimedia objects using animation, video, or sound to attract as many people as possible. These banners often appear either at the bottom or top of web pages, although some appear anywhere in the page and are usually found in web sites displaying newspaper articles or editorials.

Hackers – This is a colloquial term that refers to anyone who creates any sort of malware in order to perform some sort of malicious task to your computer, ranging from actual data damage to stealing information. By definition though a **Hacker** is someone who attempts to bypass the securities that have been put in place to protect your computer in order to gain access to it.

Key Loggers – Key Loggers tracks or logs the keys typed on a keyboard, and normally are performed without the user's knowledge. The recorded history then can help someone identify important information such as User Names and passwords. Types of these Key Loggers include both software and hardware-based types, remote access versions, and also kinds that take periodic screenshots of your System.

To combat this Kaspersky Lab ® have built into their software a **Virtual Keyboard**, which is an on-screen keyboard that you can use to enter information instead of using your physical keyboard.

Malware – This is a holistic term that refers to all forms of malicious attacks to computers and networks. Many people mistakenly refer to **Malware** as being **Viruses** but these are in their own specific class with unique properties. Malware is the more correct term to use in generic classification.

Network Attacks – **Hackers** attempt to penetrate networks on a daily basis, and several of the more common attacks deal with vulnerabilities with the computers' Operating Systems, weak password securities, weak **Network Access Controls** (discussed below), and improper email authentications. These types of attacks need to be addressed and it would be advisable to enlist the services of Certified Network Security Specialists to analyse a network's weak spots and take appropriate action.

Payload – **Malware** use different methods to infiltrate computers, and these depend on the programmer and what they would like to achieve. Once they have successfully penetrated the computer's defences, another set of code is executed which performs the actual damage to the computer. We call this the **Payload** of the malware.

Phishing – This is a type of malware that attempts to obtain personal information from bogus emails. They mimic bona fide companies who have sent out emails as a request for the user's personal information in order "to update their database" whereas in reality the email is sent back to the Hacker who extracts the information for personal gain.

Pop-Ups – When you access certain websites small auxiliary windows automatically pops up informing you of something, and they are usually related to advertising. Hackers can capitalize on this by attaching code that executes either automatically as the window opens or executes once you have performed some sort of action on the window, thereby effectively infecting your computer.

Rootkits – Rootkits are code that installs into a user's computer without their knowledge or permission, and continues to run in the background without the user's knowledge. From this code various other activities can occur such as to download other malware from the Internet.

Spam – **Spam** constitutes unsolicited, or unwanted email and is covered in more detail in Chapter 17.

Spyware – **Spyware** is a type of **malware** that installs onto computers and collects information about the user without their knowledge, and hence in most cases Spyware unobtrusively installs onto the machine and operates in the background so as to not alert the user as to its presence.

Adware that monitor your surfing habits and display advertisements accordingly is also classed as **Spyware**.

Trojans –   **Trojans** are, by definition, a type of virus that infiltrates computers, but they have special properties in that the **Trojan** appears to be a legitimate type of software but it carries a **payload** of malicious code that executes secretly and performs the actual damage to the system whilst the Trojan software appears to run as normal.

Viruses –   Although the term **Virus** has become a holistic term for **Malware**, by definition **Viruses** will penetrate a computer and attempt to duplicate themselves as quickly as possible in order to spread as wide as they can. Whilst doing this they perform various malicious deeds to the host system through their **payload**. Almost all viruses attack the software of the computer although there have been a few instances whereby the code actually does damage to the physical hardware.

Worms –   **Worms** differ from **Viruses** in that they are only concerned about self-replication, and concentrate on spreading themselves within networks. Viruses, however, tend to only concentrate on targeted computers. Another difference is that Worms do not need to attach themselves to existing programs. Many Worms concentrate on spreading, and those that do malicious damage to computers work through **Payloads.**

PROTECTION

In order to protect yourself from threats you need to implement protection for your computers and networks. The following is a list of some popular protection types and are listed in alphabetical order.

Anti-Virus – In selecting an Anti-Virus product use on your personal computer or network, need to make sure that it needs to contain protection against all the forms of malware attacks currently in circulation. Try to look at some of the independent testing companies out there to gain an understanding of the rating of the various products on the market before you purchase one.

Content Security Filters – **Content Security Filters** limits the internal network as to how much access the clients can have to the Internet in terms of which websites are allowed and prohibited. Common to these filters are such categories as **Black Lists** and **White Lists** and these contain lists of websites that are either taboo (Black List) or acceptable (White List). Many popular Content Security Filters report periodically back to some sort of centralized database facility that is housed at the vendor's offices to update their own local databases. Furthermore, the filters report any new potentially damaging website back to the central database so that it can be broadcast back to the other currently installed filters.

Most filters also include facilities whereby local administrators can further configure these lists and add or subtract additional criteria based upon their company's specific needs. Furthermore, some filters have additional features that can limit the times spent surfing the Internet.

Digital Certificates – **Digital Certificates** are virtual labels of authenticity on websites. These certificates are issued from certified companies who analyse the content of a website for any anomalies before these certificates are issued. Such websites can be implicitly trusted. Examples of such websites are those owned by banks.

Firewalls – These are either hardware or software based devices that are designed to allow authorized communications to occur within networks and between networks whilst blocking any sort of unauthorized access. There are several methods that are employed (often several are used simultaneously) to prevent access where applicable.

Another definition is: **firewalls** inspect network traffic passing through, and allow or deny the information transfer based upon a predetermined and configured set of rules.

Firewalls do not detect any sort of malware other than network attacks and hence an Anti-Virus product needs to be installed and configured on the firewall to perform that function.

Network Access Whenever a computer, laptop, or other mobile
Control – device attempts to connect to a computer network it will not be allowed any sort of access unless it complies with a specific set of rules, including Anti-Virus, Systems updates, and configuration, provided an NAC solution is installed onto that network. As soon as the device connects to the network it is scanned by the NAC system and only after it has met the requirements determined by the NAC will it be given access to the network and its resources.

Network Monitors –	**Network Monitors** continuously monitor networks for instances of failure or increased activity. Most often these monitors are physical devices that connect into the network through an Ethernet port on a switch connected into the network. They are extremely configurable and there are several different activities that can be effectively monitored.
Proxy Servers -	A **Proxy Server** serves two main functions in that it hides the internal network is from the outside world. The second role it performs is that of **caching** by storing sections of websites previously visited by users on the internal network. When these sites are revisited the Proxy Server supplies most of the code for the website so that performance is increased.
Spam Filters –	A **Spam Filter** monitors all incoming email and identifies legitimate email from spam based on a predetermined set of rules and keywords. These rules and keywords are normally preconfigured in the software itself or by Network Administrators.

Do's and Don'ts

The following is an alphabetical list of some Do's and Don'ts that will serve to protect you against most forms of malicious attacks.

Anti-Virus Products –

- **Subscriptions** – Purchased products are normally supplied with a 12, 24, or 36-month subscription that entitles you to download Virus List updates, software updates and patches, and new versions of the software.

In order to gain these advantages you need to make sure that your computer can connect to the Internet.

When the Subscription Period nears its completion the software will in some way or another warn the user that a renewal is imminent, and if the period expires, the software will no longer continue to obtain any updates from the Internet, thus eventually rendering the product useless.

- **Execution** - In order for the software to be effective it must be permanently running in the background in the computer. The background operation should not hamper the overall performance of the machine. Occasionally users disable protection to increase performance and hence Kaspersky Lab® have a **Gaming Profile** built into their 2015 products that allows the user to operate memory and graphical intensive applications without having to disable the Anti-Malware application.

In the network versions certain policies and profiles can be configured by the System Administrator to prevent users from tampering with their Anti-Malware in any way, thus preventing potential security leaks into the network.

- **Scans** - It is advisable to schedule a complete system scan at least once a week to ensure that a threat has not been able to bypass the initial protection screens and infiltrated itself into the internal system. Try to schedule the scans for when the computer will not be used, such as weekends or evenings. In a network scenario, the System Administrator will have configured this centrally.

Backups –   No matter what you do with your computer, there is a golden cardinal rule that states:

"Always backup your system!"

In business backups are normally performed on a daily basis, and in home situations it is advisable to schedule these for once a week.

By scheduling regular backups you ensure that you are able to restore most of your data if any damage to your system has occurred.

Emailing –   Most of this topic has been discussed in Chapter 17, except the following:

Firstly, before you send or receive emails ensure that your Anti-Virus software is active. Next, be careful when sending out emails with attachments. The latest versions of email clients have, by default, certain securities that prevent certain types of attachments from being opened because they might contain malware. Ensure that your attachments are not executable files in any way.

When receiving mail, your Anti-Virus software will warn you before downloading the mail to your computer. Look through the list of incoming mails to make sure that you identify the recipients and the nature of the message. If you are unsure as to either the recipient or the subject matter, rather delete the mail. And be especially aware of those mails containing attachments.

Hard Copy Disposal – From time to time we are forced to print information out (also called **Hard Copies** in the computer world) in order for it to be useful to us. Some of that printed material will on occasion contain some or all of our personal information. If not guarded this printer material can fall into the wrong hands.

Paper Shredders were invented to effectively shred paper into several small strips that, when mixed up in the paper bin, becomes almost impossible to put back together, and thus the information printed on them is effectively lost.

Get into the habit of tearing up unwanted printed documentation before you throw it away or use a Paper Shredder. And try not to keep documentation of this nature in your purse, handbag, wallet or briefcase.

Personal Spam Filters –Due to the fact that extra filtration is required by each individual user when sorting through email it is advisable to install and configure a Personal Spam Filter onto each desktop.

Most personal Anti-Virus products have one built in, and at a network level specific modules can be installed at a server level that will further assist with filtration. The filter that is supplied with Kaspersky Lab ®' *Internet Security*, for instance, is almost intelligent and, once it is trained, it identifies strains in received emails that look like Spam and will react accordingly.

Removable Media – Removable Media such as **Floppy Disks, Stiffy Disks**, **CD**'s, **DVD**'s, Removable Hard Drives, and **Flash Drives** are capable of transferring malware into your computer, so you need to ensure that your Anti-Virus software is running so that it scans these media when they are inserted into your computer.

Software – You need to be extremely careful when you download software because sometimes the software contains bugs and doesn't work properly resulting in damage to your Operating System. Still other software downloads all sorts of advertisements onto your computer. And, in the worst case scenario, the software contains hidden malware that installs onto your computer and infects it. Try wherever possible to use legitimate software that you have purchased. If you have to purchase software online, make sure that the website is secure and check its Digital Certificate's authenticity.

Before installing any sort of software, make sure that you have a recent backup of your system before you continue, and ensure that your Anti-Virus is running before continuing, especially on software you have downloaded from the Internet.

Beware of pirated software that provides "cracks", as some of these can contain some sort of malware.

Strong passwords – In order to increase security on both personal computers and networks you need to develop strong passwords.

Some basic rules to adhere to are:

- **Alphanumeric Passwords** – Use a combination of alphabetical characters and numbers combined together to make up a password.
- **Uppercase and Lowercase** – Uppercase and Lowercase characters have different numeric values and thus, when entering passwords these come into effect, so combining Uppercase and Lowercase combinations of letters in your passwords further enhances password security.
- **Punctuation Characters** – Using punctuation characters within passwords can dramatically enhance the security level.
- **Password Length** – The longer your password is the more difficult it is to hack because of the many possible combinations that are likely given the length

of the password you select. You should not limit your password to less than 6 characters/ numbers.

- **Password Rotation** – It is important to change your password from time to time because if a hacker has been consistently working at trying to crack your password, chances are that he or she will eventually succeed if the password remains static.

Unattendance –   **User Profiles** were invented so that when a user logs onto a computer their personal settings are loaded and they can begin working. Part of the profile also store the user's personal information such as websites they have visited and their documents, as well as other miscellaneous settings.

If your profile is loaded, and your account has not been secured, anybody can jump onto your computer and do whatever with it and your profile, together with your personal information, can be affected if you leave your computer unattended and do not lock your desktop.

Websites –   Before surfing the Internet make sure your Anti- Virus is switched on and running properly before you proceed. When running a search on popular search engines, try to limit your selections from the first 20 results. Results listed past that might have links to questionable websites. Try not to be side-tracked by the many advertisements you come across in your travels because some of them might contain malware.

Lastly, if you need to enter any sort of personal information make sure that the website is secured and if not, try not to give any specifics such as your address or telephone number.

Clear out your Internet History every once in a while. This clears up space on your hard drive and prevents any of your personal information to fall into the wrong hands.

CHAPTER 16.
SALES ANALYSIS AND REPORT WRITING

It's a known fact that sales people absolutely hate doing administration work, and these include preparing reports. However, in order for a Sales Manager to accurately determine a sales person's performance, they need some sort of indication of their staffs' activities and abilities.

You must understand that a Sales Manager's job is to produce profit for the company through his or her staff (the Sales Personnel) and he must answer to his Director when the Sales Department is not doing too well. In order to do that the Sales Manager must gather as much information as possible to present to the Directorship in answer to their queries.

Bearing this in mind unfortunately you will have to perform some sort of administration work to present to your Sales Manager so that they can do their job properly. It also serves to guide the Sales Manager when you are not performing well to analyze your reports and make suggestions to rectify the situation.

In this chapter we look at some of the different reports that you will need to develop and maintain for these purposes, but this list only details some of those reports, and you might find that you will be tasked with presenting other reports that I have not discussed here. It depends on what information your Sales Manager requires from you, but this should give you an indication of the types of documents you will need to prepare.

MEETING REPORT

The Meeting Report is a summary of what transpired during your meeting with your prospect, and serves a few roles.

Firstly, it serves as a reminder to you of what happened at the meeting and what you need to follow up on, including the information you need to quote on.

Secondly, it shows your Sales Manager what activities you have done, and whether your meetings quotas are on target. I cannot explain to you how many meetings you should have (although I do discuss this in theory in the chapter on Time Management) because I don't know what your Sales Manager has set as your target, but these documents serve to illustrate your level of sales activities to a certain extent.

Another aspect of these Meeting Reports is to give the Sales Manager an indication as to your performance in terms of people seen versus sales made, and if he or she notices that you are maintaining your level of meetings but your sales figures are poor, he can peruse through these documents in an attempt to find out where your problem lies.

To this end then, these reports should be filled in accurately, although you might deem it tedious. There is something else that the report can assist you with. Let's assume you have five meetings in a day, and the meetings are about fairly similar issues (they all want a new network installed, for example). It becomes difficult for you to remember the exact requirements of each client as you progress through those meetings, and at the end of the day you might make a mistake with what each client wants because their requirements are so similar.

Now I don't mean that you need to sit in your car and write out these reports neatly after each and every meeting. What I do recommend however, is to make a copy of the report and, during your meeting, take down the necessary notes and jot them down on your sheet. Then when you are back in the office use your rough draft to write or type out a proper report, and if necessary, attach your rough draft to the neat report which will be the one that you will present to your Manager. In that way you will remember exactly what is required for each client and, glancing over your rough draft again, it will trigger your memories of the meeting a little further.

I'm not going to explain many of the fields on the template I have included on the next page because they are fairly straightforward. I will however briefly discuss the following:

Quote Done – This little yes/no checkbox will aid in reminding you whether you have put together the quote or proposal for the client.

Reason for Visit – This is a summary of the reason for your visit in the first place and if filled in before you head off to your client, it will serve to remind you what you need to discuss during the event. It also helps your Sales Manager to figure out what you were trying to accomplish at the meeting and whether you achieved it or not.

Meeting Report

Company:		**Date:**	2015/04/25
		Sales Rep:	Adrian Noble
Address:		**Quote Done:**	
Tel:			
Fax:			
Contact Person:			
Email:			
Reason for Visit:			
Report:			

SALES FORECAST

From the very start of each month your Sales Manager will have presented you with a Sales Target to reach by the end of the month. Some Managers issue targets based on turnover, but most Managers will focus instead on Profit.

As a Sales Person your concentration shouldn't be on turnover. Instead Profit is your main goal in sales. You can sell R1'000'000.00 each and every month, but if you have not put a sufficient mark-up on, then there will be no profit, or very little profit will be gained from all that effort.

Too many sales people choose to reduce their profit margins in order to secure the deal, and in doing are actually hurting not only their pockets, but their company's as well.

I learnt something in my last position as a Product Manager: a tactic that my former Director employs all the time, and I have now adopted this with a good measure of success.

"What will it take to get the business?"

In this same company I worked for there were two sales guys who frequently would quote a client, then wait a few days, and then, during their follow up, when the client had questions to ask, they automatically would reduce the mark up to "sweeten the deal" without first asking the buyer what their apprehensions were. Ninety percent of the time the hesitance was pertaining to something completely different, such as the technical aspects of the solution that needed to be resolved before the client was satisfied that the solution would work for them. But, in dropping the price, the client scored an added bonus, because once offered you can never go back on your suggestion. So the client won, in more ways than one, and these sales guys lost, time and time again. One of these sales guys sometimes would even reduce the price **before** even giving the prospective buyer their first quote.

Why?

This is just plain stupid. I used to argue with these two continuously about this practice, but as far as I know they still follow the same practice today.

Dumb, dumb, dumb!!!

Never, ever, reduce your price if you do not have to. Sometimes you can even load the selling price to a much higher value than the Recommended Retail Price suggested by your company, and the client will be willing to spend that if the solution works for them, and if you have gained their trust enough to make the sale.

How this little strategy works is you ask the prospect what they want out of the deal. By placing the ball into their court you gain the privilege of knowing what makes them tick, of knowing what they are looking for or want, and then you can adjust your sales pitch to meet that demand.

In the first meeting where I experienced this in practice was with my Director. I had setup a meeting with a National Retailer and he came with me to assist me in making the sale. After we threshed around in the meeting, me touting off the benefits of the product range, and how good it would be for their customers, etc, my Director noticed that the meeting was not going anywhere, and we had basically reached a stalemate. He then popped the question to the prospective buyer: "What will it take for us to do business with you?"

Well, it just so happened in this particular case that price was an issue. Now, and remember this for future reference, not once in this meeting had either myself or my Director mentioned price. As it turns out the prospect was selling a competing brand and if we could match the price we then could have the business. Well, we matched the price and within a month our product was on their shelves, and still is today, three years later.

You see, what made this client tick was price, but it we had started throwing numbers around at the start of the conversation, we would have lost him because he would have assumed that our product was too expensive for him.

So getting back to this topic, Sales Forecasts are fairly accurate determinations of what you should achieve by the end of your sales month.

I have included a sample Sales Forecast on page 412 and I will be referring to this template for this discussion.

When you create your quotes you basically consolidate them and put them here. Right, let's go through the headings.

Date – A bit of an obvious one here. This refers to the date the quote was created.

Client – The recipient of the quote.

New/Existing – This field is interesting to your Sales Manager because it shows him how much new business you have brought in versus existing business.

Product – Again quite an important field because it shows which products and/or services have been sold. This does not necessarily tell the

Sales Manager which products are more popular; it rather tells the Manager which products the sales person is concentrating on selling at that time.

% Closed –   This percentage explains how close you are to making the sale. It is not a mathematical calculation at all. Rather it is an estimation by you based upon your personal judgment and circumstances surrounding the client and the current deal. Such things as when payments will be made to when Managerial Authorization will take place to effect the sale comes into consideration, but it generally tells the Sales Manager which are your "hot" sales, and thus which ones they should be expecting shortly.

% Mark-up –   This is an average profit mark-up on your Cost Price from your quotation and affects the next column, **Profit**, which is the difference between the **Cost Price** and the **Selling Price.** More of this is discussed in your **Commission Sheet**.

Turnover –   The last four columns displays the Turnover for the sales, and an estimation from you as to which month the sale will be made. The Totals then will give an indication of whether you are on your target for the month or not.

Some of the pertinent information in this document is estimated, but it gives a good indication as to your sales activity, whether you are concentrating on new business or not, what your average profit margins are, how close you are to making those sales, and when you expect them to be finalized.

Sales Forecast 2015 for Adrian Noble										
								Turnover		
Date	Client	New/Existing	Product	% Closed	% Markup	Profit	April	May	June	July
4/1/2015	XYZ Tools	New	Computer	50	22	R 1,760.00	R 8,000.00			
4/20/2015	ABC Shoes	Existing	Upgrade	80	25	R 1,500.00			R 6,000.00	
				Total		R 3,260.00	R 8,000.00	R 0.00	R 6,000.00	R 0.00

COMMISSION SHEET

This document is very important because, well, quite frankly, it shows you how much money you should be getting!

I personally concentrate on keeping this document as much up to date as possible, because it give me an indication as to what my personal budget will be at the end of each month.

I hope that I am not influencing you in the wrong way by emphasizing this document because the other reports are equally as important but for different reasons. This document is your personal measure as to how well (or badly) you have done.

In the template I have developed for us to look through, I have assumed a 10% commission on profit earned, but your Sales Manager might negotiate a different percentage for you.

One thing to note here: the totals you have gathered here might differ slightly from the actual money you receive because there might be some costs that you have omitted but the Accountants have calculated in, but it at least gives you a ball park figure to work with.

Another thing to note here: make sure you calculate your Commission Sheet without Sales Tax, because you can never earn commission off of Sales Tax, and it will just skew your results.

There are some obvious fields which I'm not going to explain to you, namely **Date**, **Client**, and **Profit**. Right! Let's get into the other columns! Refer to the below diagram on page 414.

Cost Price -   This is the total Cost Price of the goods and/or services that you have sold to the client. When calculating the Cost Price for Labour Charges, it does become a little more difficult (assuming you receive commission on Labour) because you need to take into account what will be paid to the Engineers, and their travelling costs, but you can at least calculate an average and put it in.

Retail Price - This then would be the Selling Price to the end user, and is calculated by adding the Mark-up Percentage to the Cost Price.

Profit - The Profit is calculated by subtracting the Cost Price from the Retail Price.

% Mark-up - The Mark-up is the percentage you place onto the Cost Price in order to obtain a suitable Retail, or Selling Price. In order to ensure that your company earns a profit your Sales Manager will have given you a minimum threshold to work with (in my experiences my minimum threshold has been 15% or above). You must remember that in order to calculate a profit, your company needs to take into account salaries of the Support Personnel, Lights and Water, rental for the offices, payments for Insurance and Security, such as your company's alarm system, and telephone and Internet costs. Once all these costs are taken into account, the minimum Profit percentage ensures that enough money has been made to cover these costs as well as your commission. If you happen to drop below this minimum you can run the risk of damaging the company financially because then it will be operating at a loss. Just bear this in mind.

Adrian Noble

The Total at the bottom of the spreadsheet is an average profit percentage over the total amount of sales. In some companies Sales Personnel might only get awarded their commission if this average percentage is over a certain threshold, so be aware of this total.

Commission - This is the money that you have earned as is calculated at 10% of the Total Profit.

Commission Sheet for Adrian Noble - April 2015							
Date	Client	Product	Cost Price	Retail Price	Profit	% Markup	Commission
2015/04/01	XYZ Tools	Computer	R 6,240.00	R 8,000.00	R 1,760.00	22.00%	R 176.00
2015/04/20	ABC Shoes	Upgrade	R 4,500.00	R 6,000.00	R 1,500.00	25.00%	R 150.00
		Total	R 28,326.47	R 17,586.47	R 3,586.47	23.50%	R 326.00

GRAPHS

It has been scientifically proven that people (and animals) respond quite readily to visual signals and it is on this basis that most of your modern marketing techniques rest.

The same can thus be said of graphs because, to some people they impart more information than supplying spreadsheets of figures, especially when those people are not accountants by nature.

It must be noted that whatever graph you create and present the finished product must be clear and understandable, and if possible, use plenty of colour to illustrate different points that you want to emphasize.

I have not included graphs in this book on purpose because I have noticed in the past that many readers do not really read examples in books, but merely glance through them with thoughts of, "oh, that's nice!" and carry on reading. The reason I think this happens is that those graphs don't mean anything to the reader even if they understand the purpose of the example. They are not important to the reader because they cannot relate to the information being displayed. You might think I'm wrong in this assumption, but that's just my opinion.

In any case, I haven't included graphs in this graph for these reasons.

Conclusion

You must remember that these Sales Reports are important because they are a gauge as to how well you are doing in Sales. They show your Sales Manager your performance and if there is something wrong a good Sales Manager will attempt to help you to better yourself.

So yes, they are tedious, and yes, you may think that your Sales Manager is checking up on you, but at the end of the day you want to make money and if these reports can help you when you are not doing well, then it's best to put in the little extra time and fill them in properly.

Summary. Chapter 16.

It is the Sales Manager's job to maintain performance from their Sales Department each month so that the company earns profit. In order to do this the Manager needs information from each Sales Person to analyse the individual performance of their staff.

In the example reports in this chapter not every field has been discussed because they should be self-explanatory. However, there are some fields that might cause some confusion and thus are explained a bit further.

Meeting Report

Although time consuming a report should be drafted after each meeting. It not only serves to illustrate to your Sales Manager that you are performing, but it help in reminding you what was discussed and what needs to be quoted on.

Quote Done –   This area is an indication if a quote has been prepared for the client or not.

Reason for Visit – This is used as a summary and a goal for the meeting so that you can prepare yourself beforehand and after the meeting look back and see if you have accomplished your original goal or not.

SALES FORECAST

The Sales Forecast allows a sales person to gauge their progress throughout the month to ascertain whether they will meet the target set by their Sales Manager or not.

It furthermore assists the Manager in determining and approximation of expected turnover for that month.

Date –   The date when the quote was prepared.

Client –   This would be the quote recipient.

New/Existing –   This serves as a marketing notification for your Manager to see if you are focusing on new business or on existing clients.

Product –   This becomes a focal point on which products were concentrated on for that month.

% Closed –   Based upon intuition and estimation, the percentages here illustrate how close you are to making the sale.

% Mark-up –   In order to earn commission you need to earn profit for the company and this field gives you an average mark-up of your potential sales. Obviously if this percentage is too low, your manager will detect this and assist you in raising your percentages.

Turnover –   Some sales targets work with Turnover, and this column shows how much turnover will be earned for the company.

COMMISSION SHEET

This report is an indication of your performance for the month and also your total earnings.

Cost Price -   This column shows how much the goods and/or services cost the company.

Retail Price -   This would be the price the goods were sold to the client.

Profit -   The resultant Profit is the difference between the Cost Price and the Retail Price.

% Mark-up -   The percentage added to the Cost Price with directly affects the profit and your resultant commission.

Commission -   As a sales person you earn a percentage of the profit earned for each sale. This percentage is predetermined by your Sales Manager.

GRAPHS

These provide visual representation of analytical data that can be more beneficial to readers as these diagrams sometimes can be easier to understand provided they are comprehensive and professionally designed.

Chapter 17.
Using emails for
Communication

Possibly, in my opinion, one of the most important and beneficial communication mediums that was ever invented other than the telephone, email communication has revolutionized the communications industry in allowing people to contact each other almost instantaneously anywhere in the world, and this medium has allowed us as sales people to be able to increase our activity tenfold smartly.

Now what do I mean by "smartly?" There is an old saying that says:

"Work smart not hard!"

And by using emailing facilities we can do just that! This chapter devotes itself into dealing with emails, how to use them to effectively get your point across, and yes, how to save money in doing so.

But you must be careful to not abuse this privilege of modern day society in much the same way as a telephone should not be abused. Think about this for a second. How many times have you had people phone you up wanting to sell you stuff, and they start rambling on in such a fast pace that you honestly cannot keep up with them, let alone get a word in edgewise? This is a common way that Telesales Operatives work – they are taught to sell so fast that you cannot answer yourself, and although has proven itself effective, I personally do not approve of this type of salesmanship, not in IT sales in any case.

I might be wrong, and there might be many people who, based on my thoughts here, would like to contact me and tell me I'm wrong. They will tell me that they have built a multi-million Dollar empire by employing these sorts of methods, but with what integrity? What respect have they gained from the average customer by using these tactics? I'm all in for earning bucks, but I abhor these sorts of methods personally. Use them, don't use them; that's up to you.

Anyway, back to the subject at hand. If emailing is used correctly it will vastly improve your overall sales, and will allow you to spend less time on the telephone, which saves money (at least here in South Africa it will because unlike other countries we have to pay for each and every call we make, whether it is local or international).

Please bear in mind that I'm not going to do an exercise in how to use your favourite email client, with all its bells and whistles; that is not the point of this chapter at all! The point here is to help you to use emailing to effectively communicate with your prospects and clients, and in some cases to get your point across!

Right, so let's get in here!

ADVANTAGES VS. DISADVANTAGES

Let's look at a few advantages and some disadvantages in using this type of communication in selling.

Language Barriers – I have often found the problem of, when speaking to people telephonically, that I honestly battle to understand what they are saying because of their accent. You will find in your travels that you will be dealing with people of different nationalities and sometimes their accents seem to get in the way of the sale. Similarly, they might also battle with the way you speak. Don't worry; I have had this problem as well whereby my prospect couldn't understand me because my accent (I was born in Rhodesia and raised in South Africa, so I have a mixture of British English coupled with South African English) is foreign to them. Furthermore, we, in every different nationality, pick up little idioms that are common to our country but that seem odd to different cultures.

Furthermore, due to the nature of what we are selling, some people do not understand the terminology we use in a technical perspective, and so much information thrown at them in one go just goes over the top of their heads and we lose the sale.

Digression point here.

There is a type of selling called **Neuro- Linguistic Programming (NLP) Selling** that deals with the human sub-conscious, the way it works, and how we apply it to everyday situations. A Sales Person proficient in this type of selling will find quite remarkable results.

Please bear in mind that I will not, and I repeat, not, get into an entire discussion about this particular subject, but I can assure you that it is quite wonderful if applied properly. What I am going to use here is the concept of the fact that there are three kinds of people with respect to NLP. There are those who react more to visual things and if they can see something it triggers in their brain. There are others who would react to auditory situations (i.e. they react to things they hear). The last kind of person reacts to things they can feel.

A person who reacts more to auditory stimuli will be quite perfect to talk to over the phone because this is what triggers in their brain – sounds. It is these kinds of people who generally have no problem at all with accents and can understand them quite easily. But for the poor visual and physical types of people (I myself for one am more of a visual type or person) they seem to battle with understanding the human voice, and hence would prefer to see or feel something before they can fully relate to it.

So back to what we are talking about. Emails can assist you in overcoming these language barriers in being precise and clear and can explain everything so that the other person understands exactly the point you are trying to get across.

Anytime, anywhere – In South Africa normal working hours are from 08h00 until 17h00. In other countries it is different. Using the telephone limits the amount of time you can spend talking to clients. It also limits the time that business can be carried out with respect to other activities that do not involve actually talking to people.

Emailing overcomes these barriers in that there are no time limits- if you wish to correspond at two o'clock in the morning you may quite easily do so knowing that the recipient of the email will receive your message when they open it.

In addition, we have a slight problem on Earth called **Time Zones**. Damn nasty things that mean your eight-to-five is not the same as Japans' eight-to-five, so whilst you have one hellava brilliant sales pitch that you want to try at 10h00 on somebody in Australia, they will not like you very much when you call them and they are sleeping!

Emailing allows us twenty four-hour communication whenever we feel like it.

And this brings me to my next point – **anywhere!**

You can send emails anywhere in the world to anyone in the world. You can be sitting in the middle of a café in Pakistan with a laptop and the Internet and communicate with somebody sitting at the beach in Brazil quite easily. It prevents us from being bound to our offices.

Documents – With the advent of email technology we can send stuff to others, be it documents, photographs, music, presentations, anything! It allows us to create that all-important yearly sales budget at home on the weekend and send it to your boss before Monday morning. It also saves on paper!

One-to-many – With this technology we have the ability now of reaching more than one person with the same information simultaneously. Emails can be created and sent to many people, ensuring that they all receive the same information. It is also duplicable meaning that an email received can be passed onto another person without any modification.

Remember the old children's game called Pass the Message, whereby a message is whispered in the ear of the one person who whispers it to the next person and so forth? By the time the message has reached the last person in the line it is so garbled and mixed up from the original that only the subject of the message remains intact (actually, I'm wrong here because sometimes even the subject gets changed as well!). How do you think rumours and legends were forme3d?

Speaking vs. Written – Some of us have difficulty in speaking properly. Let's face it; some of us become tongue-tied when speaking to people. It doesn't necessarily mean that we are bad sales people – we just don't like talking. We forget what we are going to say, and when we do say it it sounds like we have just threatened the other guy with a chair or something.

Email allows us to formulate our thoughts properly so that a carefully prepared sales presentation can be imparted as is without any deviations whatsoever.

On the other hand, we do have some disadvantages here namely: The number one on everyone's list:

Spam!!! – This will be covered in a little more detail later but for the purposes of this conversation Spam mail is unsolicited email, or mail that people don't want. It is equivalent to receiving junk mail in your post box (remember that little red post box by your gate outside where you receive letters – those paper things in brown or white envelopes that normally contain bills – remember those things???). Ok, so spam email is basically junk mail that people don't want and they normally delete these messages.

Spam has caused untold havoc in the world today and unfortunately is a downside to using email, so when you do communicate in this fashion, be sure you're not spamming!!! More on this later!

Speaking vs. Written – Conversely to above, those of us who thrive on the spoken word will find selling by email stuffy and boring. Some sales presentations require the instantaneous response from the prospect without prior thought in order to make the sale.

Emails allow the prospect time to stop and think; time to make up reasons why they cannot or should not purchase your sale and/or product, and it for this reason that emailing should augment your entire sales approach – not replace it. It is a tool that can help but it should not become a tool that replaces. The spoken word is still the best way of selling (hence the term **Word of Mouth**). In my travels I have yet to see the popular sales term **Word of Email**. Guys don't place your entire trust in emailing to get through to your clients; just rather use it to help you along.

Equipment – The use of emails unfortunately does require some equipment namely a computer and the Internet, whereas the spoken word can either be face to face or over the telephone (ok, ok, this is also equipment but is a lot cheaper and can be found almost anywhere).

Typing proficiency – Some of us just can't type fast, and some of us just can't spell, and some of us just can't write good letters. I personally can type fast (luckily) but there are those of us who have never learnt and they tend to use the One Finger Method of typing which makes it extremely tedious to write letters. I'm sure you've seen them, tongue out, finger looming like a worrying insect over the keyboard whilst they search for the correct key to depress. Well, luckily today we now have Speech Recognition Software which alleviates the need for such brutality.

Incidentally, for those or us who unfortunately are disabled, Speech Recognition Software becomes the perfect ideal for communication (thank the Lord this has been developed).

A quick story here! When I was a lecturer we had a Typing School Instructor whose job it was to teach her students the correct way to type complete with poise, etc. For three years she nagged me to take her course because she said that I type like a drunken ape! Personally, I don't think see anything wrong with my typing. I may be a bit lopsided, and I don't use all my fingers (I use all of my left hand and a finger and thumb of my right hand – I'm left-handed after all) but I get the job done. Right?

There are some of us who are not good at writing letters, and some of us who can't spell. Ok, with modern software we can correct the spelling but the letter writing ability? The only way you are going to fix this is either do one hell of a lot of reading (novels, etc) or find somebody to proof read your work before sending it out. I myself fortunately have a very good mastery of the English language and I have found that in every job I have ever been in I have proofread my colleagues' work. Even my bosses in the past have handed me their proposals to look over! I'm just one of the lucky ones.

S P A M!!!

Ok, right, mmmmmmm, here we go!!!

Now, before I go any further, there are those of you who are sitting there saying, "But I'm an IT salesman and is should be my job to understand all this technology, so you really don't need to explain all this to me!" That may quite well be, and I commend you on this train of thought, but there are people out there who have purchased this book that are not in the game of IT sales (thank you very much for your support and I hope it serves you as well as for my IT guys) and feel that I might have a few ideas they can use. There are also some of you IT guys out there that are still new to the game and are still learning much there is to know about Information Technology. And then are some of you that might have forgotten how Spam can affect us.

As I mentioned before, Spam is defined as unsolicited email, or email that we do not want. I related it earlier to junk email and this is exactly what it is. It's the leaflets and pamphlets that are placed in your mailbox (the real red one, remember? The one that sits by your gate through rain, hail, and snow. Remember?). It's the advertisements requesting you to purchase stuff and receive free gifts in return. It is the letters that tell you you've won the Sweepstakes but you can only claim it you sign up for a year's subscription. We don't want it, but we also cannot prevent people from sending it either, neither can we send a letter back to the company requesting them to stop soliciting you because then it gives them all your contact details and tells them that you have at least read the pamphlet and this then gives them the opportunity to contact you in the future.

Spam works in much the same way only much faster, cheaper, and more devastating. It has led to an entire multi-million Dollar industry just in itself whereby companies create and distribute Spam whilst other companies develop Anti-Spam Filters to block that Spam. And it has also created ways of increasing Internet bandwidth just to cope with the levels of Spam traversing the Internet on a daily basis.

In looking at the products offered by Kaspersky Lab ® the Endpoint Anti-Malware Protection has a built-in configurable Anti-Spam filter that has proven itself by Independent Testing Companies as one of the leading products in this category. Regarding these sort of results on a personal level I would want a filter that is rated at the highest percentage possible in blocking unsolicited emails. Not only do these mails contain malware (some of them anyway); they consume unnecessary network traffic and also waste time for the user in that thy have to keep on deleting these types of mails.

Anyway, I'm not going into a completely technical discussion on how an Anti-Spam filter works, or how to configure it, but I'm going to use a little discussion here just to tell you how **not** to create or distribute Spam.

There are various ways that these filters work but one of the most common is with the use of keywords and phrases. Most often these Spam messages will contain sex, various pills and drugs, swearing, specials, free things and cash, so you need to understand not to include these into your email in order to ensure that it gets through to your recipient.

Obviously you are not going to mention anything sexual (for the sake of this book I'm not going to be specific) either in the subject line, or in the body of the email. Similarly, offering drugs on special, free things, cash, or any of these will cause triggers in the recipients' Anti-Spam filter that will quickly redirect your email to the Junk Mail Folder, which probably mean that it will either never be read, or only read many days or weeks down the line when the recipient eventually decides to empty out their Junk Mail Folder.

No, you need to ensure that your subject line is clear and concise with good terminology and that the body of your email contains good Business English with a clear indication of what it is you are trying to get across.

Incidentally, some filters will block messages that are sent with no subject line at all, so be careful of this as well.

Later on we will be discussing Distribution and Subscription Lists, but generally speaking people frown upon an email that begins with "Dear Subscriber/Sir/Madam" or anything of that description. Furthermore, an empty salutation is also a no no. Always use the recipient's name in your salutation and you have overcome that little hurdle. An email that is addressed in such a way normally always suggests that the mail is being mass distributed and not personalised at all.

If you are forced to use a "Dear Sir/Madam" salutation (I have done so in the past) then ensure that you mention at least the recipient's company somewhere in the body of the email so that it becomes personalised. Let me show you a quick example of what I mean here.

Dear Sir/Madam

I wonder if you can help me. I am a representative of ABC Computer Company and I would like to

> *schedule an appointment with your IT Manager at Badger's Clothing but I am not sure who to ask for. Is it possible if you can give me the relevant person's contact details so that I may liaise with them personally?*

By using the "Badger's Clothing" in the text I am ensuring that the email becomes personalised. Got it?

On the legal side of things, because there is just so much Spam bouncing around the Internet today you might think a sender could be prosecuted for harassment. Well unfortunately because there are no boundaries with the Internet it makes it extremely difficult to track down and arrest a spammer when they are sitting in a garage in Budapest whilst you are in the USA. So what instead happens is a request can be sent to the ISP hosting the email address and that email address can be blacklisted and removed meaning that you could lose your email address forever! If you are sending out emails from your work address that you think are legitimate but others deem are Spam instead you could have your email address revoked meaning that firstly all your former clients will not be able to reach you and secondly you will need to explain to your boss why this has happened. It might go even so far as the ISP shutting the entire domain down! Can you imagine explaining to your boss why they have lost their entire domain (affecting everyone else in the company including the company's website) because you inadvertently set out a Spam email. They could even have you up on criminal charges!

According to the CAN-SPAM Act of 2003 (Controlling the Assault of Non-Solicited Pornography and Marketing Act), which came in effect on 1 January 2004, it states, amongst other things, that your email, if commercial, must contain some sort of opt out method for recipients. What this basically means is if you are in the practice of broadcasting emails (such as in news lists, described below) you must give an option of unsubscription to the service. Normally this is a link placed at the bottom of the email which sends some sort of request back to the sender so that you can be removed for their mailing list, hence ensuring the recipient does not receive any further email.

So now you think to yourself, "Hey, if I just unsubscribe to this lot of spam email I'm receiving it will stop coming."

WRONG!!!

There are legitimate companies who honour these sorts of requests but, with respect to the amount of Spam originators they are few and far between. These spammers have created automated software that goes around the Internet gathering lists of email addresses to include in the spammer's distribution list. The software even goes as far as to capture a domain and generate random names based on that domain to include. And all this is down automatically, whilst the spammer is sleeping, shopping, drinking beer, watching TV, or even working through their normal daytime jobs.

To a spammer a legitimate email address is like a goldmine because these spammers are paid exorbitant amounts of money in selling their lists to others: hackers, other spammers, and specialist Commercial Marketing Companies who use those lists in turn to promote and sell their own products and/or services (which in itself becomes more Spam to handle). This is actually the reason why Spam exists and why spammers do it – so they can sell their lists of legitimate email addresses.

Remember earlier I mentioned to you those damned telemarketers? They work in much the same way with cellphone and telephone numbers – they buy and sell lists.

Ok, so the spammer is looking for a legitimate email address and their automated software is randomly going out and looking for domains and anything that looks like an email address, and is randomly putting together combinations of email addresses in the hopes that some are legitimate and some are not.

And then you decide to respond to one of the Spam messages by asking to be unsubscribed from their mailing list and then, BAM, you're in!!! You have immediately just informed the spammer that your email address does in actual fact exist and before you know it, the spammer has sold your email address to other Spam companies and subsequently you are hit with so much Spam you can't even think straight!

This personally happened to me way back about twenty years ago when I was still a newbie to the field. I had my nice little personal email address going and I was happy. It was my first Internet account with my whopping 14'000kbps modem chugging away quite nicely and I started receiving a few of these Spam mails in my account. Irritably I started hitting the "Unsubscribe Me" at the bottom of email and before I knew it, within one month I was receiving between 600 to 1000 Spam messages daily. By the way I still have that account (yes I have had that account for twenty years) and even now I still receive about thirty Spam messages daily.

You may ask yourself "Why can't my ISP setup an Anti-Spam Filter so that I don't receive these emails?"

In a company this is a feasible option because that company is providing a service for its employees. But with an ISP it is completely different.

The HUGE ISP's (and I'm going to use Google as an example here) host millions of subscribers, each with different wants and needs. There are some warped people out there who actually want to receive all emails pertaining to sex and so Google places an Anti-Spam filter onto its server. What then happens? Well the majority of people become quite happy because they are no longer receiving the sex emails, but not the select few who start complaining because they are no longer getting their mails, and they protest, and are fully within their rights to do so.

No, unfortunately for ISP's they cannot use filters of this nature at all, so where does that leave you? Well, your company should have a filter in place and so should your own personal computer to further filter messages that you deem are Spam. That's the only way to fully protect yourself.

QUICK MECHANICS COURSE ON HOW EMAILS WORK

This little section is for those of you who are not sure as to the ins and outs of email and how it works. Again, I'm not going to get into a full technical discussion. I am merely pointing out a few things here so that you understand the whole concept.

Right! Now, there are a couple of definitions that you need to know and as I explain I will fill you in on those terms.

We start with an email **client** and an email **server.** The **client** is the application you use to create your emails. It is the *Microsoft Outlook* ® on your computer, or the Web Mail account you are using to generate and store all your emails. It is your post box.

The email **server** is the Post Office, and it is the application that collects the emails and redirects them to the designated email clients. The server can physically reside in two locations. When we talk of a **local email server** we assume that the email server is located in the client's site, perhaps somewhere in their Server Room. When we talk of a **remote email server** we then assume that the server resides at the clients' ISP's premises.

An email server uses two protocols being **SMTP** (Simple Message Transport Protocol) and **POP3** (Post Office Protocol). Incoming emails to the server come in using the SMTP protocol and outgoing emails use the POP3 protocol for transport to recipients' email clients.

What this basically means is when you send an email out you send it using the SMTP protocol and when you receive emails you receive them using the POP3 protocol.

In most cases the email server hosts both of these protocols in a single computer and generally in everyday networks the machine is powerful enough to handle the incoming and outgoing routing of both quite happily. However, in an Enterprise environment, whereby a company is dealing with thousands of email requests on a daily basis, sometimes separate computers are used for SMTP and POP3 traffic. These mail servers become known as **relay**

servers as their sole function is to collect incoming traffic and distribute outgoing traffic, with a centralised email server whose sole function is to control this flow of traffic.

When an email is sent from a client it is sent to the SMTP server which stores it in your "post box" on the server's hard drive and a request is then sent to the POP3 server to send the email out when your email client connects, anywhere in the world. These messages will be stored on the server indefinitely until you connect and download your email. The email then is transferred out of your post box on the server and into the hard drive of the computer you are using.

There is an option in your email client that allows you to keep a copy of the email on the server for a definite amount of time but generally speaking that email will only be transferred once you connect.

If you are using a Webmail account through a Web Browser then the email will remain on the server until you delete it or forward it because these Webmail browsers do not have the facilities to transfer the email to your local hard drive. They are designed to allow you to connect remotely from any computer, whether it is a public computer (such as found in Internet Cafes) or a computer in another company's network (such as the client you are visiting). This then leaves the option open for you to download and obtain email from your own computer when you are back in the office, but instead means that you do not necessarily have to carry your computer wherever you go; you can still read your email whilst being away from the office.

I hope this helps you in understanding this concept a little better.

CC AND BCC

When drafting an email you will notice two additional fields below the recipient's address field, and these become extremely useful when sending an email to more than one person.

In order to use these properly you need to understand the differences between them.

CC stands for **Carbon Copy** and sends an exact duplicate of the email you sent to the original recipient to another recipient. When the people receive your email all recipients are shown at the top of the email.

BCC stands for **Blind Carbon Copy** and does exactly the same thing but the major difference here is that all recipients are not displayed at the top of the email; only the original recipient is shown.

This Blind Carbon Copy field becomes extremely useful, especially when you distribute emails to mailing lists (as discussed below).

When distributing bulk emails it is a very bad marketing practice to display the entire list of recipients to all who receive those emails. Not only does it give those people an insight as to how many people received the email, thus nullifying the "personal" effect of the recipient thinking they are the only one to have received the email, but it also gives those recipients an opportunity of using those email addresses for their own purposes, such as sending their own emails on, or even selling those lists to other companies.

A bit of a hint here – when sending out bulk emails place all your recipients in the BCC field and then put your own email address in the To: field. That way the email is sent back to you and is simultaneously sent to your mailing list. What the people will see on the other side is your email address as the original recipient.

MAILING LISTS

It is extremely beneficial to send an email out to several people at the same time, especially if you want to impart the same information to many people, such as marketing, or a newsletter.

Gathering lists of emails for this function assumes the term of **mailing list**, and you will often come across this expression.

There are a few things to note here when dealing with mailing lists.

Firstly, make sure that the people on your list actually belong there. It is no point in sending computer-based information to people dealing with animals as this information is of no use to them. Many people will send you an email requesting you to remove them from your mailing list. When you do receive these requests then take the time to do as they request. It is highly embarrassing on your part when you keep receiving these removal requests from your client, and on the other side it irritates your client beyond belief, meaning that ultimately you could damage the relationship between yourself and your client.

Secondly, make sure you use the BCC field (as explained above) because you don't want those recipients to identify your entire mailing list database. As I said before, they can quite easily use your mailing list for their own purposes, and if that list is sold to a Spammer, then you run the risk of infecting that entire list of people with Spam.

Also, be extremely careful of using your mailing list to distribute emails of a humorous nature, or chain emails, or petition emails. Most people shrug off chain letters and petition emails, and if they identify them as coming from you, again it could hurt your professional relationship with them. In addition, one man's humour might be another man's poison, and people react differently to humour, especially when it affects race, sex, or religion. As a rule of thumb, rather do not even consider using your mailing list for any of these activities – rather keep it strictly for business-related activities and you will be safe.

Lastly, be extremely careful of the size of email you broadcast out to a mailing list. You must remember that when dealing with the BCC field the email server will treat each email individually and a 2Mb email sent to a hundred people will clog that email server up as it will try to send 100 x 2Mb emails out resulting in a traffic load of 200Mb! Try to refrain from broadcasting emails with attachments and you should be safe here.

SIGNATURES AND ASSISTANTS

The last thing we need to discuss in this chapter is the use of signatures and Assistants. Almost every email client has a signature facility and it would be worth your while to design your signature so that each and every email will contain your contact details and will form a uniformity that your clients become familiar with and hence can associate with you much easier.

Your signature should contain your name, your company, your position within the company, and the company's contact details. Other details that can be included are company logos, your email address, your cellphone number, and in some cases, disclaimers.

Disclaimers are little sections of legal text that protect you in case an email is sent erroneously to a recipient who might consider it to be unsolicited and hence Spam. I'll give you an example here of disclaimer text below. Obviously there are several variations to this, but this is just an example to illustrate what I mean.

If you are wondering why you should try to include disclaimers it is very simple. Let's say there is a person who dislikes you (either professionally or personally) and they decide that they would like to cause some mischief for you. It's quite easy. They can get hold of one of your emails and broadcast it to as many people as they like. In that way it can be construed as Spam and could result in you losing your email address.

Another common practice is to get hold of one of your emails and send it to the same person repeatedly, by placing a single recipient's email address a number of times in the BCC field. In that way a person could receive your email numerously, and if the Spammer has copied the email address a hundred times over, this could be quite disastrous indeed!

Ok, take a look at this typical disclaimer:

> *DISCLAIMER: The information in this message is confidential and may be legally privileged. It is intended solely for the addressee. Access to this*

> *message by anyone else is unauthorized. If you are not the intended recipient, any disclosure, copying, or distribution of the message, or any action or omission taken by you in reliance on it, is prohibited and may be unlawful. Please immediately contact the sender if you have received this message in error. Thank you.*

You may want to use this as is, or you may want to adjust it as you see fit. Place it at the end of your signature and you will ensure that you are legally protected.

Many email clients have an option of Assistants, which can become extremely useful in automating your emails.

One of the most commonly used assistant is the Out Of Office Assistant, whereby you can setup a standard email that will automatically be sent to anyone who sends you an email. Of course your email client will receive the email as per normal, but the person who sent you an email will receive an automated reply that will inform them of your absence, and you can place additional information in the text you choose that might instruct them to contact alternative people who can deal with their request in your absence.

Another nifty way to use these Assistants is to automatically have the email copied to another person. If you are lucky enough to have a Personal Assistant (a real, genuine human being, not a piece of computer software) who handles your meetings and your clients, etc, then it would be extremely useful to implement this facility because then you can be sure that your PA will receive everything you receive and can act on any requests when you are not around.

Conclusion

The invention of the **email** has definitely revolutionized the sales industry, and in fact any industry. It has allowed us to speed up our sales activities a hundredfold and it knows no boundaries.

Used properly you can only increase your sales performance. But used improperly and you can actually damage both your sales and your reputation quite dramatically and could even land you in legal trouble if you misuse the privilege.

So use the system wisely, and go out and sell stuff!

SUMMARY. CHAPTER 17.

Email communication has revolutionized the communications industry in allowing people to contact each other almost instantaneously anywhere in the world, and this medium has allowed us as sales people to be able to increase our activity tenfold smartly.

If emailing is used correctly it will vastly improve your overall sales, and will allow you to spend less time on the telephone, which saves money

ADVANTAGES VS. DISADVANTAGES

Advantages –

Language Barriers – Emails can assist you in overcoming language barriers in being precise and clear and can explain everything so that the other person understands exactly the point you are trying to get across.

Anytime, anywhere – Emailing overcomes time barriers in that there are no time limits when and where you can send emails. You can also send emails anywhere in the world to anyone in the world and they prevent us from being bound to our offices.

Documents – With the advent of email technology we can send attachments of various items to others quickly and efficiently.

One-to-many –   We have the ability now of reaching more than one person with the same information simultaneously. Emails can be created and sent to many people, ensuring that they all receive the same information.

Speaking vs. Written – Email allows us to formulate our thoughts properly so that a carefully prepared sales presentation can be imparted as is without any deviations whatsoever.

DISADVANTAGES –

Spam!!! –   Spam mail is unsolicited email, or mail that people don't want.

Speaking vs. Written –   Emails allow the prospect time to stop and think; time to make up reasons why they cannot or should not purchase your sale and/or product, and it for this reason that emailing should augment your entire sales approach – not replace it!

Equipment –   The use of emails requires some equipment namely a computer and the Internet.

Typing proficiency – To those who battle to type or to spell or whose Business English is not very good email is not a good medium to use.

S P A M!!!

Spam is defined as unsolicited email, or email that we do not want.
    There are various ways that Anti-Spam filters work but one of the most common is with the use of keywords and phrases.

Most often these Spam messages will contain sex, various pills and drugs, swearing, specials, free things and cash, so you need to understand not to include these into your email in order to ensure that it gets through to your recipient.

If somebody suspects you of sending Spam a request can be sent to the ISP hosting your email address and that email address can be blacklisted and removed meaning that you could lose your email address forever! It could also mean that your entire company's domain is also blacklisted.

According to the CAN-SPAM Act of 2003 (Controlling the Assault of Non-Solicited Pornography and Marketing Act), which came in effect on 1 January 2004, it states, amongst other things, that your email, if commercial, must contain some sort of opt out method for recipients, such as giving an option of unsubscription to the service.

QUICK MECHANICS COURSE ON HOW EMAILS WORK

A few definitions:

An email **client** is the application you use to create your emails.

An email **server** is the Post Office, and it is the application that collects the emails and redirects them to the designated email clients.

A **local email server** is located in the client's site.

A **remote email server** resides at the clients' ISP's premises.

An email server uses two protocols being **SMTP** (Simple Message Transport Protocol) and **POP3** (Post Office Protocol). Incoming emails to the server come in using the SMTP protocol and outgoing emails use the POP3 protocol for transport to recipients' email clients.

CC and BCC

CC stands for **Carbon Copy** and sends an exact duplicate of the email you sent to the original recipient to another recipient. When the people receive your email all recipients are shown at the top of the email.

BCC stands for **Blind Carbon Copy** does exactly the same thing but the major difference here is that all recipients are not displayed at the top of the email; only the original recipient is shown.

Mailing Lists

It is extremely beneficial to send an email out to several people at the same time, especially if you want to impart the same information to many people, such as marketing, or a newsletter. This is done using **mailing lists**.

Signatures and Assistants

Each and every email should contain your signature which should have your contact details and will form a uniformity that your clients become familiar with and hence can associate with you much easier.

Your signature should contain your name, your company, your position within the company, and the company's contact details. Other details that can be included are company logos, your email address, your cellphone number, and in some cases, disclaimers.

Many email clients have an option of Assistants, which can become extremely useful in automating your emails.

One of the most commonly used assistant is the Out Of Office Assistant, whereby you can setup a standard email that will automatically be sent to anyone who sends you an email.

CHAPTER 18.
WHERE AND HOW TO BEGIN SELLING

The start of a journey is always daunting, but exciting. Many fears and doubts enter your mind when you stand on the threshold of your door and you look at the road ahead. Your eyes can only see the horizon and you know that your destination exists past that, into the unknown.

You ask yourself, "Can I do this? Do I have the strength and discipline to go the road? What happens if it doesn't work? What if I fail? Can I turn back?"

These fears enter almost anyone's mind at some point or other, and you need to find the strength and resolve within yourself to be able to take that first step into the world. I unfortunately cannot take this step for you nor can I teach you how to take that first step either. The mere fact that you have obtained this book (I hope you bought it and didn't steal it: only joking, of course you bought it) tells me that you are at least entertaining the thought of making sales your lifelong profession, and this would be a correct choice **if** you are determined to see it through.

Although this chapter is written specifically for those who are just starting out in sales either as a career or as the start of a new job or venture, there are those veterans of you who might think that this chapter doesn't apply to you. I do however urge you to at least glance through it because we all tend to forget the basics from time to time and retracing your steps back to the beginning not only refreshes your memory but also might help you remember why you chose this career in the first place and might lend a bit of enthusiasm into your future prospects.

I mentioned at the beginning of this book that sales is the only profession in the world whereby you can generate your own income, but, this being said, sales is also one of the hardest occupations to perform.

Many people baulk at the thought of sales, but you need to ask yourself exactly what is it that scares you? Is it the thought of approaching people, meeting with them, and convincing them to purchase your goods and services, or is it the fear of rejection that stays your hand?

For most people these are perhaps the two strongest objections that are faced when considering this venture, and you seriously need to question yourself whether you are able to overcome these apprehensions in order to succeed. As I said, I cannot teach you how to do this: you need to look within yourself for the answers, but if you are able to face these negative emotions and focus your energies past them you will be well on your way to experience and enjoy one of the greatest careers in the world!

Given this then; given the fact that you are determined to make a success of sales, the next little hurdle you need to overcome is where to start, and how to start. This is possibly the most difficult part of the entire journey – how to put your foot forward.

Now this is where I can help you, and guide you into taking that first step into the unknown. After that the rest is up to you, but if you keep on applying the same techniques over and over you will eventually create a whole little business around you; one that you should be proud of because you will have created it, and nobody else. Yes of course you will have support from Managers, Support Staff such as Technicians and Secretaries, Accountants and Clerks, but realize that without you in the forefront there will be no clients at all.

So let's take a look at the different parts of this chapter and put them together in different ways to create a whole, and then you should have enough tools to get the job done.

MARBLES IN THE PIPE

Right! So you've got your desk and your nice shiny computer in front of you. You've sat down and created all the sections on your hard drive to store all your documents. You've arranged your email client and created little folders in anticipation of those hordes of clients to come rushing in. You've opened your diary on a fresh clean page and entered today's date. Now what?

First thing's first! Nobody knows you are out there. Nobody knows where you are. So you need to start telling people where you are and what you do. In other words, you need to start marketing yourself (and obviously your company) in order to make yourself known.

There are various ways of doing this. One way, which seems to be oh so common amongst new sales people, is to grab the telephone book and start from A and work your way through to Z. At least that is your intention, and I can assure you that after page three you are going to give up, or at least become demoralized in the process. That phone book is quite big and you won't know most of those people, and there is no focus there.

Ok, so this is a bad idea. Of course it is. In my experience no sales person ever has ever got anywhere with this sort of approach.

You then ask yourself, "Well what happens if I focus on a particular category of companies? Yes, that will work because then I can plan a strategy around that particular industry!" So you madly flip the pages in the phone book to that category, plan an approach, and start phoning away. Again you are going to luck out, because you are trying a straight cold calling strategy.

Earlier in this book I devoted an entire section to cold calling and how to go about it, but, and there is a big but here, this assumes that you have a point of reference. Now what I mean by this is your company is established in some sort of way, either through some of your existing clients or merely through a point-of-presence scenario. It is easier to contact people on a cold calling basis if you are able during the conversation to refer to some past clients and experiences. In this way the prospective client can feel some sort of security in that your company has performed some work in the past for other companies and that the company is not just starting out, which is always a bad thing in a consumer's eyes.

No, where your strategy should lie is in familiarity. You need to contact people who are familiar to you. Your friends, your family; people you have met in the past, that sort of thing. These people already know you, having dealt with your in the past either professionally or personally, and are thus more trusting towards you and what you have to say. Not only that but contacting these sorts of people will make you feel more at ease. You will not feel like a Public Speaker orating for the first time to a hostile crowd.

What you need to do here is create a list of a hundred names of people that you know. Now you are probably asking yourself, "I don't know a hundred people!" Rubbish! Take for instance your family – you know them, obviously. You know your friends. Obviously! Who's your doctor? Dentist? Vet? Who does your taxes? Who do you know at the local pub (or hairdresser, if you prefer)? What about sporting events? If you have children, who are their friends' parents?

Do you get my drift here? You can quite easily generate a good list of at least thirty people just off of the top of your head in this fashion. And as you go along over the next few days you will be adding to that list until you have got a good, solid database to start off with.

There is a concept here that I need to share with you, and it is called **Marbles in the Pipe**. Unless you have some marbles in your pipe, you will never succeed at sales. You must always have a list of prospects to be able to call on otherwise you will never generate any sales. If your pipe is empty, you've got nobody to call on and hence you can't make any sales. Always keep marbles in your pipe and you will eventually win.

You must remember that everyone needs to work somewhere. Clearly I'm talking about adults here, but everyone needs to earn a living. Let's take your children's friends' parents. They must work somewhere, and if they are familiar with you then you have a port of call at the company they work for. Of course they might not necessarily be the decision makers at their workplace but they can quite easily steer you in the right direction to the correct person and I'm sure they will not mind being used as a reference.

SUCCESS RATES

No sales person ever has a perfect hit ratio. What I mean by a hit ratio is the amount of success you have with new prospects. This is often the factor that leads new budding Sales People to leave this profession before they have even started. They cannot overcome the rejection that almost always occurs when approaching prospects for business.

There is one thing that you need to realize concerning this: **don't take it personally; its just business!** Too many sales people seem to think that the reason why a company doesn't want to purchase is because there is something wrong with them as people. There are many reasons why a company will not purchase: either they are currently using another Support Company, they have no budget, they are on a contract, or their branch cannot make the decision forcing you to contact their Head Office in another location in order to be successful. The thing to remember here is there is almost always a valid reason why a company will not accept your proposal – **it has nothing to do with you as a person!**

A good success rate is about 20% which means that out of every ten companies that you approach you should be able to get at least two meetings. So as a benchmark contact fifty companies. Out of those you should have at least ten meetings. If you have more then it means that you are doing well and your approach is good. If it is less then you need to look at your approach and fine tune it a bit. Try it out on one of your workmates (even better – try it out on your Sales Manager). Some people seem to get embarrassed at this exercise and prefer not to go through with this. Some people even get a bit egotistical and think that there is nothing wrong with their approach at all! What you need to remember here is your success is at stake and if you don't fix your problems early on then they will eventually become bad habit and will hamper your achievements in the future.

CANVASSING

Sometimes talking to people on the phone is just not enough. Sometimes actually seeing a company physically tends to put things into perspective and allows you to focus your sales pitch a little better.

I often use this type of cold calling to good effect. It gives me a good idea of what the company looks like and how receptive they will be to my efforts.

Ok, so what is canvassing? What this basically means is to grab an area and literally go from door to door gathering information. What you don't want to do is have a meeting right there and then with the decision maker. This is not the object of this exercise at all. The object is to visit the company and get a general idea of the company itself. In this you need to be fairly observant so that you can use the information later on.

I seem to be a bit vague here, so I am going to clarify things a little bit.

When you have a meeting with a particular company (whether it's a new client or a past client) take some time out to scope the businesses in the area. You can always use your meeting as a point of reference ("I have just had a successful meeting at company X and, seeing as I have a few minutes free, I thought I would pop in here and ask you if perhaps I could have the details of the Manager in charge of your network so that I can contact them at a later stage to setup a meeting with them."). Most often the Receptionist (the person you invariably will be talking to when using this approach) will give you those details with very few objections, and you then have another potential client to approach in the future.

What I mean by being observant is you need to notice various things about that company you are approaching. Are they big or small? What is the condition of the overall appearance of the company? Are they busy in reception? What does their reception area look like? How does their cabling look like inside the building?

This sort of information can give you a very good insight about that company. The sheer size of the company should give you a good indication of how many computers they will have. If the company is ragged and dirty, with old signboards and rusty fencing, then it probably means that they might not have a very large budget to work with. If the reception is quiet it also gives you a hint as to how much business is passing through the place. And untidy cabling is always a good starting point to get your foot in the door, provided you don't insult the company when you do finally approach them for a meeting.

Furthermore, a stunning looking reception area can also give you a good starting point when contacting your prospect; you ca always compliment them on their reception's appearance. People love flattery even if it is not personal.

In some cases you will find that, when canvassing, you meet the person to whom you will eventually need to setup the meeting with. That person just might by chance happen to be in the reception area when you do pop in. Have a brief conversation with them by all means but if you are not prepared to have a meeting with them right there and then that say so. Tell them the truth. Tell them that you were just popping in to gather some details to contact that person at a later stage for a meeting and that you are not prepared for a meeting at the present moment. They will respect you more for that and you might even be able to schedule your future meeting at that time. In any case it will give you a nice lead to work with.

When canvassing I have often come across deterrents that prevent a sales person from approaching a company in this manner. Fencing, electronic gates, and nasty little signs written in red that says thing like, "Reps by Appointment Only!" are evident with some companies. With these you will have a bit of a problem but most of them will have some sort of signage where you can get at least some of the details. Then when you phone in at a later stage you can always use this as an excuse: "I was in the vicinity but did not have a chance to visit you. I did however manage to get your details from your signage."

COMPANY SIZES

There are different sizes of companies in the business world, and these can determine (but not always) how long it may take before you manage to close a deal. Let's briefly look at these different categories:

SOHO and Home Users – These refer to home users and to offices that are generally run from home. This means that the maximum numbers of computers you will probably deal with are approximately ten. SOHO Stands for **Small Office, Home Office**.

SE – By definition **Small Enterprise** generally means an office consisting of up to fifty computers.

ME – **Medium Enterprise** will take you from fifty computers to approximately five hundred machines.

Corporate or Enterprise – These network types belong to large companies.

In knowing these categories we can structure our strategy a little better.

When you begin a venture in sales there are various aspects that will influence your choice of client. Firstly, and this has been mentioned before, you have no (or very few clients) to use as a reference. Many companies will be apprehensive to deal with you and hence some past projects will definitely be an advantage.

Secondly, being new to the company, there are several procedures that you will still need to learn so that you don't make a mistake and promise something that your company cannot or will not deliver.

Thirdly, your new company will have products that you definitely will need to learn, as discussed in the section on Product Knowledge. Knowing this then you will not necessarily know all the advantages and disadvantages of a new product range and hence you might miss out on a key sale because you are not aware of all the features inherent in a product range you are trying to sell.

Fourthly, for the first few months in a new company you will most probably be on some sort of probationary basis, and hence you will need to prove your worth to the company before they will consider you on a permanent basis. As sales depend primarily on money the best way of this proof is to bring in some sales. Granted they might not be the biggest deals that your company is looking for, but it does show your Management that you are at least trying to enter the market and will encourage them to assist you in aspiring further.

It is for these reasons that for your first initial sales you should concentrate on the smaller clients, either the SOHO market or the SME market, and leave the Corporate or Enterprise market for a later stage.

In analyzing these company sizes we will often find that in the SOHO and Small Enterprise company sizes the owner or Director is normally the decision maker. Occasionally another person might have that responsibility (such as the Operations Manager or the Financial Director) but it is fairly uncommon for there to be a dedicated IT Manager on that site.

With Medium Enterprises and Corporate environments there are almost always IT Managers involved with that company and this means that in order for decisions to be made concerning significant projects the IT Manager will need to consult with the Managing Director or similar level of Management. This invariably leads to a longer sales cycle.

REFERRALS

I referred to this earlier in the book but I am going to reiterate it here. When you contact people for business, whether they are known to you or not, always ask them if they know of other companies who they could recommend you to contact.

If you do manage to get a few names always make sure that you can use your client as a reference before you just go ahead and do this.

BUSINESS NETWORKING

This is also an interesting way of getting into the market here. There are many Chambers of Commerce (at least that's what they are called in South Africa) which basically are associations of businesses from different industries that are formed within different cities. In order to participate your company needs to become a member but there are various benefits namely:

1. The Chamber of Commerce (abbreviated COC) often hold luncheons or breakfast functions whereby representatives of the member companies get together to discuss business and generally to network with each other.
2. As a member you are able to obtain the database of all the members of the COC thus giving you a good base with which to work off of.
3. During these networking functions many suppliers perform short presentations on products their company provides. If the company you are working for has a specific product range you might get the opportunity to present it at one of these functions.

4. The COC often gets involved in various conventions and exhibitions. Being a member you are then able to tap into these conventions either as an exhibitor or a visitor and you will be able to gain more business.

Find out about your own COC in your area and, if possible, try to get your company to become a member. It becomes a valuable source of information.

CONCLUSION

You have come to the end of this journey with me, and I have been with you every step of the way as you have gone through this book.

I really hope that I have managed to teach you something about sales and I really hope that now, after having read my book, you go out there and make it happen!

Just think about it – use this stuff; apply it, and that new house or car will be yours!

So now, grab your pen and diary, put your shoes on, and get out there and sell!

SUMMARY – CHAPTER 18.

This chapter is written to assist the new sales person in starting out in sales.

MARBLES IN THE PIPE

You must always have a list of prospects to be able to call on otherwise you will never generate any sales.

You also need to contact people who are familiar to you. Cold Calling is practiced later when you are more experienced.

SUCCESS RATES

A **hit ratio** is the amount of success you have with new prospects.

When you are rejected by a prospect **don't take it personally; its just business!**

A good success rate is about 20% which means that out of every ten companies that you approach you should be able to get at least two meetings. If your success rate is less than this average then you need to look at your sales approach and fine tune it a bit.

CANVASSING

This is to visit an area and go from door to door gathering information. The object of this is to visit the company and get a general idea of the company itself. In this you need to be fairly observant so that you can use the information later on.

Once you have this information you can then setup a meeting at a later stage and use the information you have gathered to plan a strategy.

COMPANY SIZES

There are different sizes of companies in the business world, and these can determine how long it may take before you manage to close a deal.

SOHO and Home Users –	These refer to home users and to offices that are generally run from home. The maximum number of computers is ten.
SE –	**Small Enterprise** generally means an office consisting of up to fifty computers.
ME –	**Medium Enterprise** will take you from fifty computers to approximately five hundred machines.
Corporate or Enterprise –	These network types belong to large companies consisting of more than five hundred computers.

For your first initial sales you should concentrate on the smaller clients, either the SOHO market or the SME market, and leave the Corporate or Enterprise market for a later stage.

REFERRALS

When you contact people for business, whether they are known to you or not, always ask them if they know of other companies who they could recommend you to contact.

BUSINESS NETWORKING

There are many Chambers of Commerce (at least that's what they are called in South Africa) which are associations of businesses from different industries that are formed within different cities. The benefits of these are:

1. The COC often hold luncheons or breakfast functions whereby representatives of the member companies get together to discuss business and generally to network with each other.
2. As a member you are able to obtain the database of all the members of the COC thus giving you a good base with which to work off of.
3. During these networking functions many suppliers perform short presentations on products their company provides.
4. The COC often gets involved in various conventions and exhibitions.

in the United States
asters